A DICTIONARY OF
TRUE CRIME

'Evil isn't an army that besieges a city from outside the walls. It is a native of the city. It is the mutiny of the garrison, the poison in the water, the ashes in the bread.'

Charles Morgan

A DICTIONARY OF TRUE CRIME

A REFERENCE GUIDE TO THE DARK AND
CURIOUS CRIMES OF BRITISH HISTORY

STEPHEN WADE

First published in Great Britain in 2024 by
PEN AND SWORD TRUE CRIME
An imprint of
Pen & Sword Books Ltd
Yorkshire – Philadelphia

Copyright © Stephen Wade, 2024

ISBN 978 1 39903 449 4

The right of Stephen Wade to be identified as Author of this work has been asserted by him in accordance with the Copyright, Designs and Patents Act 1988.

A CIP catalogue record for this book is available from the British Library.

All rights reserved. No part of this book may be reproduced or transmitted in any form or by any means, electronic or mechanical including photocopying, recording or by any information storage and retrieval system, without permission from the Publisher in writing.

Typeset by SJmagic DESIGN SERVICES, India.
Printed and bound in the UK by CPI Group (UK) Ltd, Croydon, CR0 4YY.

Pen & Sword Books Limited incorporates the imprints of Atlas, Archaeology, Aviation, Discovery, Family History, Fiction, History, Maritime, Military, Military Classics, Politics, Select, Transport, True Crime, Air World, Frontline Publishing, Leo Cooper, Remember When, Seaforth Publishing, The Praetorian Press, Wharncliffe Local History, Wharncliffe Transport, Wharncliffe True Crime and White Owl.

For a complete list of Pen & Sword titles please contact
PEN & SWORD BOOKS LIMITED
George House, Units 12 & 13, Beevor Street, Off Pontefract Road,
Barnsley, South Yorkshire, S71 1HN, England
E-mail: enquiries@pen-and-sword.co.uk
Website: www.pen-and-sword.co.uk

or

PEN AND SWORD BOOKS
1950 Lawrence Rd, Havertown, PA 19083, USA
E-mail: uspen-and-sword@casematepublishers.com
Website: www.penandswordbooks.com

Contents

Introduction vi

A Note on the Guide.. xvi

The Reference Guide... 1

Contents 166

Bibliography and Sources 169

Introduction

A few years ago I sat on a panel with two crime novelists at the Ilkley Literature Festival. Some asked us why we wrote about crime. The novelists said interesting things about creating detectives and criminal situations. When it came to my turn I made the point that I *became* the detective, rather than having to invent one.

Over the last three years, for instance, I have researched the case of Louie Calvert, alleged Leeds murderer from 1926, whose fate was to be hanged at Strangeways. I made a vow with myself to write about her and her transgressions with an attitude, tone and narrative stance which would be nothing like the sensational 'horrible murder' approach of what I call the 'red and blacks' – the popular press.

Ask general readers about the true crime genre and they will probably think immediately of the books found in isolated and compact little shelves in the bookshop or in the library, hived off from the ubiquitous crime fiction volumes. True crime in that sense – dealing generally with serial killers, psychopaths, gangland and the mafia – relates to the beginnings of the modern genre as typified by these books. But there is far more to true crime today. It is aspiring to be a literary genre to stand alongside the acknowledged literary works. The genre has a highbrow room in its great mansion of criminal narratives.

However, it has always been difficult to write true crime that breaks away from the 'red and black' tales of slaughter. When I started writing regional crime casebooks around twenty years ago, I planned a book on women guilty of murder throughout Yorkshire history. When I researched the topic, I soon came to see that the word 'murder' was hardly applicable to many of the cases I read about. Technically, according to the criminal law of the time, most of the hapless young women who concealed a birth or found that they had a dead infant on their hands were guilty of murder. But I did not want the word 'murder' on the cover of my books. I failed. Publishers want that writ large, in any combination of stock phrases. Why? Because the true crime we have always expected is a genre of horrors. It always dealt with the unthinkable, the revolting and the beastly.

It has taken a long time to chip away at the true crime stereotype. When Thomas de Quincey wrote his influential essay 'Murder Considered as One of the Fine Arts', in 1827, he lifted the philosophical and literary interest in the act of murder into a realm beyond that found in the immensely popular *Newgate Calendar*, which had been reprinted in various forms since 1773. There, in the pages ostensibly written from the experiences and observations of the gaolers, readers found the horrendous criminal deviance one might expect in an age when the capital crimes on the statutes was rising up to its peak of 220 by the 1820s.

The Newgate Calendar did include the notion of possible redemption. The villains could admit guilt and ask for an avoidance of hell, which was surely waiting for them, as the authors believed. One compilation of crime stories, *York Castle*, published in 1829, told the tales of horror and then added a sermon as an appendage, to describe the last dying speech on the scaffold.

De Quincey enjoyed himself in his supposed 'lecture' on the art of murder by humorously insisting that there was a deeper reason why intelligent and educated citizens would take an interest in what was later to be called 'criminology'. His readers would have been familiar with the celebrated Ratcliffe Highway murder of 1811, when a family was hacked to death not far from Wapping, and they also knew that the probable murderer, John Williams, had become what we would surely call a celebrity. London had become fascinated by him, as it had been by many dramatic exits from the world during the years between the early 1790s and the 1820s, when treason and sedition prompted the suspension of *habeas corpus* at times, and the regular imprisonment of literary types such as Leigh Hunt, who settled in prison with his family.

In other words, De Quincey sensed the revisionary attitudes to the horrendous rise of crime which the British nation had seen over the previous century, when the rise of empire, commerce and property meant the creation of a succession of acts to punish murder and theft in all their forms. Within that context, he had also become aware that John Williams was a new breed of killer. He was arguably the prototype of what Edgar Allan Poe was to describe in his essay 'The Man of the Crowd' (1840):

> *He noticed me not, but resumed his solemn walk, while I, ceasing to follow, remained absorbed in contemplation. 'This old man', I said at length, 'is the type and the genius of deep crime. He refuses to be alone. He is the man of the crowd. It will be in vain to follow; for I shall learn no more of him, nor of his deeds.'*

De Quincey and Poe perceived the emergence of the alienated individual whose transgressions would be beyond understanding or explanation. As their century wore on, and the first steps in professional forensic science were undertaken, the primary aim was to find a way to identify an individual criminal. Crimes committed by gangs of robbers or vicious crooks who garrotted theatre-goers in the 1860s were open to investigation, particularly after the first real detectives were put in post in 1842 at Scotland Yard. But what about the apparently motiveless criminal?

The more I researched and wrote within the increasingly wide spectrum of true crime and crime history, the more I came to see that the lone, alienated, disenchanted destroyer of life and peace was the factor which would determine how the genre progressed.

In the last decades of the nineteenth century, when fingerprints were beginning to be understood and applied, and the methods of Alphonse Bertillon (profiles of individual criminals using precise measurement of physiology) were being developed, publications began to appear with titles such as *Romance of the Forum* by Peter Burke and *Mysteries of Police and Crime* by Arthur Griffiths. True crime became a best-selling genre alongside the spectacular concomitant success of Conan Doyle and his Sherlock Holmes. The periodicals were packed with features on smuggling, criminal barristers, burglars, murder scenes, and of course, detectives.

The eighty years between De Quincey's essay and the books on serious crime which appeared in collections such as those of Burke and Griffith had seen the impact of Jack the Ripper, the Fenian bombings, several attempts on the life of Queen Victoria, and the activities of spies and anarchists in London.

In the 1890s, the time was ripe for a new version of *The Newgate Calendar*: there was an expanding readership for the collections of criminal tales that the Regency public had so enjoyed. The popular true crime genre was here to stay. But now, I would argue, an alternative mode was created: there were writers who wanted to make true crime into a genre with a status and esteem that might sit alongside essays, travel works or memoirs. After all, the late Victorian and Edwardian years were a period in which *belles lettres* flourished, and commuters working in the booming city, travelling to and from suburbia, wanted a twenty-minute read. A 'horrible murder' story was about right for that. But what about the new readers of amateur criminology? They needed something with a professional dimension.

Enter the Scottish maestro of the literary true crime genre, William Roughead (1870–1952). He was a lawyer working in Edinburgh, and he attended many of the murder cases he wrote about. He once explained that in 1889 he took some time away from work to watch the trial of Jessie King, who was a baby-farmer. Roughead was the ideal contributor to the volumes which were published from 1905 by William Hodge, an Edinburgh firm, with the series title 'Notable Scottish Trials'. Roughead produced his first contribution, *The Trial of Dr Pritchard*, in 1906.

Roughead understood that murder as a subject for narratives of many kinds was an aspect of life that would always be attractive to the public. It was the exact nature of that attraction that intrigued him. In his book *What is Your Verdict?* (1931) he uses as an epigraph these words from Joseph Conrad: 'Murder is always with us. It is almost an institution.' Roughead realised that there would never be one universal explanation of murder; there was no common ground. Every homicide was unique. Although there are variations on certain motives, the mystery will always be there, along with the eternal question: are we all capable of taking a life, given the right circumstances?

Many of Roughead's collections of murders are about those 'right circumstances'. His rare achievement as a true crime writer is that he places the very ordinary ('Poison in the Pantry') by the side of the tough, complex reasoning needed in mysterious deaths, as in this from 'The Secret of Ireland's Eye':

> *It may be that the Court of Criminal Appeal, had such been available, might on the merits have reversed the jury's finding. Certainly, it was a narrow case; the evidence was purely circumstantial and called for very nice and cautious estimation; had the trial happened to be held in Scotland, our national via media of Not Proven would probably have been followed.*

This is slow-paced, judicious and gently educative. It places the issue in context and opens up thought. Roughead enlarges on this delight in the complexities of murder which he was to call the 'criminous' in his essay, 'Enjoyment of Murder', which was printed in his 1956 volume *Tales of the Criminous*. His reasons for this questionable 'enjoyment' are all related to that strange hinterland of the actual scene and occasion of the crime: the prurient, voyeuristic but at the same time possibly empathic territory occupied by the amateur criminologist and avid reader of the genre. He writes in that essay:

> *Many years 'acquaintance' – I hasten to add, at second hand – with divers sorts of murderers has convinced me that however disparate their methods may be, all have this common characteristic: self-conceit, so abnormally developed as to become a sort of moral cancer – an overwhelming sense of their individual importance in the scheme of creation, and a corresponding indifference to, and disregard of, the claims and feelings of others.*

I feel that Roughead's attitudes to his writing came from that amateur gathering which was originally called Our Society, and which was to become The Crimes Club, which I wrote about in my book *Conan Doyle and the Crimes Club* (2013). He and his circle of criminous enquirers came to perceive that a serious crime was never simple. Every stage of the offence from planning to action was of interest.

Roughead, then, saw the importance of making a narrative of murder multi-layered, but not confusing. He became adept at interweaving personal reflection, legal facts and the overall human situation of the crime. His friend, Henry James, became an enthusiast, and his responses to reading Roughead's books perhaps express a common stance: 'Most interesting and attaching is the book which had held my attention charmed, and your manner of presentation is so strong and skilful that one casts about with open appetite for more such outstanding material into which you may be moved to bite – or at least to make *us* bite.'

Implicit in Roughead's attitude to his subjects is the premise that the most common, everyday murder is worthy of attention. His careful research and his even-paced evaluation of each case opened up my attitudes to writing about true crime, and I would guess that his work lies at the heart of what has now become a new flowering of writing in the genre.

Recently, writing about crime fact, while maintaining the criminous attitude, has expanded bravely into new genre cocktails of memoir/murder, documentary/murder and even imaginative prose fused with murder. In 2017, Alexandria Marzano-Lesnevich published *The Fact of a Body*, which has the subtitle 'a murder and a memoir'. Here, she recounts a homicide committed by a person with an extreme learning difficulty. The approach opens up the ancient problems of culpability and diminished responsibility. The legal issues are explained but the human story takes centre stage. The mixture works wonderfully well.

Of course, Truman Capote's now classic work *In Cold Blood* (1966) stands firmly and confidently in many minds as the book which changed true crime. It demonstrated how the documentary element, the no-man's-land between fact and fiction, may be fruitfully exploited in order to 'thicken' the narrative content and to raise the complexity of the narration and its ruses.

True crime in traditional forms persists of course. We see that in the compelling *I'll be Gone in the Dark* (2018) by Michelle McNamara, which is at once a template for the obsessive search for resolution in crime writing and a commentary on the obsession itself.

Drawing together these two traditions of true crime writing – the sensational and dramatic hyperbolic style and the literary, measured, nuanced approach – I can see reflected in my own writing the benefits of allowing both into a story. When I wrote *The Girl who Lived on Air* (2014) I saw at the research stage that dealing with a story from 1869 Carmarthenshire was going to be a challenge. It required delving into the law of manslaughter as it stood at the time and also understanding folk medicine and official medicine at a time when science was eager to stand taller than the local 'wise man'. But in the end, as Roughead helps us to see, the human situation will clarify and become important as the tale is told through questioning and with empathy.

Why do I write in this genre, and why did I begin to do so? I became aware that looking into transgression shines a torch on a human community, wherever or whenever that may be. I like to think that something of Roughead's attitude is behind my storytelling, and I always aim to inject some empathy into the assessments, even when the crime is heinous and difficult to comprehend.

I would argue that the true crime genre has now proved that it can stand beside other respectable genres under the heading 'literature', rather than sitting in a rather shameful lesser place, the dunce in the class. Much of this new respectability we owe to William Roughead. But even at its best, what does the popularity of true crime tell us about ourselves?

In 1957, when the possible abolition of the death penalty for murder was in the air, an official report listed fifty homicides in Britain in the year preceding the publication of the paper. The authors noted that all fifty involved a factor which was either accidental or circumstantial: in other words, a killing with a possibility of manslaughter rather than murder. That simple difference is crucial, of course. In a murder, there have to be these two elements:

Mens rea   a guilty mind or intent (malice aforethought)
Actus reus   the elements of an offence excluding those which concern the mind of the accused.

There has to be an intent to take life or to act in such a way that death would be a possible outcome; then there has to be such an act taken.

An accepted definition of murder is:

unlawful homicide committed with malice aforethought, express or implied. Express malice exists where the person killing does do with the intention of causing death or grievous bodily harm. Implied malice exists where the person killing does not actually intend to kill or do grievous bodily harm, yet intentionally does an act which to his knowledge is likely to cause death...
(Mozley and Whiteley's Law Dictionary)

The classic definition also contains the added clause: 'the death occurring within a year and a day', which has given rise to a number of fascinating cases over the years in which the accused has waited to see if the charge might be manslaughter or murder – the noose or a long spell inside. Also, in Britain, we have the issue of the *'crime passionel'* and as Sir Harold Scott wrote as a commentary on this:

> *Thus* crimes passionels *arising out of sexual jealousy amount to murder unless the jury considers that the provocation was enough to make a reasonable man do as the killer did through loss of self-control because of what he saw or of what was said to him.*

In popular culture, though, such fine distinction hardly matters. The fact is that in a narrative in popular genres, a killer is a killer, and the nuance is of little interest. What always attracts attention is the *motive*. A true crime murder story, like all stories, is about *why?*. There are so many possible reasons for taking a life that every murder story will differ, and the common defence 'I didn't mean to kill him/her' is hard to prove and also to disprove. Even more interesting is the killing done for money – a hit. Here there is an element of 'business' and so motivations are plain and one-sided. There may well be other emotions beneath the surface, but what arises in the heart of the story is killing for cash.

Of course there are also 'firsts' and I start with the once-famous case of the murders which were solved by means of fingerprints, and for which the fingerprint evidence was judged to be admissible. There were plenty of others in that category to choose from, but few forensic firsts have such appeal.

What about weapons and methods? The *modus operandi* in the majority of cases is plain and direct – poison, the blunt instrument, the blade or the bullet. Poisonings have always been prominent in the famous cases, and many of these are baffling in their complexity. But there are also straightforward approaches, such as in the Hay case when food was poisoned, and in fact consumed in the presence of the apparently amiable and well-respected killer. Poison is in some ways the expert's chosen means: this is because there is a wide choice, each with a different method of extinguishing life. There is a huge difference between the killer wanting the victim to die mercifully quickly, as with strychnine, and the poison which will provide a long and agonising death, as has often been the case with arsenic, given in small doses. The latter was complicated in Victorian times because, as with James Maybrick, arsenic was used in tiny doses as an aphrodisiac.

There are great murder stories too: in the sense that something about them captures the public imagination, and there is a strange element to this: something that creates almost a fictional feel to the tale. Of course that is because such affairs are distant from the man in the street and that distance lends an unreal quality. In my cases, the story of Guenther Podola perhaps comes closest to this. I was eleven when Podola shot a policeman dead – Sergeant

Purdy. This was reported on television, and as it was 1959, it was in the early days of television being in ordinary homes. I have a lingering image of a phone box being involved in the story, and of the uproar at the thought of someone killing a police officer. The image was accurate, as it turned out that Podola had rung his intended victim from a phone box at South Kensington underground station. What this illustrates is the tendency for prominent murder stories to haunt the imagination, just as a scene from a novel or a film might.

I have three stories of police killings in this collection, and of course that makes sense when we consider that officers are in the front line, taking the bullets as well as the threats. They often live in very dangerous situations, and their heroism when facing a gun barrel has figured in hundreds of famous murders – many of which are unfortunately forgotten. Each creates a temporary furore until the next more horrendous killing occurs. Crime magazines tend to make lists and write from the basis of the arithmetic of death: they make copy from questions about which serial killer has carried out the most murders, or who has committed the most disgusting killings.

It is significant that as I write this book there are eighteen criminals serving life sentences without the possibility of parole who were once infamous as well as famous and who are now in all the books about murder in Britain, yet the younger generation will not know them. The man who was once a horrific and highly dangerous killer is now a zombie on drugs, harmless and aged, walking a hospital ward or watching television and sipping cocoa, safely behind a very high wall. A murder story offers the most transient fame, and yet many lust after that 'cred' and what it brings both in jail and inside the covers of true crime books. Any accidental discovery of an old yellowing newspaper will confirm this. There will almost certainly be a headline asking who killed someone, or quoting the numbers of the slain.

So why write about the famous but forgotten cases? We write about such murders because they teach us, with very special insights, about the nature of the worst transgression, one of the key Ten Commandments, an act going back to Cain and Abel. They involve intricate questions of morality and they show that morality becomes entangled with the condition of the criminal law at the time of the events. At one point in time, the moral fabric of the community will be outraged by something that, some years later, is very ordinary. The obvious example is what is known in the slang of everyday talk as 'queer bashing'. In the days of Quentin Crisp and his adventures around London clubs, when gay men were targets for cruelty and violence, there were murders that illustrate the nature of the social context: that existed before the acceptance of homosexuality within mainstream culture.

Another vivid example of this intersection of morality and law in murder cases is the murder trial involving a woman in the dock. One of the most celebrated cases in Scottish history, that of Jeannie Donald, revealed much about a specific community, its geography, its patterns of behaviour and its integration and divisions. In other words, a murder can shine the torch of knowledge into the dark corners we previous ignored or chose to forget.

There is a literary tradition of crime writing about famous murders which tends to create a line of thinkers, each adding to what has gone before and each developing a new theory. In my collection there is one outstanding example: that of William Herbert Wallace. As Douglas Wynn wrote in his book *On Trial for Murder* (1996), 'This was one of the strangest murder cases ever. The murder reads like a detective story and there have been some twenty books written about it. Raymond Chandler called it the "impossible murder"...' In writing my own contribution to the debate, I am conscious that this murder case has gone so far into the realms of literature rather than life that I feel the creative weight of previous minds at work on the enigma.

Finally, as well as writing about killers, I have worked with several in the capacity of writer working in prisons. The majority of murderers are sad individuals who made a bad choice of behaviour, lost control in a confrontation, or allowed something dark to enter their soul: something that took away the restraint, the block to action. A cold killer has no block, no filter to allow the right human feelings in at the crucial moment. The killers I have met have been people who would be horrified at the thought that some would think them 'evil'. A few I have worked with might perhaps relish the thought of that word being applied to them.

We now have a great deal of scientific knowledge about human aggression and neuroscientists have developed theories about which parts of the brain may be damaged or tend to malfunction when it comes to violence. Whatever the causes, the killers, in most cases, if we avoid ideological and religious elements, tend to fit into one of three categories:

1. The killer who is temporarily controlled by some urge that dominates the natural restraint we have from socialised behaviour.
2. The killer who purposely allows the urge to take life into his or her being, for 'kicks' or for gain.
3. The killer who places no value on human life and who sees murder merely as a business, a way of life.

Murder and memory make an interesting enquiry in this context: ever since the street ballad-singers and sellers of chapbooks sold a tale of 'a good murder' back in the Victorian period, the theme has been one of 'out of sight, out of mind': crowds of thousands swarmed to watch the hanging of Courvoisier, the man who murdered his aristocratic employer in 1840, but that was soon forgotten when the next hanging came along. The subject causes sensations but they are fleeting ones, merely passing interests. But choosing which ones provide truly fascinating revisits from a crime writer has been full of interest, and in the end, the main attraction has been that of tantalising questions.

The choice has been immense: the same problem confronted Jonathan Goodman when he edited *The Daily Telegraph Murder File* volume. In his preface he says, 'When I came to choose according to the *Telegraph* accounts of matters to do with murder for this book, the Palmer case was already chosen. Deciding what else to include was made hardly less daunting by my having decided to stay within the 113 years till the abolition of capital punishment in Great Britain: during those years [since the founding of the *Telegraph*] there were some 40,000 known murders in England and Wales...'

Writing about the crime of murder attracted its first grandly literary treatment in the hands of a writer who moved in the Wordsworth circle, Thomas de Quincey, and he more than anyone understood its appeal to readers other than those who hanker after tales of the noose and back-street garottings. He said, in his famous essay 'Murder Considered as one of the Fine Arts', 'Murder may be laid hold of by its moral handle... or it may be also treated aesthetically. As the Germans call it, that is, in relation to good taste...' He was hinting at the way in which readers of crime stories tend to divide into those who see a murder as totally serious business, related to the close study of criminology, and those who enjoy the story on a more playful level, with little to do with the dark reality of its occasion.

Gershon Legman once wrote that 'Murder is a crime. Writing about it is not'. He was noting that there is an element of the subject which relates to the way we divorce the actual facts from the relish of the drama and sensation. This, after all, is there in the so-called 'cosy' genre of crime fiction, in contrast to the direct shock of a serial killer story or explicit forensic writing.

A Note on the Guide

First, as with all reference works, my guide is selective. It is beyond the imagination and work-rate of any writer and researcher to provide in one volume a complete reference to all major true crime cases and supplementary topics. Naturally, I have been selective. What I have aimed at is a balance of those cases I personally researched and found notably interesting and significant, and the cases which are indispensable for such a topic – Jack the Ripper, Dick Turpin and so on.

As a crime historian, I have long felt that there is a need for a new guide to true crime history. There are many reasons for this, notably that updates are necessary on the select body of cases which have attracted most attention from writers. These are the 'premier league' of cases, those stories that are constantly revisited, such as Jack the Ripper, the Wallace mystery, the Moors Murders, the Red Barn, the Bravo Case and a number of others. But equally, there is a case to be made for dozens of secondary cases to be retold, and these are the ones that usually relate to the ever-present criminological subjects that lie at the foundations of the genre.

These evergreen subjects are principally miscarriages of justice, unsolved murders, dramatic trials, nationally important crimes, morally repugnant offences (such as cannibalism or baby farming) and of course true crime at its highest level in terms of the meta-history of Britain, such as the Princes in the Tower or the espionage offences during the two world wars.

Arguably, a reference work should serve many purposes: it should provide reliable and up-to-date information; it should provoke discussion and response on important subjects in law and criminology; and of course it should be a gripping, irresistible read for those who enjoy the genre. With the latter point in mind, I have worked hard to make this book a compendium of stories as well as a factual assemblage of key criminal cases.

Additionally, many topics related to true crime history must have a brief presence in such a work. I refer here to prison, court systems, important legal reform, significant biography and also some abstract terms and concepts. My view of true crime is that it offers the reader a unique insight into people and society at any given time in history. When communities contain the imbalance created by crime, when the 'time is out of joint' as Shakespeare wrote, the light shines on matters usually kept out of the focus of historical writing. The same might be said of crime fiction. Naturally, a fair proportion of the cases in these pages have been subject to fictional treatment. A typical example is the Thompson and Bywaters murder of 1922, which interested F. Tennyson Jesse, who produced the classic novel *A Pin to See the Peepshow* 1934).

There is one further element in my conception of the guide. I have always believed that readers of this genre, and of the social history of crime in general, enjoy asides and footnotes. The well-known phenomenon of serendipity is known to readers and researchers. Often in such writings as memoirs or biographies, insights will occur into mainstream narratives. In fact, with the Thompson and Bywaters case in mind, such an example would be Beverley Nichols' book *Twenty-Five*, in which he recounts going to interview the father of the hanged woman, Edith Thompson.

In relation to this point, it should be noted that classic literature also has a place; writers and biographers who have contributed prominently to the subject surely deserve a place in my pages. Some examples of this would be Oscar Wilde, whose works *De Profundis* and *The Ballad of Reading Gaol* are established classics which add considerably to our knowledge of true crime and criminology. Similarly, significant people would include, for instance, Sir Arthur Conan Doyle, Sir Bernard Spilsbury and William Roughead. In the ranks of police personnel, there are many candidates for inclusion, notably Nipper Read, Jerome Caminada and Walter Dew.

There are also controversies involved in a book such as this. By this I mean that some true crime subjects and themes are areas of disagreement; they may have moral or political consequences or perspectives. All that may be said in this context is that I have made an effort to keep to the facts, but also to include opinions and accounts of evidence that may turn out to be important.

As to models and influences for crime reference works, mention must be made of the impressive work of Oliver Cyriax, whose *Penguin Encyclopaedia of Crime* has been a standard since its last printing in 1996. Also an important influence is *Firsts, Lasts and Onlys: Crime* (2007), which supplies fascinating and eye-opening facts on the subject. More on these influences is included in my bibliography.

My own perspective on true crime writing has changed during my writing career, and in my book *Murder in Mind* (Scratching Shed, 2018) I gave a partly autobiographical account of how and why reading and writing the genre came into my life. In the process of writing that, I realised just how important such subjects as forensics, profiling, restorative justice and similar lines of thought are to the literature around crime and law.

Writing that book made me much more aware of how the theoretical thinking behind law and morality impacts on any given narrative of a true crime case, and that one should never reduce the subject to a mere spree in the midst of something horrendous, something showing the worst side of humanity rather than the best of us.

The Reference Guide

'Law? Don't tell me about that. I've got my own law, mate'
                    Comment made by a prisoner to the author

'They did not wish the property to go out of the family, so they waylaid their sister's lover, murdered him, put him in a sack and threw him into the Towy.'
                                        Kilvert's *Diary*

Note: As there are a number of 'canonical' true crime stories – cases told and retold many times – I have decided to provide minimal entries for most of these. In contrast, where there is an asterisk * next to the heading, there will be a full entry with a detailed narrative. Also: cross references will appear in italics in the body of the texts on each heading.

A

Acid Bath Killer, The

John Haigh, who stated that he had committed nine murders, was such an extreme example of a merciless killer that one paper called him a 'vampire'. His *modus operandi* was the use of an acid bath, something highly unusual and repulsive. Gerald Byrne, who had a special talent for producing publications with fascinating manuscript sources (see *Neville Heath*) brought out a book in 1949, one of the early publications on the case, that has letters and pictures and photographs. Byrne was skilled in gathering unusual details very soon after trials, and for this case, the documentary material is invaluable.

Haigh was the son of Plymouth Brethren, but high moral values had no impact on him, and by the age of twenty-five he was in trouble with the law and did a longish prison stretch. He was to be a danger wherever he went, starting with the family for whom he worked in amusement arcades. His campaign of death by acid began with the murder of William McSwann in London in 1945; in this, he was implementing the fruits of his macabre research carried out behind bars, when he somehow managed to experiment with acid on mice. Male and female friends and acquaintances became his victims; by the time he came to the killing of Olive Durand-Deacon in early 1949, whose remains were the first to be discovered by police after she was reported missing, he was adept at destroying flesh. When police eventually tracked him down and found the horrendous basement where he went to his nefarious work, they found the tools of his murderous trade: carbolic acid, rubber gloves, a revolver, and a stirrup-pump.

Apparently Haigh had always been fascinated by blood, but this passion had grown into the administering of horrible death. Finally, forensic knowledge kicked in following a search outside Haigh's workshop. Bone fragments were found in sludge, and then came the discovery of something that almost always pinpoints a murder – dental evidence. Dentures belonging to Olive Durand-Deacon were found. It comes as no surprise to learn that Haigh was hanged in August 1949 at Wandsworth. Albert Pierrepoint, the hangman, gives this account in his memoirs of the strap he used:

> It is a strap made of pliant calf-leather, no different in design from the straps I normally used, supplied by the Home Office in a box of execution apparatus, but it is personal to me. I have used it only about a dozen times. Whenever I used it I made a red-ink entry in my private diary. This is the only indication I have ever given that I had a more than formal interest in this particular execution...

Adams, Dr John Bodkin (1899–1983)

In 1956, the coastal town of Eastbourne was the centre of media attention, and crime correspondents knew they had a major story breaking. The focus was on a local doctor called John Bodkin Adams. The investigation into matters relating to what could, or should have been, euthanasia broke when a celebrity comic, Leslie Henson, phoned the police about what he thought was a suspicious death – and the death in question was of one of Adams's patients.

The patient was Mrs Gertrude Hullett, and her death initiated many questions and interviews, with Adams under constant observation. What emerged was the story of a doctor who only wanted wealthy patients, who tended to leave expensive items or sums of cash upon their deaths to their apparently caring doctor, a man who gave them time, attention and drugs.

Whilst the suspect was somehow always present when there was death, he was cleared of murder in a trial at which top lawyers went to work and overcame the police statements of evidence. After all, the thought of a GP in Britain walking to the scaffold was too extreme to contemplate. Many commentators also saw that the doctor was being hounded and victimised; the attention was so extreme that a photographer and reporter from a French magazine arrived in the town and trailed Adams around his patch as he walked from patient to patient on his rounds.

The police investigation was determined and resolute; the lead detective, D.S. Hannam of Scotland Yard, travelled far and wide collecting information. Many thought that the doctor would be found guilty. Hannam's dossier on his suspect was apparently nine inches thick. The detective was sure that his man was a 'mass murderer'.

However, Adams was acquitted. His only penalty was that he was struck off the medical register because of the effects of the scandal, although some years later that was rescinded. He continued his life of shooting, playing golf and being a local 'character'. During the investigation, there had even been exhumations of bodies as the search for forensic evidence went on. The anecdotal evidence was convincing, including the testimony of a nurse who, on seeing the strength of a dose given to a Mrs Kilgour, stated that the dose would kill her, and she told the doctor so.

For proof of how intriguing the case was (and still is), consider the massive study by Pamela V. Cullen, *A Stranger in Blood*, which is 676 pages long and contains a mass of relevant detail. When I researched the case for my biography of Herbert Hannam, what struck me as a very influential factor was the campaign for doctors' roles in euthanasia to be revised and regulated. The campaign was led by arguably the most famous and significant medical man in the land – Sir Berkeley Moynihan, who had made his name during the First World War.

Aram, Eugene (1704–59)

The record books always stress the same puzzling duality of this man from Knaresborough. They refer to him as a scholar and a killer. Such was his notoriety that his life was fictionalised by Bulmer Lytton and inspired a poem by Thomas Hood, 'The Dream of Eugene Aram'. Even in everyday anecdote, there were memories of him from ordinary people, such as some comments from those who knew him in King's Lynn, where he moved to work as a teacher. Although the murder for which he was hanged took place in Knaresborough in 1745, he was not arrested and imprisoned until 1759, and a woman, who was a little girl at the time, recalled seeing him arrested; in fact, he was her schoolteacher.

Aram was outstanding in the study of languages and it has been noted that had he not become tempted to kill and steal in order to pay debts, he undoubtedly had the ability to be a learned academic. In 1735 he was a schoolmaster in Knaresborough (where he remained until 1744), and had fallen into bad company, becoming friendly with a local rogue called Houseman. When a shoemaker in the area, Daniel Clark, went missing after obtaining goods on credit from tradesmen in the town, a search for his body ensued, and some of the goods were found in Aram's possession. After it was found that there wasn't enough evidence to convict Aram, he fled to London.

In 1758, a skeleton was dug up in Knaresborough, believed to be that of Clark. Houseman was arrested but claimed the skeleton was not Clark's and, when pressed, explained where the body was actually buried and blamed Aram for the murder. At the York trial in 1759, Houseman turned King's evidence and although Aram spoke in his own defence (apparently very ably) the death sentence was passed on him. In his cell he attempted suicide but failed; he was hanged on 6 August 1759. His skill with words was shown in a poem written in his cell before his death:

Come pleasing rest, eternal slumbers fall,
Seal mine, that once must seal the eyes of all;
Calm and composed my soul its journey takes,
No guilt that troubles, and no heart that aches;
Adieu thou sun, all bright like her arise.
Adieu! Fair friends and all that's good and wise.

For the gentler side of Aram, we have a memory from the girl, his student, who witnessed his arrest. This was described in a Victorian collection of anecdotes:

She informed me that at the time of his being arrested, she was a girl of eleven years of age; that he was put into a chaise handcuffed, and that the boys of the school were in tears; that he was much esteemed by them, having been used to associate with them in their play hours. She said that the picture of him in the Newgate Calendar is the express image of him; and she mentioned that he always wore his hat bangled, which she explained meant 'bent down or slouched.

Assizes

The story of the assize courts is a reflection of how the criminal law gradually developed into a system which would have parity across the land. The courts represent the boldest step by which central legal power began to cover the King's domains, using local and national elements. In each shire, the sheriff, who had been there since very early times, gathered the jury and the other machinery of law, ready for the visit of the assize judges, because that is what assizes were – courts done in transit – giving the assize towns distinguished visitors and a high level of ritual and importance for a few days each year.

Originally the law courts followed the King, and his own court was the *Curia Regis*. The Magna Carta (1215) included this sentence: 'Common pleas shall not follow our Court but shall be held in some certain place'. The result was that Westminster was made that 'place', but then the notion of having the top judges moving around to deal with criminal and civil cases became a workable option, with economic and logistical benefits of course, as persons accused would be retained and then tried mostly in their own counties or provinces.

Since early mediaeval times there had been assizes – literally 'sittings together' – to try causes and to gather officials in the English regions to compile enquiries and inventories into local possessions and actions. These were 'eyres' of assize, but they were not courts. The assize courts came about when travelling justices went out into the counties to try cases: the Assize of Clarendon in 1166, and the Council of Northampton in 1196, decreed that the country should be split into six areas in which the judges of the High Court would sit. These became known as circuits.

During Edward I's reign an Act was passed to create court hearings in the local place of jury trial, before a summons for the jury to go to Westminster. The people involved were to come to London unless the trial had happened before: in Latin *nisi prius* (unless before). What developed over the centuries was that serious offences – crimes needing an *indictment* – had to be tried before a jury. The less serious offences, summary ones, could be tried by a magistrate. In addition to that, the terms 'felony' and 'misdemeanour' also existed until they were abolished in 1967: a felony was a crime in which guilt would mean a forfeiture of possessions and land, so the offender's children would lose their inheritance. A misdemeanour was a less serious crime.

The justices of assize had a number of powers. First, they had a commission of *oyer and terminer* (to listen and to act) on serious cases such as treason, murder, and any crime which was labelled a felony. They also had to try all people who had been charged and who had been languishing in gaol since their arrest, and they tried cases *nisi prius*.

The assize circuits became established as the Home, Midland, Norfolk, Oxford, Eastern, Western and Northern circuits, and the records for these run from 1558 to either 1864 or 1876, when assizes were reorganised, or to 1971, when the assizes were abolished and crown courts created. From the beginning, the assize circuits covered all counties except Cheshire, Durham, Lancashire and Middlesex, the first three being referred to as the Palatinate Courts. In 1876, some courts moved from one circuit to another.

The result of all this means that a criminal who committed a crime in Leeds, for instance, after 1876, would be tried in Leeds rather than in York, the former seat of an assize for the West Riding. A useful source for checking which assizes were on the circuit at any time between the late eighteenth century and the end of the nineteenth is *The Gentleman's Magazine*, which listed assizes and the names of judges presiding at each one. This journal appeared annually. The assizes were held twice a year from the thirteenth century until they ended in 1971, and these sessions were referred to as spring and winter. A third session could be held at times if the gaols were full – as in times of popular revolt and riots, or activities by gangs.

The assizes were divided into two areas: for civil cases, referred to as 'crown', and criminal cases. Two judges would be on the road, each with a responsibility for one of the two areas of law. In the law reports in *The Times*, these are clearly marked in capitals. For instance, for the Winter Assizes in York in December 1844, we have:

WINTER ASSIZES
NORTHERN CIRCUIT
YORK, DECEMBER 5.
(Before Mr Justice Coleridge)

B

Baby Farming

At Drouet's Asylum in Tooting, babies who were deemed superfluous to requirements were 'farmed out' to solve a problem, and of course this led to significant abuse. This was in the early- to mid-Victorian years when the workhouses and asylums were the repositories of the unwanted, and inmates could include bastard offspring, for example. Babies were burdens on people too busy, amoral or heartless to care. Baby farmers were the solution here. They would take the child, who was unwanted for whatever reason, and take custody of them for payment.

Bartholomew Drouet took in a very large number of children to his asylum, and the Board of Guardians knew of him. Of course, Drouet's service was a very welcome facility in those tough times. But in early 1849 a doctor reported that 160 children were lying sick, many to one bed, at Drouet's place; he blamed the London fog. Then it became apparent that the source of the malaise was cholera – a terrible killer. There were many deaths, a trial for neglect and Drouet was acquitted. Such was the impossible and desperate situation in the 1840s for the unwanted homeless and the rejected in society. Then, later, there was Mrs Dyer.

Amelia Dyer, who became known as the 'Ogress of Reading', had a ballad about her deeds in circulation:

The old baby farmer, the wretched Miss Dyer
At the Old Bailey her wages is paid.
In times long ago, we'd a made a big fire
And roasted so nicely that wicked old jade.

There are pictures of her. With a solemn expression, she stands emotionless for the camera, a large bow around her neck, a thick shawl around her and a fancy head covering. She could be any Victorian mother in the middle of her domestic duties. But she was a killer of the worst kind: she took the lives of babies, simply for the money.

Here was a murderous monster of the first order. Amelia Dyer, in the last years of Victoria's reign, saw the potential in using young children as easy sources of cash. She advertised her services, and these included looking after expectant women, nursing and adopting babies, and any kind of caring that would appeal to those in need. Of course, as a crook she needed a 'front' – a good image. She had married in 1872 and had two children of her own, but she left her husband and began her reign of terror. In 1879 a doctor brought the police to her after one too many deaths among her charges. Dyer was convicted and did a stretch of six months' hard labour. It was not a deterrent.

In an age when there was no real supervision and regulation of social care, exploitation could bring easy money. Killing infants was also a simple matter, with the murderer needing only a pillow and enough strength to press on it. Dyer also knew something of mental hospitals as she had been subject to mental instability for some time. She could smoothly assume the front of a nurse.

Dyer was also a serious drug addict, and this became apparent after she had taken in the child of a governess. The mother wanted a visit; a substitute child was displayed and the governess recognised that it was not her child. After that, Dyer probably pretended to have her mental problems *in extremis*. She could obviously 'perform' when required. She was bound to be a mental patient in an asylum and sure enough that is what happened, but the police were on her track when she went back into her evil business. She had a new identity – 'Mrs Thomas' – and the law crept closer to her. She was charged with murder with her son-in-law as an accessory; the remains of a baby, the daughter of Evelina Marmon, were identified by the mother.

Dyer was placed in Reading Gaol, soon to be the home of Oscar Wilde for a while. She wrote a statement to the authorities in 1896 and exonerated other people who had been accused with her, writing, 'I alone must stand before my Maker'. At the Old Bailey there was just one charge – the murder of Doris Marmon. The defence could only – desperately – offer insanity as a mitigating factor, but that was fruitless.

The verdict was one of the quickest on record, taking just over four minutes. Dyer wrote a confessional narrative while in the condemned cell, and James Billington, one of a family of hangmen who were drawn to that trade, saw her from the trapdoor in June 1896. She could have presented some kind of performance, perhaps a speech lamenting her dark deeds, but she simply said that she had nothing to say.

*Bank of England Job – The American Gang

On a cold autumn day in 1872, Inspector John Shore of Scotland Yard was walking along the Strand in London with Bill Pinkerton, of the famous detective agency that never slept. Shore was a young man in his early twenties and he had started his police career in Bristol before moving to the big city. His rise was meteoric: in a few years not only had he reached the rank of detective sergeant, but he had a nickname: John Blunt. This was because of his direct approach to dealing with people. As for Pinkerton, he was visiting his brother Robert, who was a representative of the agency, based in London and living at the grand Cecil Hotel on the Strand, next to the great Savoy.

As they moved along, chatting about the crime-wave of the day – footpads and very nasty robber gangs preying on late-night theatre-goers and innocent tourists who wandered off the safer sidewalks of the metropolis – Pinkerton's gaze landed on some familiar faces: he saw the brothers George and Austin Bidwell, along with their friend George Macdonnell. The sighting was duly notedby Pinkerton; by this time a certain level of sophisticated detective communication had been established in Britain. In 1842 Queen Victoria had created a force of professional detectives, and the bobbies in uniform had been supplemented by plain-clothes sleuths.

Inspector Shore was given the low-down on the young Americans; George was thirty-three and Austin just two years younger, and they were already confident in their expertise as con-men. George Macdonnell was the youngest in the party, at merely twenty-two years of age at that time. The Bidwells had already become acquainted with the Wall Street culture and George was well connected, his parents being a respected Boston family. His father had financed a business venture for his son, George, and that had failed, so the young man was despatched to Europe, where perhaps Shakespeare's words apply: 'to follow such winds as do blow about the world/further from at home/ where small experience grows'. But then, giving this another spin, we might suspect that Mr Macdonnell senior wanted respite from a son whose brain was ticking 24/7 with questionable schemes for enrichment, often on the wrong side of the law.

Word was circulated across the city, giving a suitable warning that it was likely that some scheme of forgery or fraud was possibly imminent, and that all banks should take special care when dealing with new clients.

However, London was about to be ripped off on a very large scale. The young men seen across the Strand were not only clever and devious criminal minds, but they were also able to transform, to shape-change as adeptly as any tragic actor, and this, combined with skills in forging official documents, was to offer a challenge to the banking system at the very heart of the world's greatest Empire. The spirited young rakes, wrapped in their overcoats that autumn day, were actually more dangerous to the status quo than an outfit armed with guns and knives. They carried the profoundly effective threat of charm on the surface with the ethics of a shark beneath a smooth exterior.

Only four years before Pinkerton's walk with Shore, public executions had been abandoned, and capital offences were reduced to four, but the wind of change was bringing the kinds of threats to security and the established order which work unseen, generated by intellect rather than the force of sheer muscle. The young Americans were to create the kind of mayhem that the new dimensions of 'clever crime' were to bring before the forces of law.

By 1870 there were 30,000 police officers in England and Wales, but the CID was a thing of the future and was not established until 1878. The Special Branch was created in 1884 to deal with security matters. The CID was a response to an increase in 'white-collar' crime, while the Special Branch was intended to deal with Fenian Irish threats to bomb London. Terrorism took place out in the streets, but bank fraud did its work in silence, along business systems and in and out of accounts and credit transactions. In many ways, the new white-collar crimes were more challenging to social stability than bombs, and the American Gang would show, in 1873, that a pillar of the Establishment could be duped and robbed on a massive scale.

Macdonnell had that kind of restlessness that troubles rebels like a pain around an old scar, the kind that nothing but newness, fresh starts, and open roads will ease. It was of the robust intellectual kind: the fidgets were cerebral and the hunger for another kind of challenge was going to gnaw at him all his life, but in 1872 he was young, eager and ambitious. He had no specific aims or objectives, but he would sense the right kind of challenge when it came along, like a prairie dog sniffing the wind. It would have to be something on a grand scale. Morality was never in the reckoning either: the challenge could as easily have been to walk across Siberia as to steal the Mona Lisa.

Macdonnell was tall, hearty and restless; he found standing still to be an impossibility. He breezed through his studies and demonstrated repeatedly his ability to absorb knowledge. Foreign languages he absorbed like a sponge, and the classical ones had settled in his vocabulary from his early youth.

Think of a successful group of crooks, neatly defined by the media as a gang. There will be the 'brains' and the 'muscle' and personnel will include a planner and a doer, with an executive at the very heart of the crew. But the notion is to be organic. Not that Jesse James or Cole Younger would have used that word. More likely their method of ensuring cohesion was a pistol to the temple and a firm threat of using a bullet as a means of executive action. Still, the thinking has always been the same: have all members gel smoothly together and make each guy's expertise a source of both pride and usefulness.

In Britain, when they arrived, gangs usually preferred to agree that desperation was their motive for highway robbery or for property theft. But when the Bidwells and George arrived, London and other British cities were in the grip of a very particular moral panic. Crooks seemed to be more interested in assault and murder than in bank accounts

However, that sighting in 1872 marked an early warning for what was to be crime on a new, global scale, something that was always going to happen in the place where the great first industrial revolution of Europe had occurred. London was the hub of an Empire that ruled the seas and which was represented by continents all coloured pink on the maps. What could have been more perfect for a springboard into white-collar crime at its most impertinent, bold and daring?

The American Gang was ready to carry out a never-before thought of scam on the Old Lady of Threadneedle Street, the Bank of England. In hindsight, Inspector Shore must have wished, from the bottom of his heart, that he and

Pinkerton had crossed the road that day and put a few searching questions to the young Americans.

The Bank of England had been created in the last years of the seventeenth century, and for the first thirty years it operated from premises in Mercer's Hall and then at Grocer's Hall, but the land at Threadneedle Street, at the eastern end of Cheapside and Poultry (two main thoroughfares through lawyers' London, not far from Newgate), was bought in 1724 and the fine building of today was gradually built, with the most impressive section designed and made between 1788 and 1833, the work of the great architect and collector, Sir John Soane.

The Bank, when Austin Bidwell walked into its Western Branch, had suffered a severe crisis in the recent past, and it had tightened up its administration. In 1866, there had been a panic and the Governor at the time, Henry Lancelot Holland, had consulted the economic leaders in Gladstone's government and decided on a massive extension of credit to try to put things right. In the USA, Congress passed the Contraction Act, which gave the Treasury the power to recall a large proportion of the greenbacks issued under Lincoln. In 1866 there were $1.8 billion of the notes in circulation, and in the following year this shrank to $1.3. Then, by 1872, when the Bidwells left her shores, the USA was in recession.

Then, as now, a recession in America affected the rest of the world. Ernest Seyd of the Bank of England went to the States to help with the work of demonetising silver and making gold coins the sole currency. In both Britain and America, fears were based on the consequences of inflation and economic depression. The banks of both nations faced the problem of how to help the economy out of the misery. It has always been the same dilemma: whether to back and extend credit and so back business and create jobs, or to hold everything in and hope that austerity achieves something like stability in the end.

The Old Lady of Threadneedle Street was run by a formidable board of directors. These twenty-four men, in 1872, constituted the movers and shakers of the commercial and cultural world in Britain and beyond. At the centre was Alfred Charles de Rothschild, born in 1842 and at thirty years of age actively involved in the Bank's business. He was a close friend of the Prince of Wales, and he had started work in banking when he was just twenty-one, becoming a director of the bank of England in 1868; he remained in post until 1889.

The records of the meetings of the board of directors through the Victorian years show what the nature of the human element was, and they make it clear that the board had little time for niceties and delay; it helped employees in cases of real distress and personal tragedy, but slackness was not tolerated and staff were constantly checked and observed. When the board met in 1872 it had responsibility not only for Threadneedle Street, but also for fifteen branches. Its appointed agents at these branches were essential to the success of the great smooth-running machine that was the Old Lady, at the hub of British civilisation.

However, within this great immovable symbol of power, with its classical architecture and seemingly infinite resources, there was a human element, and the directors, not long before Austin Bidwell walked through the doors, had faced some glitches in the systems: in May 1872 they were concerned with a problem in the handling of coupons. These were yet another variety of promissory note – a piece of paper stating that a payment will be made on the presentation of the coupon. In May the board had enquired 'into the circumstances attending the loss of 19 coupons amounting to £102 10 shillings'. These came from loans to the Cape of Good Hope and to New Zealand. What happened was that the Bank had a sequence of actions in which coupons were processed, and it was clumsy. On this occasion, a part-time worker ruined the process: 'On the present occasion it appears that Mr Davis, who was appointed pro tempore to assist the ledger clerks' collected a parcel and took it, 'without examination' to the Bill Office.

The result was that 'the committee feel that great laxity must have existed in the system of check or this loss would have been discovered...' In other words, the great Bank was not faultless. It was a warning of what was to come, but clearly the criminal fraternity would be constantly looking for such weaknesses, and this simple and perfunctory note presages the kind of frauds that were to come.

So what was the Western Branch, to which Austin Bidwell came to initiate his criminal plans, and who was the man in charge, on whom all the gang's designs and preparatory work depended for success? Bidwell, in the persona of Mr Warren, entrepreneur, walked into the Branch with the air of a man who knew his own importance, and who had presence. He fully expected that the Bank's man in charge would be equally assured and confident. After all, Britain had a global reputation for being beyond comparison in the professionalism of the men who generated and sustained their invisible exports, and it was invisible exports, such as Lloyd's marine insurance and the flotation of railway companies, which was expanding the Empire and turning the world map red.

Branches were opened, from the late 1820s onwards, largely to increase the bank's control of paper money. Before that date, smaller provincial banks had printed their own notes, and gradually the government had marginalised these through Acts which restricted their expansion. The Bank Charter Act of 1844 stopped all new banks from issuing notes, and any bank which had more than six partners could not issue paper money either. The result was that

Threadneedle Street was the absolute heart of money circulation, along with other methods of transaction such as post bills, bills of exchange and cheques.

The Bank of England opened the Western Branch on 1 October 1855, to work as an ordinary banking house, that is, with practically no accounts relating to the government. There was to be close co-operation of course, between the Old Lady herself in Threadneedle Street and the Western Branch. The latter was situated within the magnificent Uxbridge House in Mayfair. Uxbridge House had been built for Lord Uxbridge in the 1790s, situated around the corner from Bond Street and the Burlington Arcade, still some of the grandest and most stylish shopping areas in London today.

As soon as the Bank of England had been established, back in 1694, the creation of branches was suggested, but things moved very slowly, and it was not until 1826 that the first provincial branches were opened in three towns: Gloucester, Manchester and Swansea. In London itself, there was no branch until the Western one, the only other city bank being the later 1881 branch dealing with the Supreme Court.

In 1855 there was no excitement about the opening of the new branch. *The Times* devoted one sentence to it, announcing that the branch had opened 'under the management of Mr C. Tindal'. But it was a magnificent location for the kind of large-scale commercial transactions it was destined to deal with. A wide stone Doric portico had been built in the 1850s, and then the old dining room was converted into the main office. There was also a large and stylish committee room, and the upper parts, as one report noted, 'will be appropriated to the residences of Captain Tindal R.N., the manager, and Mr Miller, the sub-manager'. The other main conversions from Lord Uxbridge's huge residence involved, as one writer noted, the creation of a 'south-west ante-room… united with the truncated great drawing-room to form a large office with two compartments. In other words, the Western Branch comprised two vast floors of the opulent Georgian building, which was celebrated in an 1855 feature on the opening in the *Illustrated London News*, a typical exercise in relishing yet another part of the great foundation in the city which was in the hub of the British Empire.

Into this impressive new extension of the Old Lady came Colonel Peregrine Francis. His arrival was noted in the Bank's journal records for 23 May 1872:

> It was recommended to the Court of Directors that Colonel Peregrine Madgwick Francis, Agent at the Hull branch, be appointed agent at the Western Branch with a salary of £1,500 a year on the retirement of Mr. Robert Ruthven Lyon…

That was indeed a handsome salary: in the values of 2014, his £1,500 would be around £60,000. Such a man would be exemplary; he would carry massive responsibility and he would have to embody the essential qualities of style and moral probity.

Francis was born on 1 July 1818 and baptised at St Leonard's in Shoreditch, London. The church is immortalised in the rhyme 'Oranges and Lemons' – 'when I grow rich/say the bells of Shoreditch' – and Francis knew London in his childhood and formative years. His father was a wealthy merchant and his home was in Brunswick Place, Marylebone, not far from Regent's Park.

Francis had started his career in banking in East Yorkshire, after his army days. He had been an officer in the army of the East India Company, which had been the major factor in controlling India and regulating all Britain's commercial interests since the beginning of the seventeenth century. He had been trained at the military training school at Addiscombe in Surrey in 1833–34, afterwards going out to India, where he married Emma Thomas in Madras on 22 August 1849. When the Company ceased its control and handed over responsibilities to the Army of India in 1861 he retired and came back to Britain.

When he was recruited for London Francis was based in the city of Hull, the great fishing port on the Humber estuary, with its mass of trawlers and freighters. It was a port facing towards Europe: those escaping religious persecution in Eastern Europe passed through Hull, many on their way across northern England to Liverpool, where they could board a ship bound for New York and new lives as Americans.

There were all kinds of reshufflings of staff across the branches of the Bank of England at the time. Just a few weeks after Francis started, Captain Percy Lempriere, who had been sub-agent with Francis at Hull, was moved to Leeds. He had had the misfortune to lose two of his children to the common killer diseases of the time, typhus and TB. The Bank took a close interest in its employees and was generally humane and considerate in its attitudes to their domestic circumstances. After the relocation of staff, Colonel Peregrine Francis, by 1872 the father of six children (so he would need that large salary), was obviously someone who impressed his superiors at Head Office in London.

Colonel Francis and Captain Lempriere were military men. It was the policy at that time to place ex-officers in many important professional positions: they manned the prisons, led the police force and found new careers in all types of public administration. At Northallerton prison in the north of England, for instance, the Governor had been one of the famous officers of the 'six hundred' in the Charge of the Light Brigade in the battle of Balaclava in 1854, during the Crimean War.

It was the policy of the Bank to employ as their branch agents men who had two essential qualities: local knowledge and sound business knowledge. The latter quality comprised both fiscal knowledge and a strong ethical trait in their character. Being an employee of the Old Lady meant having moral rectitude and displaying the right kind of behaviour at all times. The records of the Court of Directors show a continual monitoring of any staff, from clerks to senior managers, who might be falling short of the mark. Colonel Francis, although he had been based in Hull, had the right moral sense, being an army man, and he knew London. It would have been hard to find an army officer at the time who did not know London. As memoirs of senior officers often show, the general trajectory of the training arc they had was one in which acquaintance with London clubs and theatres was *de rigueur*.

Francis, by the time of Bidwell's arrival, had been running the branch for only four months, but he was every inch the sophisticated, cultured type required by that responsible post: he was articulate, charming yet precise; he was a good listener, and he clearly had the skill of close observation and knowledge of the world so essential in transactions involving large sums of money. He had seen service in India earlier in life, and was a practical man as well as a man of affairs. But in one sense, the entire success and viability of the Bank depended on knowing the ways of officials and businessmen.

In mid-1872, just as Peregrine Francis was settling in at his new desk, and no doubt taking in the wonderful grandeur of his daily surroundings, which contrasted sharply with his much smaller and more workaday Hull office, there was action being taken to control and regulate the discounting of bills of exchange. These documents and transactions were at the very hub of the commercial world around the Bank. These bills are defined in the legislation as 'An unconditional order in writing addressed by one person to another, signed by the person giving it, requesting the person to whom it is addressed to pay at some fixed or determinable future time a fixed sum in money to or to the order of a specified person or bearer'. In other words, it operated like a cheque, but it normally had a defined period in which it had to be used, and the point is that it allowed time for the issuing person to gather cash or assets, or alternatively, it confirmed his credit standing with the bank concerned.

The bill of exchange therefore committed the bank to part with the sums of money accrued as the bills were taken at the cashiers' counters. Why did the banks do this? The answer is, quite simply, profit. They charged a discount – a fee – for the transaction, and it was the source of considerable profit. During the middle months of 1872, when Francis was the new man at the Western Branch, the Court of Directors minuted a sequence of reductions in the percentages of discounts on such bills. In early May, the records noted: 'Amended… that the minimum rate of discount on bills not having more than 95 days to run be raised from 4 to 5 per cent'. A bill of one thousand pounds would earn them £50 – a large sum in the 1870s. That was for a bill with a short time in which cash had to be paid on it. But later that year, for bills with

95 days to run (which the Bank preferred of course) the discount rate was lowered in stages down to 3%. But a bill with less than 95 days had the rate increased to 6% by July of 1872.

All this meant that, as Colonel Francis was meeting and interviewing customers, the directors at headquarters were working out profits; yet they were doing much more. They were aware that bills of exchange needed to be carefully supervised and checked. There was always a threat. That vulnerability to fraud may be seen in the accounts presented to the Court from their solicitors, Freshfields, which is today an international law firm with 2,400 lawyers around the globe. When they presented their bills for services rendered in August 1872, it included this item:

Charges in connection with the measures taken to detect and punish forgeries
Upon the Bank   £14.13.2

In fact, the cost to the Bank for legal services in the short period of six months in that year was over £380. Peace of mind is expensive, as the value of that sum today is around £30,000.

In 1872, then, the great bank at the centre of the British Empire was full of confidence, enjoying almost a complete monopoly on credit in the larger, most prominent areas of the world markets it dealt with, and its Board of Directors, through their regular court meetings, checked and regulated everything that happened, almost down to the last paper-clip in the smallest office. Yet beneath this apparent assurance and self-esteem, there was that worm in the apple, the possibility of there being a criminal smart enough to exploit the Bank's systems and protocols.

The heart of the fraud plan was then put into action. Austin, as Warren, visited Francis to tell him that he would be often in Birmingham overseeing his Pullman project. This was to set up the credibility of that business in Francis's mind. Austin asked if his bills would still be discounted, and Francis replied that they would be if they were 'of the very best paper'. It is incredible from today's perspective to see how lax the system was then, relying on the personalities of the people involved. It was a system open to exploitation by the best con-men on the scene.

What happened next was that from Birmingham, 'Mr Warren' sent registered packages to Francis and a pack of bills drawn from well-known financial houses in Europe was discounted by Francis – a sum totalling over £4,000. As this was happening, George was setting up another 'business' in the name of Horton, and Noyes was introduced to the people who mattered as Horton's clerk. Everything was set up and what was needed then was a bill from a really top-notch institution. What happened was so bold and ambitious that it was incredible even in its conception. George asked Austin to go to Paris and secure a bill of exchange from the Rothschilds.

In this astonishing story, there is nothing quite as dramatic and fortuitous as the adventure that Austin had in France. Fate stepped in and ensured his assignment was destined to succeed. He was involved in a train crash. He recalled later that he saw the expedition as futile: 'I expect an expense of a thousand dollars, a delay of two weeks, and nothing accomplished at the end'. How wrong he was. As he slept, his carriage was jolted and thrown onto an embankment; he had been severely cut by glass and as he woke up he became aware that his legs were trapped by the collapsed carriage roof. As he struggled to be free, the door fell on him. He was taken for medical help and as he lay recovering at the nearby station he saw a notice on the wall listing forbidden railway behaviour. The name appended was Baron Alphonse de Rothschild, president of the railway.

This was an amazing stroke of good luck in the guise of a misfortune. Brother George had made notes for him in a notebook and Austin checked the facts: in 1846 the Rothschilds had opened the north-south *Chemin de Fer*. Austin seized the moment and, as he was well enough, he went to the Maison Rothschild in Paris and spoke to the manager, Gatley. He told the story of the rail disaster and when reparation was offered he asked for a three-month bill for £4,500. At first he was refused, but after a highly emotional performance, he was asked to return later. Unbelievably, Austin, as Warren, spoke to the Baron himself later that day. After that meeting, he set off home with a bill for over one hundred thousand francs in his pocket, signed by Alphonse de Rothschild.

Everything was now in place and bills were presented, including the Rothschild one. George knew that they had a month before the fraud was discovered, so they all had to think of a quick escape. But there had been emotional entanglements, notably by George. It became imperative that they destroy all their paper evidence and then go their separate ways, planning to meet in America later. The frauds were accelerating and even duplicate bills were presented, so the profits were mounting up. It was too tempting to not destroy the last few forged bills, and that was to be their downfall.

The last forged bills were posted from Birmingham in February 1873. The total profits from forgery then totalled £100,000. But it was all about to crumble, as Colonel Francis was told by his clerk that two 'Warren' bills had no date of issue. It was essential to check this with the issuers, Blydensteins, so a bank messenger was sent to check out the issue date. There was no date and no record, so the terrible word 'forgery' was then in Colonel Francis's mind and he had to act quickly. He went personally to the Bank of England in

Threadneedle Street to report what had happened. Mr May, Chief Cashier at the Bank, checked the Warren file and things began to become clear. Would the process of enquiry, and then the police intervention, happen in time to catch the crooks? Francis must have felt the resonance in his head of those fatal words he had spoken when giving Bidwell access to funds and credit status: 'You are now a client of the Bank – you may deposit as much as you like!' Of all the characters in this incredible story, Colonel Peregrine Francis comes across as one of the most tragically duped. If only he had pressed 'Warren' to tell him more of the details of his Pullman scheme, the fraud might never have been possible. He must have had many sleepless nights since that discovery of the undated bill.

The first man to be apprehended was Noyes, posing as the clerk to Mr Horton. He was to be held without charge as the first detectives on the case started their chase for 'Mr Warren'. The City Police moved into action; the Commissioner himself appeared on the scene as Noyes was taken to a cell. The hunt for Warren/Bidwell was then top priority at the Mansion House and at Old Jewry. *The Times* summed up the situation well: 'It was discovered on Saturday that bills to an enormous amount had been forged upon all the principal houses in the City of London and that these bills have been discounted by the Bank of England...' George Bidwell planned to escape with his lady friend, Nellie, and they arranged to meet to catch the night train at Paddington. But the detectives were closing in and he became aware of that. The detectives had also traced Macdonnell to St James Place where he had his rooms. Macdonnell was on his way to Paris, and he was the member of the gang who was to test the police force to the limit.

Bidwell slipped past Sergeant Smith, the man appointed to watch for him after Nellie was taken into custody. He managed to get himself to Holyhead and then on the ferry to Dublin and his pursuit by detectives was to be a narrative as exciting as a Hollywood thriller. He went to Cork, and then north again to Belfast, where he could cross to Scotland. He was thinking of locations that would be least likely in the minds of the pursuing police.

At one point in his escapades, at the beautiful Irish town of Lismore, George engaged in a long drinking session with the express intention of making the cabman who had helped him so intoxicated that he would not be able to answer police questions. In that same Lismore hotel, he knew that he had been recognised by a travelling lawyer, and he slipped out of the place in the early hours, knowing that the man was alerting the local police to his presence. He managed to hire a cab and head north.

The alert was out all across Britain and Bidwell's description was everywhere. In Edinburgh, where he finally stopped to take stock of the situation, he posed as a Frenchman, Monsieur Coutant, and as he settled into his lodgings, across the seas, Macdonnell was arrested on board the SS *Thuringia*. He had tried to bribe a New York detective in one last desperate attempt to escape by virtue of his wits, but failed.

George Bidwell was hiding out in a working-class area of Edinburgh in Nicholson Street. He made a few mistakes that aroused suspicion, mainly ordering the London papers every day. A local bank engaged the services of a private detective, James McKelvie, who traced and observed George. The detective got his man after a chase through the back streets and a last desperate attempt by George to elude them.

The City police had brought out all their resources from the very beginning of the hunt. As Ann Huxley wrote in her account of the story:

> The headquarters at Old Jewry were almost deserted. The manhunt for the forgers had depleted the small force of personnel. The City of London police numbered 780 men... And it was vital to the pride of the City police that the forgers should be found, and quickly. It is hard not to underestimate the importance to the City men of the resolution of this case; their rivalry with the Peelers was legendary and there was always a sense of inferiority, often down to sheer lack of manpower and resources when compared to their neighbouring colleagues.

But the drama in this amazing story was still not ended. Even as they languished in Newgate, the Bidwells and Macdonnell still tried to work their escape. They bribed a warder named Norton and he gathered some more corrupt allies from the prison staff. The plan was to have the Bidwells' brother John come across from America to organise an escape via a ship at Tilbury. There were to be guns involved and a rush out of the courtroom at the Old Bailey by the whole gang. But the City police were taking no chances. It is in this last act of the drama that the detective force is at its most impressive. John Bidwell was tailed by an officer as he went to an omnibus and on that journey the officer saw Bidwell meet and converse with the Newgate warder, Norton. It was clear that an escape plan was in process. The City officers were well prepared when the court resumed.

All it took was a nod – from George to brother John – and the police thwarted everything. Security in court the next day was at the highest level. There was a solid body of men acting as a police escort around the gang, and earlier eight armed policemen had trapped and arrested the warders. Chief Superintendent Bowman was well in control. Two other warders had been shadowed going to John Bidwell's home, so intelligence was full and accurate. There was to be no escape.

As was reported at the time, 'The evidence for the prosecution was so conclusive that the counsel both for Macdonnell and for George Bidwell declined to address the jury...' The summarising comment from the reporter at *The Times* was 'Such is generally the end of all vast schemes of fraud. They need so long a strain of attention, that, sooner or later some slight blunder is nearly sure to be committed by which the whole design is frustrated.'

Perhaps the most telling detail at the trial was the fact that Macdonnell translated the words of the proceedings into Greek as he sat in the dock. That men of such intellect could be criminal minds was a sign of the times, and was something that Conan-Doyle would bear in mind in the creation of his arch-villain, Moriarty. Crimes in which the police were pitted against such fine minds were to be a feature of the whole process of crime investigation from that time onwards, and led to the creation of specialised police departments within the force.

But the tale of the Bidwell gang does not end there. After the savage sentence of penal servitude for life was handed down, there was a clamour for clemency. These were young men, and they had not committed a violent crime, and for a crime against property rather than against the person to have such a draconian sentence attached was seen as too extreme to be allowed by some factions in society. However, the gang had committed the most outrageous fraud imaginable and had struck at the very heart of the British financial establishment. From the point of view of the City police, it had been a crime of huge proportions right at the centre of their 'patch' and was a source of profound embarrassment.

It was George Bidwell who stole the limelight again, at least as far as the media were concerned, and in terms of how this truly remarkable story survived and was retold through time. This was because he refused to do any labour at all after his arrival in Dartmoor. He said that he would not do one day's work for the Queen; a report of 1881 assessed his situation: 'Long disuse of his legs had reduced him almost to a cripple. The muscles were extremely wasted, both hip and knee joints were contracted... so that he lay doubled up in a bundle.' Due to extreme ill health, he was released in 1881.

The Bidwell gang had not only brought off the greatest forgery in the chronicles of crime; but they had also been able to infiltrate a highly complex financial structure of relationships and business networks and exploit them for criminal activity and massive profit. Yet they had not been astute enough to consider certain consequences of a practical nature, such as the necessity of turning notes into coinage before the frauds were discovered and note serial numbers traced; nor had they thought about the practicalities of handling and carrying such heavy weights of coins. This failure had been part of their downfall.

*Baretti and Dr Johnson

Samuel Johnson was a humane, warm and loyal man; he made friends easily, and had a wide circle of literary and political friends, as well as ordinary working folk. If these friends ever needed his help, he was always there for them. When his Italian co-author, Baretti, was accused of a serious crime, Johnson went to his aid.

In 1769, Johnson had been away in Brighton, where he had met the Corsican patriot Pasquale Paoli, but he was soon to hear what had happened to his friend Baretti. The Italian was walking back to Soho when he was stopped by a prostitute, and as he rebuffed her, she grabbed his testicles and Baretti instinctively turned to strike her. This attack was seen by three roughs who were loitering nearby and they set about him; the woman had screamed and so they assumed Baretti was assaulting her, so they pursued him. In self-defence, surrounded by what must have seemed like a gang intent on doing him serious harm, Baretti took out his knife, and in the struggle the blade stabbed one of the men and he died of the wounds.

The facts were not clear. The trial transcripts suggest that witnesses were unsure of the basic events; a witness, Elizabeth Ward, gave an account that made Baretti seem very aggressive, saying that she was sitting with the girl who accosted him and that he hit her (Ward) with 'a double fist'. But the barrister questioning her suggested that she had spoken of retaliating by being 'clove down with a patten' – meaning that he should be struck with a wooden over-shoe. She saw Baretti being mobbed by the young men but did not see him draw the knife. This was a crucially important testimony.

The court tried to establish whether or not Ward knew the young men who were after Baretti's blood, and she only knew one, who had kissed her the previous night. This all happened around the Haymarket, a place notorious for gatherings of 'women of the night' and for all kinds of sexual liaisons. Ward followed the gang to see what they might do, and she told the court that after that, she saw the knife drawn, describing the alleged offence in these words, accounting for Baretti's actions: 'He ran quite fast, about eight or nine doors up Panton Street, the way where he ran into the house, only the house was farther on; then I saw his head over their shoulders, turn back. This was when he was gone eight or nine doors up. They all kept close to him. I believe it was then the deceased was stabbed'.

In the affray, Baretti had stabbed a man called Morgan, who had been the aggressor, with his friends to help. A man called Clark gave confused testimony.

Another bystander, called Patman, joined the affray. He had been stabbed and panicked; he felt the blood run down his face. Morgan ran after a man who by that time was clearly desperately afraid. The self-defence approach to the events was looking likely then. The other man was John Clark, who seems to have held back and let the other two do the most active shoving and grabbing at the Italian. Naturally, both he and Patman claimed that their 'shoving' had been 'light.' But it became clear in the questioning in court that Clark had only a vague idea about what actually happened, and his statements were confused and contradictory. The counsel reminded him that 'the jury are to depend upon something when a man's life is at stake. Have you not declared upon oath that Morgan was the first that said he was stabbed?' Clark's answer contradicted what he had previously told the coroner.

The constable who was called and who took Baretti along to the magistrate at Bow Street, John Fielding, gave a dramatic account of the arrest: 'I immediately sprang to him, seized him by the collar and took the knife and knocked it against a tea-chest to force it in; it was not quite in, and bent the point of it as it is now'. The fruit knives in use then had a short blade, around three inches, and folded like a pen-knife. Clearly, they had to have a sharp blade to peel an apple, so they could do serious harm. The constable ascertained that Baretti was 'a gentleman, and secretary to the Royal Academy and so they went quietly to Bow Street'.

The witness from the hospital where Morgan was treated gave information which seemed to refer to a frenzy rather than a stroke in self-defence, saying that there were three wounds: 'The wound he received in his abdomen was the occasion of his death'. Then the surgeon did some of his own detective work, reporting that Clark was indeed an associate of the women who had been slapped. Clark gave the surgeon two stories, and the surgeon made sure that everyone present heard that fact.

In court, Baretti was allowed to give his own account of the facts of that night. Earlier in the day he had gone to a coffee house to see if there was any mail for him, after working on his English-Italian dictionary. He set off back to the club in Soho where the Royal Academicians met, and he described his meeting with the woman: 'There was a woman eight or ten yards from the corner of Panton Street, and she clapped her hands with such violence about my private parts, that it gave me great pain. This I instantly resented, by giving her a blow on the hand.' The woman, seeing he was a foreigner, swore at him, and then a man struck him forcefully. There was then a chase, and as Baretti said, 'A great number of people surrounded me presently, many beating me and all damning me on all sides… I could plainly see that my assailants wanted to throw me into a puddle so I cried out murder.'

Baretti begged to be taken to Sir John Fielding, and then Sir Joshua Reynolds and other men went to him there, to help and advise. Injuries done to him were observed and noted. He was arrested and detained in Newgate. He could have been tried by people of his own country, but declined, as he told the court: 'I chose to be tried by a jury of this country; for if my honour is not saved, I cannot much wish for the preservation of my life.' Then a key witness told something of what was surely the truth, in complete contrast to the tale told by the three men earlier in court. This was Ann Thomas, and she saw 'a crowd of people' at the end of a street by the Haymarket, and she saw 'a gentleman run from among them on the side of the way I was… they all ran after him, they were all in a great bustle: I saw but one woman among them…' She made it quite clear that Baretti was running in fear of his life.

When Peter Molini gave an account of Baretti's injuries after that night's violence, the court was in no doubt that Baretti must have acted while in extreme fear, desperate for self-preservation. Molini said, 'As he was complaining of pain in his body, I asked him to strip, that we might see. In looking on his back, I observed a bruise under one shoulder, on the left side, and one a little lower… I also saw swelling on his right cheek. Two of the bruises were very visible. His jaw was swelled…'

All that remained was to present the court with character witnesses, and so Dr Johnson, along with other notable men of the time, attended the Old Bailey to have his say. James Boswell, in his famous *Life of Johnson*, explains: 'Never did such a constellation of genius enlighten the awful Sessions House, emphatically called Justice Hall; Mr Burke, Mr Garrick, Mr Beauclerk and Dr Johnson; and undoubtedly their favourable testimony had due weight with the court and jury.' Boswell adds that Johnson gave his evidence 'in a slow, deliberate and distinct manner, which was uncommonly impressive.' Thanks to the wonder of the internet and the easy availability of the Old Bailey Sessions papers online, we can read those impressive words today, imagining the 'Great Cham' of literature speaking to the court. After Reynolds and Beauclerk had spoken, Johnson's interchange with the lawyer was as follows:

Dr. Johnson: I believe I began to be acquainted with Mr Baretti about the year 53 or 54. I have been intimate with him. He is a man of literature, a very studious man, a man of great diligence. He gets his living by study. I have no reason to think he was ever disordered by liquor in his life. A man that I never knew to be otherwise than peaceable, and a man that I take to be rather timorous.

Q: Was he addicted to pick up women in the street?

Johnson: I never knew that he was

Q: How is he as to his eye-sight?

Johnson: He does not see me now, nor I do not see him. I do not believe he could be capable of assaulting anybody in the street, without great provocation.

Baretti could not have had a better speaker on his behalf: Johnson was always interested in law, and had an extensive knowledge of civil law, as well as a great deal of common sense regarding the practical workings of a trial. The Italian scholar was acquitted of the charges of murder and manslaughter and a verdict of self-defence was returned. But he had tasted the miseries of Newgate and he had a nasty side to his character. As Mrs Thrale, wife of his patron, said in a letter in 1784, 'Yesterday received a letter from Mr Baretti, full of the most flagrant and bitter insults concerning my late marriage with Mr Piozzi... he accuses me of murder and fornication in the grossest terms, such as I believe have ever been used, even to his old companions in Newgate.'

Yet the friendship of Baretti and Johnson was close and often full of fun, as at one point on a journey to France, the two men had a sprint, and Johnson won. Baretti died on 5 May 1789, and Mrs Thrale wrote 'He was a manly character at worst, and died as he had lived, less like a Christian than a philosopher, refusing all spiritual or corporeal assistance... He paid his debts, called in some singular acquaintance, told him he was dying... bid him write his brothers that he was dead, and gently desired a woman who waited to leave him alone.' She was told that Baretti's papers and manuscripts were burnt by his executors. But we do have his books, notably *The Italian Library* of 1747 and *Lettere Famigliari*, a book of travels. His collected works were published in Milan in 1838. However, he also has the dubious distinction of appearing as a chapter in the classic work of criminal tales, *The Newgate Calendar*, in which the comment on his trial is that 'Those who would consult their own safety should avoid giving offence to others in the street. The casual passenger has, at least, a right to pass unmolested; and he or she that would insult him cannot deserve pity, whatever consequences may follow.'

The year before the trial, Johnson had praised Baretti to Boswell, and his words give us no doubt that Johnson's testimony for his friend was genuine and honest. He said of Baretti: 'His account of Italy is a very entertaining book, and sir I know no man who carries his head higher in conversation than Baretti. There are strong powers in his mind. He has not, indeed, many hooks, but with what hooks he had, he grapples firmly.' He had spoken slowly and carefully in court in order to have no doubt or ambiguity in the reception of his words by the jury. Surely, this was a hint relating to Johnson's potential as a man of law, had his career taken a different path.

Bentley, Derek (1933–1953)

This is known as the 'Let him have it' murder in some quarters, and that phrase could fruitfully be used in any context to illustrate the perils of ambiguity in our language. Was the order something that suggested 'give him the gun', or was it an instruction to kill? The title of John Parris' 1953 book, *Scapegoat*, says it all. In Croydon, in 1952, sixteen-year-old Christopher Craig and his friend, nineteen-year-old Derek Bentley, committed an armed robbery that went wrong: a police officer was shot and killed, and whatever the truth of the events, Craig was too young to face the noose, if indeed it was even he who fired the gun.

John Parris shows that there was very likely a mix of bias and questionable evidence in the case. Derek Bentley was only nineteen; there was what might be called a 'chapter of accidents' in the robbery. The police account was that the dead man, Sydney Miles, was one of a group of officers who had arrived at the scene of the robbery (Barlow and Parker's warehouse) and a policeman called Fairfax had confronted the lads; on the roof he arrested Bentley, who said 'Let him have it, Chris,' and Fairfax was wounded in the shoulder. After that, Miles emerged from a room and Craig shot him in the head.

Both robbers were culpable for the murder, though it seems clear that Craig committed murder. The jury found them both guilty but recommended mercy for Bentley, who it was reported had the mental age of an eleven-year-old following an injury. It had no effect: he was hanged on 28 January 1953, whilst Craig was ordered to be detained at Her Majesty's Pleasure. After years of campaigning by Bentley's family, he was granted a royal pardon in 1998 (after forty years) because aspects of diminished responsibility ten been put aside. Christopher Craig, who had been released after serving 10 years in prison, issued a statement, saying, 'his innocence has now been proved'.

Bill's O'Jacks Murders

This has to be one of the top twenty unsolved British murder cases in the chronicle of serious crime. The date is 1832 and the location is Saddleworth Moor, later to be infamous for not only another unsolved case in 1902, but also for the Moors Murders. The graveyard at Saddleworth Church gives basic information about the horrendous killings in this dark tale: 'Those now who talk of the far-famed Greenfield Hills/will think of Bill o' Jack's and Tom o' Bill's.' The fame came from an attack alleged to have been perpetrated by five men, and these rogues left old eighty-four-year-old Bill and his son Tom Bradbury dying from major traumatic wounds to their heads and bodies.

The scene was the Moorcock Inn, and its position out in the wilds of the Yorkshire/Lancashire border at that time was of great interest to all enquiries and investigations.

By the time Bill's young grand-daughter arrived on the scene, the killers had fled. There was gore everywhere: up the walls, on the floor, furniture and on all available surfaces, so extreme had the struggle been. Tom Bradbury was a young, very strong man; he put up a determined fight.

There are three possible groups from which suspects might be drawn: Irish workers nearby; a family of reprobates also known as Bradbury, and some of the lowest underclass of workers known as 'burnplatters'. There are arguments in favour of any of these. But perhaps over-riding this is the plain fact that Red Bradbury had to walk to stand before the magistrates at Pontefract the day after the murders, and Tom Bradbury was to speak against him. That seems to be the most productive motive.

This is further supported by the curious fact that after a very early start in order to walk all the way to Pontefract, Red Bradbury seemed to know all about the crime scene at the inn. One would have to be receptive to the notion that he should be the main suspect.

The case has often been in the news and in crime history publications. At the centenary date, in 1932, G.H. Whittaker published a booklet which included a short play on the story; then, in 1959, the Saddleworth History Club set to work on the case. The *Yorkshire Post* described the outcome, after more than a hundred people turned out for the 'inquest' set up, along with a 'jury':

> It was a strange and fearful sight. The room was blacked out. Five candles and a couple of oil lamps provided the only light... When a dog started howling in the yard outside, the time seemed ripe for anything.

By the time there was a need for a verdict, it was all too frustratingly familiar: 'When the jury returned in half an hour the foreman announced a unanimous verdict: "murder by a person or persons unknown" – the same as that returned by an inquest jury 127 years ago'.

Blackout Ripper, The

If a serial killer wished for the ideal patch for his deadly work, he would very likely imagine a landscape rather like London in the Blitz of the Second World War. The man who became known as 'The Wartime Ripper' or 'The Blackout Ripper' took advantage of such an environment. We have to imagine the kind of mental atmosphere in which life is so tenuous that death may await the individual at any time. This was the case roughly between 1940 and 1944 during the period in which Nazi bombers came over from Germany in huge numbers, intent on destroying England's capital city.

This situation meant that underground locations in particular, along with locations where bombs had created a landscape in which crimes could be undertaken in what sociologists used to call 'defensible space.' In other words, this is an instance of crime done in the dark or half-light, in corners, beneath cover and in any place where a murder will be undisturbed.

Streets were blacked out of course, as air-raid patrols biked around streets telling people to 'put out that light' so that the bombers could see only pitch black. Then, within just five days in early 1942, six women were attacked in London, and four of them died. They were mutilated, prompting readers of the daily papers to think there was another 'Ripper' at large. But top detectives were on the track of the killer; the famous fingerprint expert, Fred Cherrill, was one of them.

The first victim was found in an air-raid shelter in Marylebone. She had probably been robbed, as her handbag was on the floor and its contents spread around; she had been strangled. The next day the body of Evelyn Oatley was found in Soho, again, strangling was the modus operandi. Worse was to come, with two killings in the same day, and both had been, as early commentators supposed, working as prostitutes. The second woman had been strangled with a scarf and also cut and wounded. But the next attack was thwarted, and the police had a lead; a belt and a gas mask were left at the scene, and soon the police were to get their man: Gordon Cummins, an RAF officer cadet. His prints matched some taken by Cherrill and his experts. The killer was doomed.

Cummins was hanged at Wandsworth in April, 1942, by Albert Pierrepoint and Harry Kirk. The trial had only lasted two days and it took the jury only thirty minutes to decide on a guilty verdict. This was in spite of what seemed like a solid alibi for three of the deaths, but he was condemned for the murder of Evelyn Oatley due to the fingerprint evidence, as by this time the presentation of prints in evidence was notably sophisticated and accurate.

Blazing Car Mysteries – Solved and Unsolved

Alfred Rouse (1894-1931) was very fond of women. In fact he had affairs with dozens of them, and married two, wedding the second while still married to the first. He was a travelling salesman and his lifestyle afforded him a girl in every town. He was clearly a criminal with a motive of fun and kicks, delighting in his work. However, matters escalated when mothers of his illegitimate children expected marriage and he faced several impending child support order cases. He was in a very tight spot and by 1930 he had a plan. In November of that year, the day after Bonfire Night, he was seen walking on a road in Northamptonshire by two men in a car, and he had called out, 'It looks like someone is having a bonfire up there!'

In fact, the blaze was his car, and inside was a poor victim who was soon to be a very charred corpse. Unfortunately for Rouse, the car's number plate survived, and he was tracked down; at his home in Finchley, his wife could not tell them where her husband would be. When he was eventually located and questioned, Rouse had a yarn to tell: he had given a lift to a man, and then Rouse had stopped the car so he could urinate. The passenger, he claimed, had accidentally set fire to a canister and that was the explanation.

Rouse was charged with murder after his philandering life across the country was revealed. Desperation had led to his wish to 'disappear' and live under a new identity, planning to stage the burned corpse as his own. It had all gone sadly wrong. Forensics established that he had planned the murder, and he was hanged in March 1931.

In contrast, just two months after the Rouse incident, there was another blazing car story and this has remained a mystery to this day. Evelyn Foster was found seriously injured and burned, near a car, by a bus conductor on the Jedburgh to Newcastle road. The tale told was that a man had attacked and raped her, but questions were asked about other possibilities.

She was dying when she managed to give a description of the assailant. He was short, young, slim and wore a bowler hat. He had a local accent. A full account of her last day was given – driving a new car belonging to her father, she had given people a lift and then started driving home. She made the fatal mistake of giving a stranger a lift. The man had hit her, pushed her onto the back seat and then driven the car to an isolated location.

The man had tried to set fire to the car and then left, being sure that she would perish. Evelyn had not been robbed: her handbag was close by, with some cash inside. Speculation has grown concerning the details of the murder, and there have even been suggestions that this had all been an attempt to destroy the car in order to gain insurance payments.

There was even a line of thought saying the death was suicide, and the coroner spoke about that. Forensics on the bone burning patterns opened up the insurance theory, as it was said that the positioning of those burns was consistent with Evelyn standing on the mudguard in order to throw the petrol across into the car. But in the end at the inquest it was the too common verdict of 'wilful murder by person or persons unknown.'

Blood, Colonel Thomas (1618–1680)

In the annals of crime, anywhere in the world, one would be hard pressed to find a more adventurous, bold and enterprising rogue than Colonel Thomas Blood. In March 1671, disguised in the habiliments of a parson, and with some accomplices, he went to the Tower of London. He and his gang were there to do the impossible: to steal the Crown Jewels. Blood had a mallet and he clouted the guard, Edwards, with whom he had previously become friendly as part of his plot, and with that, then they set about the jewels, and soon found a problem: the sceptre was too long to be held under cover and so they set about cutting it in half. It just could not be done, and in their panic they dropped it, taking the famous orb and the special crown alone.

Insufficient planning was their shortcoming, however, and they were seized at the gate, where they knocked out a guard with a mallet, which indicated their rashness. The offence was unthinkable. They were bound for a long and agonizing death at the hands of expert torturers. That would be the general opinion. But the King, Charles II, decided on a pardon, which seemed senseless. What could his motive be? To make matters worse, Blood was given land in Ireland, so that seemed like a reward. Had the King arranged the whole heist, in order to raise funds? It was unthinkable. Either way, Blood was the last person to attempt the theft; no other person has since tried to copy his crime.

Bloody Assizes, The

The key player here in this 1685 event held at Winchester is Judge Jeffreys. He was a judge when judges were supposed to be hard on the king's enemies. Christopher Hibbert explains the man in terms of judges in general: 'Most of them considered it their duty to browbeat everyone except the prosecuting counsel; and Jeffreys, after all, was made Lord Chancellor by the king when he returned to London ...'

Jeffreys was born in Wales, and was appointed to the bar in 1668; in 1685 he was made the first Baron of Wem. In that year there took place one of the most important battles on English soil – at Sedgemoor. The Duke of Monmouth, a protestant son of Charles II, gathered an army ready to march on London and stage a coup, to kick out the Catholic regime. The royal forces were decided victors and Monmouth's forces were now open to all kinds of abuse, being in effect an army of traitors. Enter Judge George Jeffreys.

Macaulay, the Victorian historian, in his great history of England, explained the situation:

> At every spot where two roads meet, on every green of every village which had furnished Monmouth with soldiers, ironed corpses clattering in the wind, or heads and quarters stuck on poles, poisoned the air, and made the traveller sick with horror.

Here were the results of the Bloody Assizes. But of course the word 'assize' implies that there were trials, and that they should be trials in accordance with the right and proper legal process. But there had been no such thing. In Somerset, the staggering figure of 253 people were hanged, drawn and quartered. The King initially promoted Jeffreys to Lord Chancellor, but the judge's ultimate fate was as a guest of the Tower of London, where he died.

*Boot Fetishist or Not?

Louie Gomersal was born in either 1895 or 1896, on 11 January. The records of her disagree on this. But we do know that her father was a woollen weaver called Smith, and her mother was born Annie Clark. They lived in Gawthorpe, close to Wakefield. Louie was very small, the fourth of five children. She might have been tiny, but she was spirited - clearly quite a handful.

In her teens her criminal career began, when she appeared before the magistrates at Dewsbury for theft. A year later she was in court again, and this time her destination was Borstal. In 1912, the Borstal institutions were quite new, appearing in political debate at about the time of Louie's birth, when the idea was explained as a 'halfway-house between the prison and the reformatory.' In 1908 the Borstal notion came into being as an actual statutory existence in the Prevention of Crime Act. Young Louie would have found the regime tough and Spartan of course, but it didn't deter her from further criminal adventures.

She moved to Leeds during the First World War and joined the ranks of the street prostitutes, living in extreme poverty. In the square mile around The Calls, Mabgate and Water Lane, radiating out from Leeds Bridge and into the area now encompassing the market and the area behind the Corn Exchange, the street workers plied their trade.

Richard Hoggart, writing on the Hunslet area in his classic account of working-class culture, *The Uses of Literacy* (1957), explains the contemporary attitudes to being 'on the game.' He wrote, 'A friend of mine from a nearby street was an only child and seemed to have no father... It was only in my teens that I discovered that his mother was a prostitute... most nodded at or talked to her as to anyone else... "After all, she's got to live" they used to say...'

What cannot be underestimated is the degree of deprivation poverty entailed. This author's mother was born a short distance away from the man who would be Louie's next householder-partner, Arty Calvert, in Hunslet, in 1928. She had memories of her family living on such sources of cash as the pawnbroker, and of course with the small pension which had been instituted back in 1909. Destitution and the workhouse were the fate of those who could not scrape together enough money to live on. In my childhood, growing up in the 1950s, there was still the fearful reference to 'the workhouse' as if such a place was an adjunct of hell.

From the early 1920s however, Louie Gomersal, now married, became Mrs Louise Jackson, and was working as a housekeeper at Mercy Street, near Wellington Lane in the city centre. This was to be her first step into a life which was founded on a sequence of jobs taken, sometimes simply for survival and at other times, for the sheer crazy joy of being someone else. What began in that first employment was a taste of the fun involved in stepping into another's shoes, and she has been branded 'the shoe fetishist' in the popular literature of crime, after stealing her victim's boots, as well as their valuables.

The work of a housekeeper then was something that made transparent the gap in class and status of owner and skivvy, but the title 'housekeeper' does add a perspective of dignity: something well above the description of 'cleaner' or 'maid.' Mercy Street was a red-brick terrace of the two-up and two-down variety, with no garden at all, neither at the front or the rear. There was simply a tiny walled front just a few feet square. Pictures of the street at the time show the stereotypical working-class dwelling with washing on the line across the narrow street.

As housekeeper to Mr Frobisher in Mercy Street, Louie had a certain level of security, but it didn't take long for high drama to enter into Louie's life when Frobisher was found dead, floating in the Leeds-Liverpool Canal on 12 July 1922. The coroner decided that there was no foul play, and it was a case of 'death by misadventure', in which the deceased is understood to have undertaken some risk that led to their death. But this death was to be stuck to Louie, as later events provided fuel for accusations of murder.

Louie was on the move again by 1924, when she was housekeeping for Arty Calvert, a night-watchman in Pottery Fields, Hunslet. Louie's need to be on the edge of life, to take risks and to fight for a wilful freedom, led her to invent a pregnancy; she fooled Arty into believing this to marry her and then decamped to another part of Leeds. Arty believed that his wife was with her sister in Ossett, being cared for in her supposed pregnancy.

In fact, Louie was loose, on the streets, looking for adventure and change. As the new year of 1926 arrived, the General Strike came with it. The desperation of the times can be ascertained by the report in the short and cheap strike issue of the *Daily Telegraph* for 10 May, which included this: 'On Saturday a great convoy of flour-laden lorries was escorted from the docks to Hyde Park, whence the flour was distributed. There were 104 lorries, 16 armoured cars, cavalry and mounted police, and the procession extended for two miles.'

But by that time, Louie had managed to schmooze her way into life under yet another roof. She had a fatal encounter with Lily Waterhouse which was to lead to one of Leeds' most notorious criminal tales. Lily had property in Amberley Road, Wortley, an area a little way north of Holbeck, over the Great Northern railway line. It was a streetcar ride away from the city centre, and although there was then a chemical works along it, Amberley Road was also close to a cricket ground and open ground by woollen mills. The two women appear to have met at the end of February. After a month together, living by prostitution, it seems that we encounter something puzzling; before the last day of March, when Lily went to report thefts from her property to the police, the relationship of the two young women seems to have been very close and cordial. The most acute insight into this comes from the statement given on 1 April by William Byrne, a bookseller in Shepherd's Lane, Leeds.

Mr Byrne and his lengthy statement are interesting, partly because of the location of his home and shop. He lived close to Harehills Lane, a considerable distance from the Leeds Bridge and Calls area, and he had his shop on Park Lane, which is a main arterial road north, going to Kirkstall and beyond. He had a lock-up shop in better-class area of Leeds, and somehow Lily and Louie found the place. Lily arrived at the shop in mid-October and for several months she was a frequent visitor to Mr Byrne, who took an avuncular, caring interest in her wellbeing. At that time, before she met Louie, Lily was estranged from her husband and was struggling to pay her rent at Amberley Road. Mr Byrne certainly saw a sad case before him- someone in dire need of help. For several months, Lily came on her own to Byrne's shop, and she was, as he saw, 'Very dirty.' Hr told the police, 'I told her I could not keep her in food and longer. From October to December 1925 she was at my shop practically the whole day and she ran errands for me. After this time, during January 1926 she would call at my shop about two or three times each week.'

It was in early March that Louie first appeared at the shop with Lily. Byrne's account records that the two young women were close and that matters between then were amicable: 'Lily Waterhouse told me that Louie was going to live with her as she had no home and no shelter... she told me that Louie and her were living quite happily together and that when she did call at my shop she had left Louie looking after her house whilst she was away.'

Here we have a glimpse of Louie in her adventures: she loved the freedom of being cut off from any family ties, and to be a free spirit, living wherever she could lay her hat. The two women were living on the poverty line though, as becomes clear when Byrne mentions Lily's health. She clearly had little food, and it looks more than possible that what money she earned went on drink, not on dinner. Byrne gives a unique insight into Lily's condition:

> One day last week [late March] Lily came to my shop and said, 'Will you give me half a crown as the Board of Health want me to have a special bath.' I gave her half a crown out of eleven shillings which I was saving for her. She had a sulphur bath on account of having the itch... she was also suffering from some deformity and she wore shoulder irons for this complaint and she showed me a portion of these...last Friday having this particular bath, she said they had broken it at the sulphur bath...

Lily and Louie then, were on the game, earning enough to pay the rent at least most of the time; without a lodger, Lily was clearly not capable of paying her rent. She was separated from her husband, but he was still in touch with her, as we know that he was allegedly the one who told her to keep an eye on Louie and to check on pawn tickets in one of her handbags when suspicions about Louie were first aroused. She told Mr Byrne this, but actually, her husband had died a year before these events. Who was lying? Certainly Lily was not exactly to be trusted. But there was a close friendship; later witnesses speaking to the police recalled how Lily and Louie had been seen walking closer to the town centre, looking for a good time, and the scenes described suggest something similar to today's media images of girls 'out on the lash' on a Friday night. They were far from being simply landlady and tenant.

Now we need to look at Fred Crabtree, a Barnsley miner and friend of Lily's. The Leeds police certainly did. Inspector Winstanley, Assistant Chief Constable in Liverpool, wrote to Leeds on 7 April to report that he had had a phone call from Leeds about Crabtree and that passenger manifests had been checked and that 'should Crabtree attempt to leave the country through this port, the necessary action will be taken, or in the event of obtaining any information which will lead to tracing his whereabouts... a further report will be submitted.'

Before the phone call to Liverpool, police had tracked down Crabtree. He made a statement on 6 April. If the call was made to Liverpool the next day, where had he gone? Why could they not contact him again? The fact is that he disappears after this interview. In this long statement he gives a very full and detailed account of his movements, and what is particularly strange is that a whole batch of other statements, made by family members and friends, real in exactly the same way. One might almost think that they had been briefed on what to say. Reading them all, in one sitting, leads to the conclusion that someone wanted there to be a firm alibi, particularly for a wound on Crabtree's face.

Was the Crabtree that Louie referred to the same Crabtree? Whoever he was, Lily knew his name and had an address in Canada. He was supposed to be going to Canada that coming weekend. Here we have to look at what Louie said in that prison notebook about the events around Lily's death:

> ... last Sunday I was there this woman brought a man home supposed to be a soldier from Becketts Park hospital for wounded soldiers and after he had been there a few days we began to quarrel about him– she wanted him and he wanted me but I wanted neither. I wanted to leave them and go home as it was beginning to get a bit too hot... the detectives were on our tracks and we could not go out without them pulling up... Well on the Wednesday night, the day I was going to leave her, we went out and had a few drinks with this man... we all started to quarrel and it got to fighting... oh the drink...he said something nasty to her and she landed out with her fist to him and they both rolled on the floor... when she got up and struck out again, I picked up the poker... my intention was to strike the man and make him leave off hitting her...

Now, Louie adds to this that as she swung the poker, Crabtree dodged out of the way and the poker struck Lily. Louie then said that Crabtree 'went mad' and then took a belt and strangled her. That coat belt was the nearest to hand, and was left there, as the detective noted when he came and found the body.

At the trial at Leeds Assizes, Louie did not speak. Since 1898 there had been legislation that allowed, for the first time, the accused to speak and give a statement. Most criminal defence lawyers did not want this to happen, as in virtually all cases, the accused would say something that would incriminate or at least, be legally naive, in terms of understanding how to 'play' in the court drama.

Returning to Fred Crabtree, he was interviewed on 6 April. The phone call to Canada was made the day after. Had he disappeared, or did the Leeds detective seem sure that there was another Fred Crabtree? As Louie makes a definite reference to his name and to Canada, it seems a very strange thing if Lily and Fred had not met. Fred claimed he was travelling from Barnsley to Becketts Park to have treatment on his eye (he was hit by gun-shot in the war when he was in the Barnsley Pals). We know that Lily had to attend hospital for the sulphur bath, but she would have gone to the Leeds Dispensary on North Street. There is very little possibility that they met in hospital while receiving treatment, as the Becketts Park work was run by the Ministry of Pensions, and the Dispensary was for poorer patients and outpatients. I attended it twice in the 1950s.

It seems highly likely that Fred Crabtree did call on Lily and Louie, in need of female company and sex. If the Crabtree who was allegedly in the fight at Amberley Road was the Fred Crabtree from Barnsley, we need to consider his statement given on the 6 April. Becketts Park hospital confirmed that Fred had attended for treatment on the 30 March, so he could have gone to Amberley Road after that and stayed for a few nights, leaving after killing Lily. In his statement he is meticulous about times and events. But then, a whole tranche of other statements are remarkably alike. A very important note is that he said that on 1 April, there was a fall from the roof at the mine where he worked. This allegedly hit him in the eye and this swelled. The son of the Rising Son pub's licensee told the police, 'I noticed that his right eye was swollen and I asked him what he had done to his eye... he replied, "I've got a bat on it at work..."' He was referring to a pit prop which had fallen, before the roof caved in according to one witness.

The odd thing is that every witness expressed themselves as if they had been briefed to tell precisely the same tale. We are left with a main suspect, if we allow that the prison exercise book is accepted as giving a true account of the fight and killing. Why would Louie have spun any kind of web of lies? She was condemned. To her friends on their last visit to her, she asserted her innocence, at least with regard to the murder charge.

The trial at Leeds was in front of Mr Justice Wright. The court learned that for the two years before she moved in with Calvert, she had lived hand-to-mouth, but had realised that there were ways of exploiting poverty and existing in various roles and guises. Possibly one of the most interesting and informative of these was her time as a Salvation Army woman. But it is futile to seek for any deep religious feeling in this woman; the feeling generally is that they looked after her, and the organisation was easy for her to exploit. She went to Alpha Street Hall meetings, but it was all a front. Often small details speak volumes and in this case, it has to be noted that she had even stolen her bonnet from a proper Salvation Army member. The author of the most exhaustive account of this case has mentioned a neighbour who knew Louise well, and she testified that the little woman had violent tempers, and that she was capable of changing her mood rapidly, and of using bad language. The witness said that the obscenities from Calvert were so extreme that she had banned her from coming into her home.

The result was that the death sentence would be passed. A Leeds City Councillor said at the time that he felt pity for her and added, 'She was a thin, wan-looking creature only weighing a few stone. I should never legislate on the lines of hanging a woman.' But others soon realised that there were two Louise Calverts: in the dock she had been quiet, restrained and polite. But down in the cell she shouted abuse at her husband, trying to say that he was to blame. All he could say was, 'It can't be helped lass.' Other interpretations of her actions and responses to graphic descriptions of the attack on Waterhouse, and of the corpse, indicate that she was unfeeling and mentally distant from any sense of the events unfolding being in any way 'real'. But the woman who was seen by some as undersized and pathetic had done the awful deed, and of course she had also been wily and cunning in the extreme. Her actions in court and before the magistrate when first charged show an amount of guile too. She dressed in black and to the local reporters she became 'the woman in black.' It has been noted that she fussed over her appearance, as if she were still putting on clothes to be someone else – to project a persona which was not really her. In the magistrate's court, even as evidence was being spoken, she changed her hat, putting on a black silk one instead of her everyday mauve.

There was an appeal. In London, she was again dressed all in black, and the context at the time was a difficult one with regard to the hanging of women; since the notorious Thompson case in 1923, the eight women given a death sentence had all been reprieved. It must have looked to many that this was going to be the case yet again, as a petition had been signed by 3,000 people. Much was made in the press on the topic of her child – the question of what would happen to it and who might adopt it was something that sold papers.

Finally, this enigmatic woman who had fuelled her life on lies, confessed the crime to the warders, and she also said, after clearly being troubled by something that was on her conscience, that she had murdered another victim- an old man she used to work for as his housekeeper. It comes as no surprise to us now, with hindsight, that this man was Frobisher, the man found in the canal, without his boots. Some might argue that this was a lie, though; that she was again fantasising. The whole question of why she removed boots from the bodies of her victims relates to this same deep personality in which complex problems existed, maybe even to the deviance in the removal of the boots, with a sexual undertone. But more likely, boots were some kind of comfort in a harsh world of pawnbrokers and poverty.

Of course, if she did kill Frobisher, there must have been a way to overcome to obvious obstacles to achieving this; after all, if he was thrown into the water at Monk Bridge on the Aire, then she would most likely have killed him close to the river, or how could such a tiny woman have conveyed the corpse to the river? If he was killed next to the river, he could have been rolled in after his boots had been removed. Alternatively, if she killed him in Mercy Street and then somehow had the corpse taken to the riverside, that would not be totally impossible, but most unlikely. Though it has to be pointed out that Mercy Street was only around four hundred yards from the water, off Wellington Street

Louise Calvert was said to have gone to her death 'more bravely than many men.' One has to say that surely there was something manlike in her;

as Shakespeare said of Lady Macbeth, ' Bring forth men children only...'
There was an element of Louise Calvert that had that quality of brutal, unfeeling detachment we see in serial killers, but very rarely in women, even of that category. Her reasons for killing were very different from the example of Aileen Wuornos in Florida, who had some kind of recognisable reason for the urges behind her killing. In that comparison, it is Louie Calvert who is the enigma.

Louie is noted in the crime history books as a 'fetishist.' This is probably utterly untrue. Boots and shoes were guaranteed to fetch a good price at the pawnbrokers' shops. They were light to carry and easy to enjoy in between spells in hock. Louie earned three shillings and sixpence on average from hocking boots. What is far more interesting here is her yearning to be someone else, to find ways of escape from the set pattern of married life, a slave to the husband and kids, house-locked and static. The books containing short accounts of her do at least suggest that she at one time dressed as a Salvation Army woman.

Bottomley, Horatio (1860–1932)

Horatio Bottomley has to be one of the most amoral conmen and schemers ever to have perpetrated frauds. Here was a man who was an M.P. and also a newspaper owner. He developed a rare skill in exploiting the gullibility of the public, and his plans and scams extended to several areas of life and culture in Edwardian Britain. He did a stretch in gaol, after being convicted of fraud, perjury and false accounting.

In 1909 he published *Bottomley's Book*, which recounted his adventures and misadventures on the wrong side of the law. He even extended his talents into poetry, with a booklet, *Convict "13" A Ballad of Maidstone Gaol*. In this work he indulges in his usual appeal for sympathy, as if he is one of the world's great sufferers: 'I will venture to express the hope that my verses may be found to possess at least one merit of ringing true, for I can honestly say that they were minted in the raging furnace of human emotion.'

Even behind bars he managed to stir up controversy, his actions even being discussed in parliament, as a Hansard report shows. In this, the Home Secretary had to face questions about special treatment received:

Mr Davies: Bottomley was received into Wormwood Scrubs prison on the 29 May 1922 and removed to Maidstone prison on the 2 July, 1923. In addition to ordinary visits to which he became entitled under the rules, he had to be allowed numerous special visits from solicitors, secretary, accountant and other persons...The visits were allowed by the Commissioners, or by the Governor, in pursuance of general directions given by the Secretary of State, or in some cases by a special permit...

In other words, Bottomley was playing the system, and he caused problems wherever he washed up in his troubled and troublesome life.

What sums up his nefarious achievement is the fact that he managed to steal the immense sum of £60 million from public funds, and such was the sense of seedy enterprise in his criminal career that even in old age he toured the variety theatres, still desperate for renown and adulation.

He was a wonderfully talented speaker. On one occasion, Sir Richard Muir was prosecuting Bottomley at the Guildhall; Bottomley conducted his own defence. Michael Gilbert, in his book on legal stories, refers to Bottomley's closing speech and comments that it was clever and impressive. It was also so grand and rhetorical that the great writer Samuel Johnson would have been proud of it. This is the last part of it: 'And I say in conclusion, Radical and Democrat as I call myself, I am one of those who honestly has always revered the traditions, the prestige and the power of this Corporation and I do not hesitate today, hunted, hounded and harassed on all sides as I am, to come to you, as not the least respected and one of the senior members of its Aldermanic Bench, to give me sanctuary.'

For a glance at his personality, we need look no further than a light-hearted guide to the law written by Ronald Irving, in which he has this contribution to the Bottomley archive: 'During one of his numerous libel actions Bottomley was heard to remark to a friend on leaving the court with a verdict in his favour, "What a nice old gentleman the judge is! He let me say what I liked. I think I shall retain him to hear all my future cases"'

Bow Street Runners

One of the least known aspects of the development of the police force in Britain is the impressive and largely successful work of Bow Street police office and the Bow Street Runners. Bow Street began as a centre for crime investigation in 1739, when Colonel Sir Thomas de Veil was based there and he started the office, and an elite force of detectives was created, small but effective. They had been constables, and worked in plain clothes initially. Later, the Fielding brothers, John and Henry (author of the novel *Tom Jones*) became the magistrates there. The establishment ran on two runners always on duty, day and night.

They had to confront and try to beat the street gangs and the night robbers, and progress and expansion happened, though slowly; in 1792 their numbers expanded, and arguably the most celebrated Runner, George Rutven, won wide acclaim. He was involved in the capture of the infamous Cato Street Conspiracy of 1820. When the Peelers, the Metropolitan constabulary, were established in 1829, the Runners were no longer required.

The main point to grasp about the Runners, and in a similar way, the King's *Messengers,* was that they were emergency investigation officers, and could be sent into the shires if need arose. In a similar way, the Special police played roles in support but often found themselves involved in major events. Without a regular, well-manned and professional group of constabularies, there was always going to be a need for ancillary corps of officers. The Runners generally had a sound reputation and were capable of some astounding detective work. Bow Street itself was a key element in the criminal justice system under the Fieldings, who issued a gazette with essential information for anyone involved in tracing criminals across London.

Brides in the Bath (George Joseph Smith)

Had they only known the dark and dangerous habits of George Smith, the women whose lives ended by being drowned in a bath would have heeded the warning of life with a dangerous and violent man and ran off to freedom.

This monster murderer, born in 1872, began as a petty thief, and was always iniquitous; his life of crime graduated from offences that led him from reformatory life to the really threatening stage, when he was around forty, of being willing to kill people simply for money. In 1898 he married Caroline Beatrice Thornhill – this did not work out, but from his experience, he concocted the notion of changing his name and starting out as a man who could attract women and then apply power over them to exploit their wealth. The first marriage led to his being known to the world as 'Mr Love'. Never was there such a misnomer, as the man turned out to be an amoral killer. He had eight wives in total, and seven of his marriages were bigamous, with marriage certificates usually carrying aliases.

Whilst most of these women were deserted after a short time (once Smith had taken their possessions and money), Edith Pegler, who he married in 1908, was his wife for seven years, and was not remarkably wealthy. Did he have some affection for her?

His first real victim was a woman who gave him a second chance after he had robbed her. This was Bessie Mundy, who married him at Weymouth in

1910. He left her not long after, and then, with a piece of bad luck, Bessie bumped into the man who had stolen her money again over a year later. She forgave him and returned to live with him once more. They were living in Herne Bay when she had made a will leaving Smith her wealth. That was the perfect formula for her exit from the world; when he found Bessie's body in the bath, one week after her will has been altered, Smith claimed to be out at the shops at the time of her death.

Then came Alice Burnham, and Smith struck again in the same fashion; the death was called 'death by misadventure' and nobody noticed the similarity to Mundy's demise. Then, shortly after the First World War broke out, Smith married again, this time to Margaret Lofty. Such was George's charm and persuasion that she also left a will in his favour. Not long after his wife went to the bathroom, George was out to buy food, taking his usual post-murder trip to the shops.

But now came the advent of newspaper reports, and a pattern of deaths was noticed by reporters, and then by police. The former 'Mr Love' was arrested in February 1915. As it turned out, there was only one murder charge that would stick: that of Bessie Mundy because there had been no signs of violence on the bodies of the earlier victims. But it was enough to condemn the monster. Edith Pegler was one of the witnesses and these words were most important in the case: 'I told him I had tried to find him at Woolwich and Ramsgate, and he was very angry about it and said he should never tell me his business again…he remarked to me that if I interfered with his business I should never have another happy day…'

The great lawyer Marshall Hall had the hopeless task of defending Smith, and the challenge of trying to find some tiny vestige of human feeling in him. He failed, and Smith was sentenced to death; it took the jury only twenty minutes to find him guilty. He was hanged at Maidstone in August 1915.

One of the most dramatic events in the trial process was something organised by Bernard Spilsbury, the famous forensic expert. He arranged for a demonstration to show how the bath drowning was done. The baths the killer liked best were those models with a sloping back; Spilsbury wanted to show the jury how a person who perhaps simply fell asleep in such a bath could not slide down and drown. Spilsbury had a nurse sit in a bath to show the method of killing. She sat with her knees up, and then one report notes that Spilsbury forced her head downwards. She faded into unconsciousness and there had to be emergency measures taken. But there is another view of the event.

In a biography of Spilsbury, what happened is described: 'A nurse in bathing costume got into the bath. Inspector Neil grasped her feet and pulled her head under water. She immediately showed signs of distress, and when hastily pulled out, had to be revived by artificial respiration. It has been said that Spilsbury helped in this, but he has always denied being present, and is believed to have discouraged the experiment.'

Smith was executed by the Rochdale hangman John Ellis. Smith insisted that he was innocent of the crime, and said so, speaking from inside the white cap which had been slipped over his head as he stood by the trapdoor to eternity. Smith had made a will and left £150 to Edith Pegler.

Brodie, Deacon (1741–1788)

As William Donaldson wrote in his magisterial work on rogues and villains, Brodie, '...though highly regarded in society, his taste for gambling, and a private life that involved several mistresses and many illegitimate children soon brought about financial difficulties.' In other words, he was a desperate man in desperate need of cash. The result was a campaign of burglary across Edinburgh, and nasty relationships with the worst of the criminal underclass. In the classic of Edinburgh literature, *Traditions of Edinburgh* by Robert Chambers, we have the essence of his criminality explained:

> It was then customary for the shopkeepers of Edinburgh to hang their keys upon a nail at the back of their doors... Brodie used to take impressions of them in putty or clay, a piece of which he would carry in the palm of his hand. He kept a blacksmith in his pay who forged exact copies of the keys he wanted... He thus found opportunities of securely stealing whatever he wished to possess. He carried on this malpractice for many years...

The fact that here was a man who lived a dual life – one of a good citizen and another as a night-time villain – has been said to have influenced R.L. Stevenson in his conception of what became *Dr Jekyll and Mr Hyde*. Before that, in 1878, his friend Henley had reminded him that he meant to write about Brodie and R.L.S. replied: 'I find you a hell of a fine fellow to complain about my idleness with this cursed Deacon...' As a boy, Stevenson confessed that he had written 'a hugger-mugger melodrama' on Brodie.

To the end, in the condemned cell at the Tolbooth, Brodie was far from typical and suitably upset. One friend called to find him singing a song from *The Beggar's Opera*: ''Tis Woman seduces all mankind.'

Brodie became one of the favourite subjects of the great true crime writer and lawyer, William Roughead (see entry on 'Roughead'). The notable writer and man of law owned a mahogany cabinet which he described in this way: 'The workmanship is wonderful, and proclaims itself the work of a master craftsman, and sure enough, upon an inside panel of its double doors is cut in quaint script this legend -

Made by William Brodie
For Jean Wilson spouse to
John Carfrae, coachmaker
In the Canongate, 1786

Roughead also confirms that Stevenson had seen that the Brodie case was 'a fine bogey tale' and indeed he had written about the serial burglar before he wrote the story of Jekyll and Hyde.

*Burke and Hare and Resurrection Men

In Liverpool in the 1830s, gangs of people, in family groups, stood at the end of hospital wards where their loved ones lay dying, ready to fight off the resurrection men. They took such desperate measures because after the famous cases of Burke and Hare in Edinburgh, criminals of a nefarious turn of mind saw body-snatching as an easy way to earn money. Many northern towns were in the grip of cholera in the 1820s and 1830s, and York and Liverpool had particularly extreme problems in that respect. But the emergence of the 'resurrection men' was something that could happen in any part of the land.

Burke and Hare have stolen the limelight in terms of crime history. William Burke, an Irishman, found work in Scotland working on the canals; he met William Hare in Edinburgh, and they first had a body to sell to the doctors after a lodger died in their digs. Dr Robert Knox bought the body for £7 and so there was a new trade opening up before them, much easier than being a navvy digging canals. It wasn't until 1828 that anyone was suspicious enough to report them to the law, but then they were caught and tried; Hare turned King's evidence and was saved the noose. Burke was doomed to hang. Dr Knox may not have been prosecuted, but a mob attacked his home. So a new word entered the language: a *burker*.

There were so many cases of graves being robbed that an inventor with an eye to the main chance invented a coffin in which the corpse was fixed to the base, and the coffin itself was impenetrable by any normal type of hand-tool.

This epidemic of grave-robbing developed for a very simple reason: the schools of anatomy in the universities needed corpses so that their young medical students could practise their skills on 'the real thing' rather than on the study of drawings and models. But it was hard to come by corpses of good quality of course; if the bodies were being dug out of the ground, where they had been six feet under, all kinds of interferences had happened to them, not the least of which was the presence of maggots, of course.

The logical outcome of this was that doctors and professors really wanted newly-deceased bodies. From that came the moral problems, to say nothing of decorum, common respect and sensitivity. But Burke and Hare realised that it was easier to get a victim drunk, then lead them into the dark, murder them and take them to the anatomists' back door at night.

In the new cities, conditions were just right for this trade: they had a population concentrated in a confined area with a very large number of beer houses and inns, and they had medical fraternities with drive and ambition to succeed.

Leeds, like most other places, had its resurrection men. One of the most well recorded cases is that of Thomas Daniel, who died in 1826 and was buried in St John's churchyard. His body was found in Newcastle a few weeks later when someone went to collect a box addressed to an Edinburgh resident. The man who collected the box and body was arrested and eventually sent to prison for six months. Then there was a similar occurrence when Tom Hudson hanged himself in 1831. But after burial, he surfaced later, this time at a pub, the Rose and Crown, as a body to be sold to the doctors. On that occasion a whole gang of snatchers was involved.

The whole nasty business became a fine art, as they often had to work quickly if they were bringing out newly-interred bodies. The trick was to leave the grave plot exactly as they had found it so that no suspicions would be aroused. Therefore the neat way to operate was to dig down to the lid, prise it off smartly, and deftly lift the body up and straight into a large sack. It was an easy matter then to put the soil back and then replace anything else around the grave such as memorial stones, flowers or objects of remembrance.

But the temptation of the cash payments brought in others too – many who were definitely not experts at corpse-removal. An instance of this was when children would be removed: something that may have seemed an easy task but was not, as in a case in Whitkirk in 1828 when the coffin was not even put back but simply left in a nearby lane.

Good citizens acted to try to stop this menace, of course. They often formed Grave Clubs: these groups of very desperate and distraught folk would work out a shift system and have people posted on guard in cemeteries through the night for the period in which the corpse would rot to such an extent that it would be worthless to any body-snatcher.

Of course, some medical men would break the law in this horrible trade because they would encourage the snatchers to speed up the goods to meet demand. In Leeds a certain surgeon called Robert Baker was engaged in such criminal acts, spurred on by the thought that he could gain a good reputation as an anatomist. He paid a gang the handsome sum of four pounds – as much as they might earn in a month – to exhume a corpse. The difficulty for Baker came the next day when mourners went to the grave and found it empty. The snatchers had not cleared up after their dark deed. All a man could do in that dilemma was to try to pack the body off to Edinburgh, the centre of medical study, and so a place that regularly received 'medical supplies.' Baker had to have the box and body left at an inn where it would be collected en route to the north, but the smell gave the game away; the box was opened and the doctor traced and arrested.

The trail led to the main snatcher, Armstrong. In court it was suggested that the doctor intended to sell on the body and make a profit – not to use it for medical purposes at all – but he denied that. As usual, it was the snatcher who got the rough end of things and Armstrong was sent to prison in York for six months. Baker was acquitted; there was always the defence, perhaps slightly acceptable to some of the middle classes, that the study of anatomy had to go on and that Baker was engaged in necessary and essential research, but there was always a dark shadow over any surgeon who was found out in this nefarious practice. His name was linked to a stigma of reproach from that time onwards. Even some of the ruffians and desperate characters who became involved in the trade dared to state a similarly educational basis as their defence, as a man called Hodgson did in 1831, when he said in court:

> I was connected with a medical man in the taking of this body and it was for the purpose of mutually dissecting it. I could not give up his name without utterly ruining him, and if you send me to prison you will ruin my prospects for life...

The plea had some kind of beneficial effect because his sentence was only six weeks in York. The body Hodgson had provided for the medical men must have given them an extra challenge as they worked: the man who died had fallen into a dye-pan full of hot liqueur; no doubt forensic evidence on the limbs of the snatcher was not difficult to notice and use against him.

The cases recorded and described in reasonable detail in the papers of the time make it clear that the circuit of the trade was well established: corpses exhumed in Leeds, taken with haste and in darkness to an inn that was a posting-house, and so would be placed close to the Great North Road, and from there collected and taken to Edinburgh. The essential elements in that process were secrecy and speed.

What changed all this was the 1832 Anatomy Act which made it easier for doctors to access corpses: it was legal to dissect bodies after that. The key words in the law were that a surgeon could arrange matters with patients so that : 'Any person could direct that his body after death be examined anatomically.' It was a sensible move that should have been done many years before, in fact, as soon as the Burke and Hare case became public knowledge. The impact of those two Edinburgh killers was profound; in fact the word 'Burker' as a term for that 'profession' stuck and was part of the English language, and in regular use, for many decades after the man's end on the scaffold.

Burning at the Stake

It is very hard to understand today, but the fact is that, until 1790, a wife could be burned at the stake as a punishment for murdering her husband. This came from the categorisation of offences. If a husband killed his wife, he would be hanged if found guilty; but if a wife killed her husband, she had committed petty treason, whereas the man had committed murder. Petty treason also applied if a servant murdered a master. Lord Wilson explained this in a lecture in 2012: 'The usual sentence for all types of treason was to be hanged, drawn and then quartered, but because it was thought inappropriate for a woman's body to be cut into four pieces, the sentence for a woman was, until 1790, to be burnt at the stake.'

This is barbarous in the extreme to the modern reader. Another repulsive aspect of all this is that, as an act of mercy, the hangman might strangle her before she was taken to the stake. In my own research into some cases of petty treason, I came to experience the feelings associated when reading and reflecting on actual cases of this burning. For instance, the murder of John Aikney illustrates this.

Elizabeth Aikney and her lover Thomas wanted her husband dead. Thomas came to the door, armed and dangerous. He attacked and killed the husband who came to see what the disturbance was. Thomas ran off, leaving the knife still sticking in John's stomach; the report of the incident says that John staggered out into the street and called for help. People found him 'holding the bloody knife in one hand and the other supporting his bowels, which were dropping to the ground.' He died the following day, and both Thomas and Elizabeth were charged and arrested. Thomas was hanged and his body given to the surgeons for dissection, while Elizabeth was led through the streets on a hurdle to her place of death. There, she was strangled as she was tied to the stake, and then the fire was lit. The usual disgusting scenes followed, at which people gathered her ashes as macabre mementos of that now notorious criminal. Death was swift for both Thomas and Elizabeth, but she had the accompanying terrors and humiliation that the rituals of burning entailed.

A notable case of pressing, another equally repugnant judicial torture or execution is in the repulsive and brutal tale of two felons back in 1723: William Spiggott and Thomas Philips. Their tale is included in the *Newgate Calendar*. They were indicted for a number of robberies on the highway, but refused to plead. It was not a wise move. The Calendar spells out the nature of what was in store for them: 'He shall lie upon his back, his head shall be covered... Then there shall be laid upon his body as much iron or stone as he can bare...' This was read out loud to them, but still they persevered with the course of action, avoiding what was certainly a sentence of death in the court. They went to the press. Phillips tolerated the weight for a short period, then begged to be returned to his cell. Spiggot was tough enough to stand the pain for half an hour. Both were then sentenced to death and were hanged. Phillips had served in the navy, and he was a riotous and amoral character. The Calendar notes that 'while under sentence of death' he behaved 'in a most hardened and abandoned manner' and 'swore or sang songs while the other prisoners were engaged in acts of devotion. Even at the scaffold, 'he did not fear to die, for he was in no doubt of going to heaven.'

C

Chicken House Murder, The

This is the case of Norman Thorne, a teacher at Sunday School who became a chicken farmer and who brought Elsie Cameron to a brutal end in December 1924. They were lovers, and on that date she disappeared on her way to see Thorne at his farm in Sussex. There was the usual search for her, and eventually her suitcase was found at Thorne's place. Two men had stated that they had seen her walking with the case, close to the farm. Thorne had a story to tell, and it was one of suicide. He claimed that Elsie had arrived, said that she wanted them to be married, and that she would remain there until that was agreed.

Worse was to follow. Thorne said that he went out and, on his return, there was the grim sight of Elsie's dead body dangling on a rope tied around a beam in one of his sheds. But was this suicide, as he stated, or murder? Fortunately for the police, Bernard Spilsbury, the great forensics expert, was there to help. He studied Elsie's corpse and found evidence of violence applied to her, but nothing to suggest that she had been hanged. However, there was a second autopsy on Elsie's body and in court, when Thorne was tried for her murder, the doctor who had conducted the second study stated that he had found grooves in Elsie's neck, suggesting suicide. Nevertheless, Spilsbury had put together a convincing argument for murder, not suicide. He stressed that Thorne had made a statement that when he found the hanged body, the eyes were open, but Spilsbury demolished that and gave an account of what they would have really been like if Elsie had in fact committed suicide. This was enough to convince the jury.

As with any sensational murder, the public had been drawn to the farm to look at the scene of the macabre death. Photos exist, showing men lined up along a barbed wire fence, probably trying to figure out how to get inside to peep into the shed with the beam. It was a notorious case, and it ended with the hanging of Norman Thorne on 22 April 1925. There was an appeal, based on a request that the medical evidence should go to arbitration, but this failed. Suicide was argued, but the forensic expert, Sir Bernard Spilsbury, proved that suicide was out of the question because her neck had no evidence of that manner of death.'

Cotton, Mary Ann (1832–1873)

There has been some questioning of Mary Ann Cotton's criminal life in recent years, but the established view, maintained over the centuries, is that she poisoned probably fifteen people by arsenic; the victims included her own children, as well as two husbands. She was born in Durham, and from a life of poverty she saw, as a young woman, that there were gains to be made from a marriage in which the husband died. The standard works on the case, such as that by Arthur Appleton in 1973, follow this narrative (see bibliography). David Wilson, criminologist, also sticks to this line and conforms the media label of her as 'the first British female serial killer.' Other studies have covered the familiar ground: a beautiful woman with a penchant for using arsenic to remove the hurdles in her way to wealth and survival. The records of her buying arsenic sealed her fate.

She had the misfortune to be hanged, but with the added horror of being hanged by William Calcraft, a notoriously unpredictable character. The execution was bungled, and one may only imagine the terror of the situation.

Was Cotton insane? Did she have a mania? Katherine Watson, in a full-length study of poisoners in British history, concludes that is is an invalid reasoning to apply modern mental health concepts here: 'She, and others of her kind, seem more akin to the modern psychopath, a person who displays amoral and antisocial behaviour but whose mental 'instability' is controlled.'

Courvoisier Case

Courvoisier was valet to Lord William Russell. He was Swiss, and earlier in life had drifted from job to job, before settling in London, where he managed to gain employment with the aged Lord Russell in early 1840. He had not been there more than a few months when the maid came to him to say that the house had been burgled. The pair began an inspection of the rooms, and of course they arrived at their employer's room and there was his corpse, on the bed, with the poor man's throat cut.

It was found that some items had been stolen, and there were clear signs of a forced entry at the rear of the property. But the following investigation was hardly demanding, as blood-stained clothes were also found and soon linked to Courvoisier. He had tried to hide these, along with valuable missing items such as silver spoons. His motive was simply theft. The trial was set for June 1840.

Courvoisier had been unhappy from the start. He told another member of staff that His Lordship was 'too fussy' and he already was thinking of leaving and looking for another post. In fact, the killer's reaction on seeing the body of his employer would not stand scrutiny. It was clearly a reaction meant to clear himself of suspicion, as he exclaimed, 'My God, what shall I do?... I will never get a place again.'

The case has entered popular imagination partly through Dickens's responses, because the novelist was there to see the valet hang. That event soon came, as no less a person than Richard Mayne, one of the founding fathers of the Metropolitan Police, was involved in the investigation. There was no detective force then, apart from the Bow Street Runners, but Mayne soon saw that the physical environment had ample signs of a failed attempt to create a crime scene that led to a burglary conclusion. The trial came along and the noose was waiting for Courvoisier. Dickens was there, along with thousands of others, and his comment that it was 'a ghastly night in Hades with the demons' sums up the general response.

Thackeray was also present, and he wrote about the occasion, giving this account of the valet: 'He opened his hands in a helpless kind of way. He turned his head here and there, and looked about him for an instant with a wild, imploring look. His mouth was contracted into a sort of pitiful smile.'

Another man who saw the valet was the diarist, Charles Greville, who noted that 'Just after I got back from Newmarket intelligence arrived of the extraordinary murder of Lord William Russell which has excited a prodigious interest and frightened all London out of its wits.' He went to see the prisoner: 'He is rather ill-looking. A baddish countenance, and his manner was calm though dejected and he was civil and respectful and not sulky. The people there said he was very restless and had not slept, and that he was a man of great bodily strength.'

Courvoisier's death was mercifully swift. Geoffrey Abbot describes this: 'In two minutes after he had fallen, his legs were twice slightly convulsed but no further motion was discernible excepting that his raised arms... sank down from their lifeless weight.' His death mask was later taken to Madame Tussaud's wax gallery where he was to become a criminal celebrity along with other villains. Much of all this sensation was down to the fact that the murder would have been, just a short time before, petty treason, and the valet would have been hanged, drawn and quartered. In 1828 that excessively cruel punishment had been abolished, following the 1790 abolition of the burning alive applied to wifely killings of husbands. (*See Burning at the Stake*)

There is an interesting addendum to the case, in that a crucially important part of the Wallace case was that Julia Wallace was found with a partially burned mackintosh by her body; one line of thought is that the killer of Julie used the same approach as Courvoisier, being naked except for an overcoat when he killed, hence any forensic material would be on the coat only.

Crippen, Dr. Hawley Harvey (1862–1910)

Although the events of the Crippen wife murder happened in 1905, even as recent as the 1960s in my family the name 'Crippen' carried connotations as dark as Dracula or Frankenstein. In fact, although this is one of the most notorious murder stories in British history, it is undoubtedly a story of love as well.

The facts seem straightforward: Hawley Harvey Crippen, an American doctor, set up a business in London, and had a home at 39, Hilldrop Crescent, Camden Town, where he lived with his wife Cora. She was a music hall performer, entertaining with the name of Belle Elmore. She was also a member of the Music Hall Ladies Guild and so she had a wide circle of friends.

Crippen was 48 at the time of the murder was ; he was described by J.P. Eddy, a lawyer who knew the case close up, as: '... a slight figure...with thinning hair and a thick moustache.' He had a secretary called Ethel Le Neve, 'a brunette, with a slight figure, a finely-chiselled nose and expressive eyes...'. The beginning of the tragedy is all too familiar: Crippen was smitten by Ethel, and he was very romantically attached. Then came the fatal night. A party was arranged, with two guests at the Camden home: Mr and Mrs Martinetti. As Eddy puts it, 'The part that Crippen played was that of the devoted husband, which perhaps was not unimportant if he then had murder in his mind.'

The world around Crippen, after that, was told that Cora had disappeared into America, as there was a family illness. When Mrs Martinetti said goodnight to Cora after the party, it was the last the two friends met. After that night, those around Crippen were told that Cora had gone to America, as there was a family illness. In actual fact, Crippen had poisoned Cora with hydrobromide of hyoscin, which he had been able to buy from a chemist friend. Not long after this, Crippen spread the word that Cora had returned and was very ill, and then after that he announced that she was dead.

The way was open for Crippen and Ethel to be together. It could have developed into nothing more than the usual sordid tale of a murder in order to have the desired 'mistress' in the affair but Scotland Yard became involved, in the shape of detective Walter Dew; he enquired into life at the business address and then visited Hilldrop Crescent. As Crippen gave jewellery to Ethel, in particular a brooch set with diamonds and a ruby known as The Rising Sun, there were reasons for suspicion. But posterity has been interested in Dew, as he missed several chances to get his man, most notably when he conducted a search at the Crippen house, where the body of Cora was actually buried under the cellar floor, and it was missed.

The case stepped up once more as Ethel, dressed as a young man, travelled to Antwerp with Crippen on board the Montrose with Crippen, who was now a wanted man. The body was found on a second visit to Camden by the police. Then came a telegraph wire, making this the first case where a killer was arrested after the use of this new communication. Dew went in pursuit, and Crippen and Ethel were eventually tracked down in Canada.

The Crippen trial was no problem for the jury; they made their decision in less than half an hour. He was to hang. After the sentence there was a petition and, as Ethel had been acquitted, the love of Crippen's life would have to go on without her lover. J.P. Eddy met Ethel and formed a strong opinion that indeed she was innocent. She had stated that she had no knowledge of the murder, and had believed that Cora had died in America. Eddy gave his opinion, which is the one which has remained: 'There is no doubt that Crippen was devoted to her. He had a photograph of her in his condemned cell.' Crippen wrote a passionate last letter to her which included the words, 'How am I to endure to take a last look at your dear face?'

As for Ethel, Eddy found out about her later life: 'She met her future husband and their marriage was a happy one. They settled down in the Home Counties and brought up a family of two.'

Cutlery Eater

Robbers and burglars through the centuries have often shown strange habits and traits. Sometimes these involve 'calling cards' and 'signature acts' but as well as these features, there have been cases of extreme oddity, beyond explanation, and one of the strangest of all has to be the case of Allison Johnson, a burglar tried at Lincoln Crown Court in 1992.

Johnson was fond of a good meal, but his preferred diet was cutlery. He enjoyed a good banquet of shiny silver, and so had acquired the moniker of 'the cutlery man.' He was what is familiarly known as an 'old lag' having clocked up over twenty years of stir time. There is no doubt that he stood out in any list of trials and cases; the question in front of everyone concerned was why would anyone do that? In court, his barrister claimed that it stemmed from low self-esteem, and that as the accused stood before the court, he had in his guts a quantity of knives and forks. Would there be any sympathy for the man?

The sympathy might have been present when the jury learned that Johnson had undergone, over the years, thirty operations to remove cutlery from his stomach. HMP Lincoln is just across the road from Lincoln County Hospital, and so the logistics of this would have been easier than in many other cases. He was jailed, and there he would receive psychiatric reports. Johnson was a vagrant, and no doubt would have thought of Lincoln prison as the nearest thing he had to home.

D

De Quincey, Thomas (1785–1859)

If historians of literature have to search for the first analysis of the true crime genre, in a way other than a journalistic or commercial voice, then Thomas De Quincey has a large claim. This is down to his classic long essay, *Murder Considered as one of the Fine Arts* (1827), which was published in *Blackwood's Magazine*; this was followed by two more papers on the same theme. With the notorious and terrifying slaughter perpetrated near Wapping in 1811 now known at the Ratcliffe Highway murder as the focus of his sustained irony about murder, as it had become for the press, he broke new ground in the genre of crime writing.

De Quincey had burst onto the literary scene in 1821 with *Confessions of an English Opium-Eater*; this was about lots of other things besides addiction to opium, and it was staggeringly honest and direct about his family and education. He had started out in life, after sporadic education in Manchester and beyond, as an impressive scholar, but had then taken to a wandering life, and in his street travels around London, he became very close to a prostitute whom he cared for and protected. After that his literary career was launched and he succeeded in writing for some of the most prestigious journals of his time. This led to his befriending Wordsworth and Coleridge, who had been his literary heroes since he was very young. But it was his strikingly original autobiography that won him fame, at a time when the Regency was generating waves of fresh talent across all the arts, in the face of government repression and the fear of France across the Channel.

His essays on murder were truly original. He adopted an ironic narrative voice and tone, writing about the savage murder committed by John Williams (alleged but not proven) when he entered the premises of Timothy Marr, a hosier, and killed Marr, his wife, their child and an apprentice. This was followed shortly after with the murder of the landlord of the King's Arms, his wife, and a girl called Bridget Harrington.

De Quincey's lecture was based on his imagining a society, described in this way: 'In tendency it may be denominated a Society for the Encouragement of Murder but...it is styled The Society of Connoisseurs in Murder.' What he had understood was that educated and learned men, in addition to popular writers and commentators, were beginning to take more than a passing interest in serious crime. In 1827 the *Newgate Calendar* provided plenty of talk for the coffee houses and taverns, but as the reporting became more widespread and more detailed, interest in the actual facts of homicide grew apace.

John Williams had indeed shown the extremes of nasty, amoral murderous rage (if in fact he was the culprit); he had taken his own life before having to face the noose, and so there were unanswered questions, and that is the basis of the irony – that writing and speculation on such things as motives and methods when it came to taking a life was almost infinite. We see that now with the continued interest from writers and historians on the Jack the Ripper case and on the phenomenon of serial killers.

The piece is written as a lecture. He begins with a disquisition on murder and comments by famous writers and philosophers; then he moves to some case studies of murder, arriving eventually at the Williams story. His account makes the Ratcliffe Highway killings special: 'With respect to Williams' murders, the sublimest and most entire in their excellence that ever were committed, I shall not allow myself to speak incidentally.' The account is full of praise, as if he is discussing an outstanding artist – and so he is. He writes: '...the blaze of his genius absolutely dazzled the eyes of criminal justice. You all remember... that the instruments with which he executed his great work (the murder of the Marrs) were a ship carpenter's mallet and a knife...'

The essays dwell on all the circumstances that would engage the connoisseur of murder, and De Quincey is foreshadowing the kinds of amateur criminological societies which would come later, such as the Crimes Club, to which Conan Doyle and dozens of other aficionados of crime supported. In other words, the pleasures of the criminous, as William Roughead called these activities, were created by the strange, highly individual imagination of De Quincey.

He died in 1859, after a long struggle to survive and make ends meet, still trying to live by his pen, against mounting debt.

*Detectives: National and Local

The first professional detectives, as an official part of the constabularies in Britain, were established in 1842. But officers in such bodies as the *Bow Street Runners* did detective work, as did the *Kings' Messengers*. The first full-time detectives, after the 1842 measures, became a special 'band of brothers' at first, and they worked in an atmosphere of fear and suspicion. The public thought of them as evil spies, as they worked in plain clothes for some of the time. To many it seemed like a European thing – a step too far when it came to that notorious British fair play. The early sleuths attracted Charles Dickens, and he knew some of them as friends and, of course, used them as sources of information in his research for his novels.

Those first detectives were soon characters in print, thanks to Dickens and other writers. In 1996 Peter Haining collected short pieces about these men, and he focuses on Dickens' achievement: 'It was with the character of Inspector Bucket, who appears in *Bleak House* (1852-3) to solve the murder of an unscrupulous lawyer, that Dickens created the first significant detective in English literature.' Yet Dickens was interested in detectives long before *Bleak House*. Haining points out that Bow Street Runners, Blather and Duff, appear in *Oliver Twist* (1837). It was with an essay called *The Metropolitan Protectives*, published in the journal *Household Words* in 1851 that Dickens really showed his knowledge of this fraternity. In the *Road Hill House murder*, Jonathan Whicher came to prominence as one of the most impressive sleuths of the first wave of professionals.

Before the advent of the professionals of Bow Street and then Scotland Yard, serious crime across the country had to be dealt with ad hoc. Sometimes the militia would be called out, or even the *Messengers*. Even individuals would act in a detective's capacity; much responsibility fell on the local magistrates, who were often targets for riots and revenge attacks. One favourite case from the chronicles of local true crime has to be that of a magistrate in Yorkshire who pulled off a stunning piece of detective work. I have written about his case more than once, and still the events of this work of detection are so impressive that the man should be better known.

The years from the middle of the eighteenth century to the end of the nineteenth century were years in which forgery and counterfeiting of all varieties were widely practised. Not only were coins forged and clipped, but banknotes were forged; in the first decades of that period, there were numerous regional banks issuing their own notes, in spite of the fact that we had had a Bank of England since 1689. In other documentation such as bills of exchange and drafts forgery was also rife. The tendency was for criminals to work in networks and use local craftsmen for different skills, as required by particular activities. It was a tough job for the forces of law, trying to crack the nefarious tricks and cons of these men.

But there has been at least one exception to this stereotype, in the Bradford and Halifax area between 1751 and 1769. This was Samuel Lister, a formidable man to have as an enemy, and unluckily for the men involved in the yellow trade of coining and clipping at that time, and in the risky activity of forgery, he was more than capable of going out to make things happen, and to play detective when needed. Lister was based at Horton House, and he had been trained as an attorney, doing thirteen years in that profession. He had to suspend his legal work if and when he was needed to act the magistrate.

There was a family tradition behind this; his father had served on the bench for the West Riding, and as the area covering Bradford and Calderdale was vast, mostly wild and empty, and in the first stages of an industrial revolution, a magistrate was sure to be kept busy. Where there are rich and poor within visiting distance, there will be much crime. At that time, the answer to crime was repression: there were around two hundred capital offences, and also plenty of local lock-ups. Stocks and houses of correction to keep the less serious offenders out of circulation for a while. In 1764, in the Halifax parish of Lister's area, there was most likely a population of approximately 40,000 and there was no magistrate in local residence when Lister stepped into the role. Bradford had three justices in the 1750s. But we are dealing with a remarkable man here, one who was highly regarded by the Marquis of Rockingham, the outstanding legal figure for the West Riding, always busy at York Castle.

Lister had plenty to occupy him in the activities of thieves and robbers, and in this work he averaged about twenty-six sittings each year; but it was in the coining circuit that he really came out from the usual role he played to become a detective, out to get his man. The man in question in his most important case was one William Wilkins, who had been arrested and brought to the court for not paying bills at various hostelries throughout the West Riding. He had been searched and interrogated and on his person were found letters, one with a Gloucester postmark, and more astonishingly, a promissory note for the huge sum of £1,100 – a massive fortune at the time, and around £350,000 today.

Wilkins said that he was from a place called Painswick in Somerset; but the letters and notes he had were not actually signed by anyone of note. They were more than likely forgeries and, if guilty, Wilkins would hang. But the problem was, how to prove that he was guilty? It was going to take extraordinary measures to achieve this, notably trying to communicate with the Painswick authorities, and this was something usually far too strenuous and time-consuming for your average magistrate to bother with. But not Samuel Lister though: he was a determined man with a relish for such a daunting challenge. He was a terrier when it came to grabbing hold of a problem; there was no letting go until it was sorted.

The first step was to enlist some qualified assistance, so he turned to a Leeds man, the Recorder, Richard Wilson. At that time, a recorder was a barrister permitted to act as a justice of the peace at Quarter Sessions, so he certainly knew the law, and he knew the ways of criminals. The two men decided to keep Wilkins locked up while information was gathered; they put items in London newspapers and sent messages to Gloucester. They were pushed for time: Wilkins was due to appear at the Lent Assizes in the South West – and in quite a short time. He could have had friends there to stand bail as well, so they moved fast. This is where the alacrity of Lister in using the 'grapevine' around Bradford paid off, as one of his regular contacts knew of a West Country man visiting the town, a certain Walter Merrett. He advised Lister to write to a clothier at Uley near Painswick, to ascertain some information.

It was a triumph: 'Wilkins' was in fact one Edward Wilson from Painswick, wanted for forgery. Matters were very soon finalised and in a short time Wilson was sent for trial at Gloucester on 20 March 1756. There he was sentenced to death. Lister also began to act against the local clippers. This trade involved filing or clipping coins down to an acceptable weight for local use, and so actually creating more coins from the clipping. It was very lucrative and very risky. The dangers were acute and it made criminals act with desperation and resolve, even to the extent of murder if they had to, as in the case of the killing of the excise man, William Deighton, in Halifax in 1789. But the Bradford men still acted against the coiners, perhaps urged on by this murder. It was no easy task to work against these rogues, though: the trade enjoyed considerable popular support. Lister was a part of the crusade against these coiners from the distant and inaccessible valleys towards Lancashire.

The best way to search out the men involved in coining was to employ *agents provocateurs*, men who would work their way into the confidence of the criminals, and then betray them. Lister, together with John Hustler in Bradford, did this most successfully, their work leading to the arrest of two men on an inspector's evidence, and they were packed off to York Castle. Lister must have known the risks he was taking. Deighton had sent men to York Castle to await the noose, and he had paid for it with his life.

Samuel Lister was indeed a remarkable man. He saw the magistracy as something opening up opportunities to act not only on behalf of the law itself, and civil order, but as a means of reinforcing the authority in economic and commercial contexts also. The action against the 'yellow trade' was done partly because he had links with local industrialists and he represented their interests, of course, in protecting the value of coins in circulation. His principal biographer, John Styles, appropriately quotes Lister's own words as an explanation of his motives: 'I think it my duty not only as a magistrate but as a private person to do all that I am able to bring villains to justice.'

The battle against the forgers went on, and even as late as 1820, there was a ring of counterfeiters, a group linking Hull men with a gang in the West Midlands. It is interesting to note that similarity to the 'Wilkins' case. Clearly, the criminal craftsmen were around Birmingham and perhaps Yorkshire was perceived as distant and 'primitive' in terms of communication. How wrong they were in the case of detective Lister.

E

Eliza Armstrong: Bought for £5

In 1885 there was a scandal that rocked the nation, and it was to open up a horrendous social malaise; Eliza was the daughter of a chimney sweep, and such young women very often went into domestic service, in an age when even comparatively poor people could afford one or even two home servants; but in fact, Eliza had been bought for £5. The story opened up this dark trade in children, and it was little short of slavery.

The most dramatic development from this case involves a journalist called W.T. Stead, who was later to perish on the *Titanic*. Stead set out to shock the press and public by campaigning on the theme of children being bought in order to be taken into the sex-worker industry. He was editor of the popular journal, *The Pall Mall Gazette* and so had a sizeable following; he became chairman of a group called The London Committee for the Suppression of the Traffic in British Girls for the Purposes of Continental Prostitution. Activist Josephine Butler, and then Stead himself, bought children as part of their campaign; in Butler's case she pretended to be a procurer. They were determined to open up a repugnant trade in people.

Stead went too far; he wanted to shock and he did so by buying Eliza for what would be around just £792 today. However, Stead had broken the law and his actions misinterpreted. He was sent to gaol for three months for abduction. The public soon became accustomed to seeing images of him in the prison uniform; the campaigner had probably achieved more than he expected.

Euston Square Mystery, The

Endsleigh Gardens back in 1878 became notorious as the location of the Euston Square Murder. In the cellar, the body of Matilda Hacker was found, and she had been missing for two years. It did not take long for the sensational killing to hit the press, and in 1879 an anonymous publication promised 'harrowing details' and an extraordinary statement by one Hannah Dobbs. She had been the main suspect in the murder investigation.

Matilda was at the time known as Miss Uish, and she was renting the home from a family called Bastendorff. When Matilda went missing, the family stated that she had left without any communication, and strangely, they do not appear to have been grilled with any degree of energy and purpose. Maybe it was because they had learned that the dead woman had lived a shiftless, transient life, not staying long at any of her homes, so her disappearance from one home wasn't particularly unusual. Dobbs entered the narrative when it was learned that she had some items belonging to the dead woman in her possession.

Evidence was slim when Dobbs was tried and even the witnesses who appeared against her were of no use to the crown. The mystery remains. Such was the stigma acquired by the address that in late 1879, the metropolitan Board of Works were asked by the Saint Pancras administration to rename the place Endsleigh Gardens. The stigma was removed, as was the case with 10 Rillington Place.

F

Family Massacre (Ratcliffe Highway, 1811)

This was the horrendous case of the probable mass murderer John Williams in 1811 in which the Thames River Police were involved, and that the writer *Thomas De Quincey* used as the focus of his seminal essay, *Murder Considered as one of the Fine Arts*. Williams, who took his own life, was the likely killer, and his victims were two families near Wapping. The maid of Timothy Marr's shop on the Highway went out to buy food on 7 December 1811. In her absence, the family were slaughtered; later, at the King's Arms, others were killed. The alarm was sounded. The constable did his best but this was a crime for which huge resources were needed.

It appeared to be a series of killings done by one single person; a few weeks later a suspect was apprehended and he stood before the magistrate charged with these crimes. He used to be a sailor, working with Timothy Marr, and he was also known at the King's Arms. But he had not been identified, not even by a man called Turner, who had survived the massacre in the public house. However, when tools associated with the murders were found in the tool-chest of a German seaman called Peterson, these were linked to Williams. He was known to use a specific tool called a maul.

'We are not yet certain we have proved the man' wrote a magistrate, and when a charge was imminent, Williams was found dead. Oliver Cyriax gave a succinct summary of the case's importance: 'The murders... made it very clear that London – still safeguarded by the antiquated system of decrepit watchmen – was unsafe for law-abiding citizens and the idea of a "police force" was hotly debated in the press.'

Several studies of the crime have been published, notably *The Maul and the Pear Tree* by P.D. James and T.A. Critchley (see bibliography).

Flasher to Killer: The Birth of DNA in Forensics

In 1983 Narborough in Leicestershire and the Carlton Hayes psychiatric hospital were to become names forever associated with the advent of the forensic tool that has revolutionised the pursuit of serious criminal offenders. Here it was that Dr Alec Jeffreys of the nearby university conceived of DNA and made it possible to produce individual, virtually unique identifiers of a person from physiological samples such as mucus, sperm, hair follicles and blood.

The engrossing story of how this DNA work emerged starts with the rape and murder of two teenage girls by Colin Pitchfork, a man who started out as a criminal by flashing girls on footpaths. He had graduated to murder and serious sexual violence, killing Linda Mann and Dawn Ashworth between 1983–86. After the first murder there had been a huge search, but after the second it was apparent the two deaths were by the same perpetrator. Then along came DNA and the police sent a letter to all males between the ages of seventeen and thirty-four, the age range they suspected the murderer to belong in. They were asked for a blood sample, and if the culprit was evident from the sample by means of the DNA, then a net around Narborough, Enderby and Littlethorpe would have a good chance of a positive result for the manhunt.

Pitchfork actually managed to find someone to take the test in his place, and so he was not traced, but as so often is the case in such operations, a small footnote to the narrative produced results. Someone overheard the substitute donor confess what had happened; this was reported to police and so they had names to work on. Interviewing the substitute soon led to Pitchfork, who had a criminal record for flashing. He was arrested. The DNA test proved positive.

Pitchfork was sentenced to two terms of life imprisonment for the murders, and ten years for each rape. He became the first person to be convicted of rape and murder using DNA profiling. The discovery and application of that momentous work on body cells and identity ushered in the modern era of DNA figuring in police investigations

Flogging

In 1896 the classic work on the history of punishment by a stick or whip was published: *A History of the Rod*, written by clergyman William Cooper. He covered its use in religious orders, on thieves, in prisons and in the forces. He also included the rod applied in schools, which, of course, had been *de rigueur* in the teaching of Latin since the days of Quintilian.

Flogging was widely used in the military services over the centuries. It was officially abolished in prisons in 1948 but continued after that for such matters as attacks on prison staff. The Criminal Justice Act of 1967 finally erased the practice, and the last recorded flogging was in 1962.

G

*Garotting Panic

In the 1860s the robbers of London began to develop a new version of the standard mugging approach to attacking the good citizens of London. They started to work in twos or threes, with one crook approaching from the front of the victim, and another being behind. There would be a distraction – perhaps a question or an appeal for something – and then the villain behind would set about the hapless victim. There would be a robbery, and this generally all took place in the dark. Theatregoers were especially vulnerable, as they would often be walking home alone, late in the evening.

Up to 17 July 1862 there had been only fifteen robberies with violence in the city of London. But then a Member of Parliament, one Hugh Pilkington, was 'garotted' in Pall Mall. A new and terrifying crime against the person had been noted.

In its chronicle of November 1862, The *Annual Register* reported that there had been a 'garotte terrorism' in London and in the provinces that year. The word 'garotte' was beginning to strike terror into ordinary people and newspapers were selling on headlines about this new version of street robbery. The report expresses the crime in this way:

> For some years past there have been occasional instances of 'garotte robberies' – a method of highway plunder, which consists in one ruffian seizing an unsuspecting traveller by the neck and crushing in his throat, while another simultaneously rifles his pocket; the scoundrels then decamp, leaving their victim on the ground writhing in agony...

The popular magazine, *Punch*, covered the menace with its usual acuteness and dash; one cartoon shows some middle-class theatre-goers venturing out into the streets with a platoon of soldiers guarding them, and defensive measures such as sword-sticks were used. It was nothing less than a reign of terror and it gradually became much more widespread than simply London's theatreland.

This 'modern peril of the streets' was first described graphically as 'putting the hug on' and it had its own jargon, with the gang members having particular roles. First, the man called the *front stall*, a look-out; then the *back stall* who was going to grab the booty, and finally the *nasty man* who would move in from behind to take the victim's throat. At the time, it was seen as a variety of crime that was somehow not 'British' and journalists tried to blame it on foreigners. It was often written about in terms linked to activities by Italian mobs. But soon it was realised that this heinous crime was becoming a speciality of the new criminal underclass of the expanding towns across Victorian England.

The terror even entered the realms of popular song, with lines such as:

A gentleman's walking, perchance with a crutch,
he'll suddenly stagger and totter;
don't think that the gentleman's taken too much,
he's unluckily met a garrotter....

In the provinces the new crime began to take a hold towards the late summer of the year. 1862 was destined to become a proper *annus horribilis* for people on the city streets, and northern towns were no exception. In Sheffield, one of the first notorious garrotters outside London was Edward Hall, a man who was apprehended after a desperate struggle with police. It was reported at the time that he was 'the leader of a gang of ruffians who garrotted and nearly murdered Mr Burnby, Earl Fitzwilliam's coal agent.' He was cornered and surrounded, then jumped from a high window in his home in Sheffield to escape. He absconded to Birmingham, where he was grabbed and almost killed by a huge police officer who punched the villain relentlessly until he gave in.

Garotter gangs in Bradford were not so lucky when the full weight of the law fell on them. William Holes and James Lynas were in court for their garrotte attack on William Dawson late on a Saturday night in Market Street. Dawson, an engine tenter, yelled for the police to help, and an officer came to the scene to see the two robbers running away down Kirkgate. Holmes was trapped in an alley. Lynas was taken in Collier Gate by a detective called Milnes. They had taken a few shilling and a silk handkerchief. At York Assizes they were to pay dearly for that attack with a long prison sentence and hard labour.

In Calverley, on the moor, a Mr Summerscales was having his constitutional walk when he was set upon by two thugs called Elvidge and Hainsworth. They had used the established methods of one man behind to choke the victim while the other approached face to face, and they had taken his silver watch. But on this occasion, the victim could not positively identify the men and they lived to attack again.

Two hardened toughs called Lockwood and Murphy were one of the most successful garrotting teams around Leeds and Bradford, and they became adept at the nefarious business; they had a cover as street hawkers, one sold oysters and the other sold nuts. They trod the streets around the whole conurbation, and were finally tracked down after an attack in Hunslet, though they had been active in Armley and Bingley. Murphy was the 'nasty man' and appears to have been extremely threatening and dangerous. It is not difficult to see how this crime would catch on in the criminal ranks; it reached the proportions of being a 'glamour' offence in that it took skill, a brazen attitude and a total lack of fear. Lockwood and Murphy almost beat their last victim to death, and they took a trip to York Assizes where they were due to suffer physical punishment and years inside.

The press began to speculate about how the most likely recruits to the garrotting craze were ticket-of-leave men. These were convicts whose terms of sentence had been lifted after good behaviour, so that they could go into society to work, thought they were required to attend musters, just as today we have a licence system in the current penal code. A ticket could be granted after the prisoner had served at least three years. Penal servitude had replaced the use of the prison hulks in the Thames estuary after 1853, and men who had only served three years of a seven-year sentence could be released under this scheme. Ordinary folk started talking about all criminals as 'ticket of leave men'. The popular journals enjoyed creating this moral panic, making their readers envisage the local streets filling up with desperate and hardened criminals waiting to strangle them as they strolled to the Sunday band-stand concert.

All this led to the passing of the Garotter's Act of 1863. In some quarters people raised a glass to the villains because their actions had introduced extreme and repressive punishments back into the criminal law. In Bradford, the vogue had been just a small part of the life of a very violent and brutal community. One way of seeing this is to note that, while thugs were robbing in the dark streets, hundreds of men were gathering to watch bare-knuckle fighting, as they did at Cottingley Cliffs when Laverty and Curlly fought on a Monday morning in this violent year. Two officers found the men fighting 'near the bottom of a small secluded nook near Cottingley Moor, the ground around rising up in the form of an amphitheatre'. There were six hundred people in the crowd, and the boxers were fighting for a prize of £10.

The year 1862 was one of living dangerously in most English cities. In London, street crime was obviously at a peak of atrocious violence, but the north was certainly not exempt from this 'new crime.' As so often, *Punch* saw the heart of the matter, and in their cartoon, 'Jones is not afraid of his shadow' they summed up the nature of this particular fear. The little man with top hat and umbrella sees the giant shadow of a garrotter with a huge club on a wall as he walks along. But the good citizen in the picture, ironically, carries a revolver.

Ghost in the Nick (Fred Nodder)

'Missing from her home... at 11, Thoresby Avenue, Newark, since Tuesday, 5 January, 1937, Mona Lilian Tinsley, aged 10 years (rather short for age), dark hair (bobbed with fringe) rosy cheeks, four prominent teeth at front... It has been established that this girl was seen at Hayton Smeath, near Retford at about mid-day on Wednesday, 6 January, 1937.'

(Text from a police poster)

Frederick Nodder moved into new lodgings in Newark in 1935, where his landlady was Mrs Tinsley. He didn't stay long, but he made a mark with the children. To them he was 'Uncle Fred.' He was difficult to live with though and when he moved on to East Retford, he proved to be a handful for the landlady, with his bad habits and tendency to create a mess. Nodder appeared to be a man with a mission – to destroy everything and everyone around him that could be classified as weak or vulnerable.

But back in Newark, the large family of Tinsleys was now one short of the usual number. Little Mona, aged ten, was missing. Her father, Wilfred, was frantic with worry. Mona did not return home from her school on 5 January 1937. The search began. Her school was not far away and he began his search there. Mona's poor father was distraught with anxiety. After the police were called, the description went out: she was wearing a knitted suit and wore Wellingtons. But a boy called Willie Placket recalled seeing Mona talking to a man and said that he would recognise the man if he saw him again. A Mrs Hird had also seen Mona with a man 'who was a lodger with the girl's mother.' The net was closing in on the person described as 'a man with staring eyes.'

Nodder had a hook nose and his moustache was ginger. Nodder seems to have been memorable, as lots of people remembered him on that journey with little Mona. A bus conductor recalled him. The police traced him to Retford and he was picked up. He had been living as Hudson, and was the father of a child living locally.

Mona had been seen with 'Uncle Fred' and consequently, as Mona was now officially missing and the anxiety increased, Nodder was interviewed. His story was that he had given the girl a lift to Sheffield, and then put Mona on a bus to her aunt's in Worksop. It was all highly suspicious and he was arrested for abduction. There was no body, so there was no murder charge. In court, the abduction still stood and he was sent to prison. As he was in custody and there was a feeling that Mona had been attacked or even killed, and so a massive search began; 1,000 people joined in to search areas between

Retford and Newark. It was such a wide stretch of land that the police from Nottinghamshire, Lincolnshire and Derbyshire all spent time and manpower on the case.

Scotland Yard now sent men to step up the campaign: the Chesterfield canal was dragged and only three months after Nodder's trial, Mona's body was found in the river Idle close to Bawtry. Mona had been strangled. Nodder, who was tried for abduction in Birmingham was in court again, this time facing a murder charge in Nottingham, and trying to tell tales to escape the noose. Nothing he could say did him any good. The presiding judge, Mr Justice Macnaughton, said, 'Justice has slowly, but surely, overtaken you and it only remains for me to pronounce the sentence which the law and justice require...'

The great barrister, Norman Birkett, had spoken for the prosecution; it was to be his last trial, appearing for the Crown. It was a terrible case, with a widespread sense of outrage around it, as Nodder had sexually assaulted Mona before killing her. 'Uncle Fred' had turned out to be a monster. The photos of him show a man with a matching flat cap and scarf of small check pattern and a thick overcoat. His eyes are piercing and he shows a face to the world that expresses nothing substantial. 'Something is missing in him' as is often said of these types of killers. Here was a twisted personality who enjoyed inflicting pain on helpless children. It had taken Mona five minutes to die. Ironically, this man who had inflicted so much pain and torment to others lived in a place called 'Peacehaven.'

He was sentenced to hang. A few days after Christmas, 1937, he was in the hands of the hangman and left this world. Or did he? He was hanged in Lincoln Prison on Greetwell Road, and his last moments would have been on the wing of the execution suite. He would have fallen through the trap to dangle and die – very quickly – taking less time to die than his victim had done. The corpse was taken down and buried, with quicklime, as was the custom. But was that the last of Fred Nodder inside the prison walls? Some think not.

Since then, there has been development in the prison, as there has with almost every other Victorian building. Staff report sightings of a man walking the corridors, a man with a dark overcoat and flat check cap. One report is of turning a corner to see a man with piercing eyes coming towards you. Some have merely glimpsed the profile, with the hooked nose and moustache.

There are many dark roads and corners around Greetwell Road. A spirit could wander those streets, a restless, evil entity like Uncle Fred. If the tales are true, then this evil man is as restless now as he was in life – always open to do some horrible mischief. In fairly recent times, when building work was done on the prison site, the graves of executed prisoners were taken up and carried to the city cemetery. The more serious ghost hunters date the appearances of the ghost of Uncle Fred to that time. When the ground opened up, his nasty spirit walked into the world again, out to disturb the unwary. The man with the staring eyes, if he exists in spirit form, will still try his hardest to unsettle the unwary night-walker. Nodder was always a man who haunted, loitered, and watched people.

Even if the Lincoln walker through Greetwell Road has no belief in ghosts, a glance at the forbidding high and dark walls of the prison there will do enough to suggest that this killer had no pleasant stay in his last hours on earth.

H

Half-Hanged Smith

In addition to the tale of *John Lee*, whom the hangman failed to kill with three attempts, we have the redoubtable Yorkshireman, John Smith. Surely, of all the London Tyburn tales, this is the most staggeringly unbelievable. Smith, from Malton, went to London and joined up in the Second Regiment of Foot Guards, but he was soon creating problems and in 1705 he was tried for the theft of several items such as silk and shoes. He was bound for Newgate, and he managed to argue away some of the charges, but two was enough to send him to the gallows.

There was a slender hope, as the *Newgate Calendar* wrote: 'While he lay under sentence he seemed very little affected by his situation, absolutely depending on a reprieve, through the interests of his friends.'

He was set into the death cart and trundled through London to the noose, and at that time, the drop used was quite short, so a felon could take some minutes to die. That was the case with Smith, and as he hung, a messenger appeared on the scene with a reprieve. It looked as though this was too late, but still there was a slender hope, and he was taken to a tavern. There, after a struggle, he came round and recovered well. That caused a media storm; he was a celebrity. In an account of the near death experience, it was said that he described the ordeal: '... my spirits in a strange commotion, violently pressing up to my head, then a great blaze of blinding light seemed to come out of my eyes...'

Years later there was Smith again, in serious trouble, and this time he escaped the noose again, as he was transported to America. He was then an old man by the figures of that time, in his late sixties.

Hall, Edward Marshall (1858–1927)

Edward Marshall Hall was one of the most charismatic of a tranche of top barristers in the first decades of the twentieth century. In fact, in the first fifty years of that century there were several lawyers who provided the Old Bailey and many assize courts with their flair and rhetoric. Some of them had great charm and powers of argument. Hall had every quality one might wish for in that profession, and at a time when the death penalty was still in full flow, and the new court of criminal appeal had appeared (in 1907) there was more drama in court than at the Old Vic.

His name is attached to the court processes involved in many of the major trials between his first brief of 1882 and the mid 1920s. His first significant work in court was in the defence of the notorious Jabez Balfour, who was tried for fraud. He had a group of companies and in 1892 one of these folded with immense debts. It was the beginning of the end for Balfour and consequently, 25,000 investors in his concerns suffered from the string of failures. He stood in the dock at the Old Bailey in 1895 and Hall could do little to stem the flood of disaster. Balfour was given a sentence of 14 years penal servitude. He died of a heart attack in 1912.

In contrast, in the Seddon murder case, his defence of the accused, Frederick Seddon, was indeed a tough task. The Seddons were charged with the poisoning of their lodger, and after inquest and police court proceedings, the case went to trial at the Old Bailey. As Hall's biographer commented, 'He would have to conduct this case without that passionate personal belief in his man's innocence.'

Seddon was a man of many occupations; his room let out to lodgers was merely one of his many activities. His main line of work was in insurance; he had a large family and his home at Tollington Park was his base, where he had an office. A woman called Eliza Barrow called in the summer of 1910 with a child, asking about the room to let. Barrow was a hoarder of cash, and a miser. Her wealth was all around her, and Seddon, used to talking people out of their money, went to work. She became ill, and when she died, a doctor was persuaded to make out a death certificate stating that the cause of death was epidemic diarrhoea.

Relatives became suspicious. Gradually, the Seddons were investigated; there was a large amount of arsenic in the corpse of Eliza Barrow. Seddon was to be defended against the charge and of course, the familiar slow death of arsenic poisoning over a period of time provided the scenario. The defence rested on the fact of the doctor's written statement on the death, and also on the only indirect evidence that the prosecution had to work with. This was mostly related to Seddon's parsimony and preoccupation with money. It was a long and exhausting trial, and Seddon was a vibrant and articulate person to have in court. On the ninth day, it was time for Hall to address the jury. Though tired, he ran through all the scientific evidence, making it appear fragile; in opposition, another great barrister, Rufus Isaacs, was just as powerful.

Mr Justice Bucknill summed up. It all came to the usual final question: had Seddon anything to say? He had. He was a mason, and he knew that the judge was a mason, and so in his last words he said, 'Before the Great Architect of the universe, I am not guilty, My Lord.'

It did no good. He was sentenced to hang, and then the appeal failed. He was hanged, and not long after, as the biographer notes, 'His wife married again and suffered much persecution...'.

Hall had a fair number of failures like this, but plenty of victories in court. He died in 1927.

Hanged, Drawn and Quartered

Crime historians and writers of all varieties need a strong stomach to explain this brutal and callous method of legal execution. But one writer who never shied away from descriptions of this way out of life was Geoffrey Abbott, who died in 2016. He was the author of books on Calcraft the hangman and on the dire punishments of times past. His standard work, *Execution*, contains all one needs to know about this barbarous method of killing. Abbott, a former beefeater in the Tower of London, was without doubt a world authority on heinous and repulsive judicial punishments.

In his volume of executions he explains the process of extinction involved in such things as being buried alive, being burned internally, flayed alive and impaled on stakes. But England surely vies with the worst culprits in the hierarchy of brutal exits from life brought about by officers of the law. One of these exits – hanging, drawing and quartering – is grim in the extreme. Here is the wording of the sentence as expressed in court:

> That you be led to the place from whence you came, and from thence to be drawn upon a hurdle to the place of execution, and then you shall be hanged by the neck and, being alive, shall be cut down, and your privy members to be cut off, and your entrails taken out of your body and, you living, the same to be burnt before your eyes, and your head to be cut off, your body to be divided into four quarters, and head and quarters to be disposed of at the pleasure of the King's majesty. And the Lord have mercy on your soul.

The example of the poor soul from historical record who had to endure all this is arguably Major General Thomas Harrison. He was one of the men who had ordered the execution of Charles I in 1649. Then, at the Restoration in 1660, there was vengeance. Charles II was present to see what he considered to be justice done. Harrison was there for him to see, with a noisy public clamouring for his slow death, and Abbott describes the most repulsive detail in the whole bloody affair: 'Harrison was allowed to swing from the gallows... Half choking, he was then stretched on the boards for the executioner to slit open his stomach and pull out his entrails. Whereupon, it was reported, the appallingly mutilated Harrison leaned forward and hit the executioner across the head. Within seconds his own head had been deftly removed...'

Other nations applied their own inhuman methods of execution, such as having horses tear apart a person suspended between them (a French speciality) but this method was treasured by the Tudors in particular, along with burning at the stake. Whenever a tourist walks along London Bridge, he or she might imagine the time when heads of traitors were placed there on spikes as a warning, after being hanged, drawn and quartered.

*Hangman Tales

Perhaps surprisingly, what statistics we have from the long eighteenth century (Augustan and Regency) suggest that not every sentence of death was carried out. There was a steady process of commutation and, of course, transportation to Australia was always an option by the last years of the eighteenth century. Roger Hudson has printed some figures showing this kind of trend. He notes that in 1814–1820, for instance, 1,765 people were sentenced to hang for burglary, but only 111 were in fact executed. In the years 1828–1834, 628 were sentenced to die for horse stealing but only 14 actually were.

Nevertheless, when hanging did take place, the spectacle was horrific, and the trade of public executioner was hardly a line of work for the faint-hearted. As well as hanging felons, the hangman had to conduct floggings and branding.

Sadly and horrifically, the most dramatic hangman tales tend to be concerned either with bungled jobs or with fights to restrain and control those about to die. There are also numerous accounts in the autobiographies of executioners concerning the particular malaise of the occupants of that unenviable public post. Some took their own lives; most took to drink in a determined way; some were saved from suicide by religion, and a few managed to return to reasonably ordinary working lives. The post of public hangman was always part-time, but a few took the role so seriously that they were true professionals.

Perhaps the most notable and successful of the breed was Horncastle man William Marwood who was the origin of a popular joke: 'If Pa killed Ma, who would kill Pa? Marwood.' He took the role so seriously that he experimented with sacks of meal, working on the more humane operation of the 'drop' from the scaffold or death-cell trapdoor.

When Marwood was starting to take an interest in the subject of execution, the hangman with most national responsibility was William Calcraft, and he had a bad reputation. He was fond of a drink and was not always able to help a villain swiftly to the next world. For centuries, the business of hanging had been carried out with no real thought given to the humane exit of the criminal. It would normally take a while to die, and hence the expression 'hangers-on' as a man's friends would hang on his legs to hasten the death.

In an interview given in 1879 he stated that 'My system is humane... my object is to spare suffering. The old plan was to kill by strangling; mine is by dislocation.' It is hard to fathom why a man following a trade in a rural community would take an interest in such things, but he did, and the more he read accounts of hangings, the more his self-belief grew. He started writing letters, attempting to argue his case in the right places. It is very difficult to see this quiet man, a craftsman born in Goulceby in 1818, developing such interests. His background was against any such notorious and responsible work; his father was an illiterate shoemaker, with ten children. It seems likely that William himself was not outstanding as a wordsmith: but he had basic literacy, as he was able to write letters, many of which have been preserved.

By 1872, he carried out his first execution: this was on Francis Horry, a man who had killed his wife. Marwood's humane method had given the man a quick death. The shoemaker had a new career. According to recent research and publication, Marwood carried out executions of 167 men and 9 women. This is far above his won claim, that he had done almost 400.

Marwood had a flair for what we would now call 'spin.' He had a card made, stating that he was 'executioner', giving his address. People would buy shoe laces from him and be happy to pay more than usual for the celebrity angle. Marwood enjoyed this; he made his workshop at 6 Church Lane, Horncastle, something of an attraction. When he wrote to prospective employers in his new trade, he sent some cards. Descriptions of him talk about him having eyes that were 'quiet, resolute and penetrating'; the interviewer who met him in 1897 said that Marwood's hands were striking: '... knotted, twisted, vigorous hands, the hands of a man who had worked with them for years at some severe manual labour and who could use them with Herculean strength and tenacity if required.'

There is a story of Marwood meeting a man on a train, and the man asked if they had met before. Marwood's reply was, 'It couldn't have been at eight o'clock in the morning.' He travelled extensively in his role as executioner and was very well organised. In one letter written to his wife he gives a clear idea of a typical schedule; he had come back from Clonmel in Ireland and now:

> ... arrived at about three o'clock this morning for Birmingham, arrived about eleven o'clock today. I am now in Birmingham with the Governor. waiting to see the Governor at Bristol at half past two today, then I leave for Cambridge... if all well I shall return on Monday night or Tuesday morning. I hope all is well at home. Tell my poor boy Nero [his dog] that his master is coming home...

On his travels, he earned well; for a job in Galway the sheriff wrote to him, confirming that the charge would be £20 for the day. He attracted such attention that people wrote to him, asking to be his assistant. Overall, he was very high-profile, and some of his clients are notorious names in the history of crime in Britain.

Marwood knew Lincoln well, and often came to the city to perform his work. The new prison at Greetwell Road had opened in 1872, just a few years after he took up the execution work, and in 1876 he was still working at the Castle as well; a letter from him to the Castle Governor gives us a good idea of his meticulous attention to detail and his professional attitude, as well as his fondness for spending time in Lincoln pubs:

> Please this is to inform you that I have received your kind letter this morning in regard to a prisoner under the sentence of death ... I will engage with you to execute the prisoner at the time appointed; I will arrive at Lincoln on Saturday 16th of December. I shall go direct to the Black Boy inn near the castle. You may depend on me to be at Lincoln at the time appointed...

But in May 1882 an event happened that was to put his name in front of the nation: in Phoenix Park, Dublin, Lord Frederick Cavendish, the Irish Secretary, and his secretary, Burke, were attacked and stabbed by Fenians. Marwood was called to hang the culprits. Four men had jumped from a black cab in the park, overpowered the two politicians, and stabbed Cavendish in the heart. The killers called themselves the 'Irish Invincibles.' Marwood would soon prove that they were not so. Superintendent John Mallon tracked down five men, and all were to hang at the hands of the Lincolnshire executioner.

Marwood also hanged the arch-villain Charles Peace, a famous and well-publicised killer, who had, ironically, been born the son of a shoemaker, in Sheffield in 1832. Peace had been on trial for the shooting of a Mr Dyson at

Banner Cross, Sheffield. Marwood's hanging of Peace became a major feature with illustrations, in the popular magazine, *Police News*.

But not long after the Phoenix Park hangings, Marwood became ill. He had been for a drink at one of his favourite Lincoln pubs when he became ill. He died on 4 September 1884, aged sixty-four. There had been some talk that his death might have been linked to the Fenians, as they had vowed retribution on him, and he had received some threatening letters, but the verdict was natural causes; he was buried at Holy Trinity on Spilsby Road. He had no living kin; his dog, Nero, was sold after his death. It says a lot about the notoriety attached to William Marwood that it is not possible now to locate his grave; so many 'true crime' souvenir hunters had taken parts of the stone that it is now unmarked.

What were his views on his trade? He said that he was proud of his work. His words on hanging were: 'It's all as stops murder. The fear of the rope keeps many a man's blood down, and his temper cool; and it is only another way of keeping down vermin – vermin have a mortal sting, and as such should be put out of the way of doing harm.' Statistics say that hanging is indeed no deterrent in many cases, and that states with a policy of execution experience no reduction in murder rates. But William Marwood, Lincolnshire hangman, in some perverse way was fulfilled by this profession. Such was his fame that Madame Tussaud made a waxwork of him. He liked being called a 'public executioner' because it made him someone distinct from a mere 'hangman.' After all, in one notable case that went wrong in Calcraft's time, an unfortunate criminal took four minutes to die on the end of the rope.

Of all the tales of hangings gone wrong, apart from the case of *John Lee*, one experience of hangman Bartholomew Binns in Liverpool maybe takes first place. This was in 1883, and the con in question was Henry Dutton, who had killed his wife's grandmother. At the appointed time of the judicial death penalty being done, the dour procession of under-sheriff, prison staff and other officials walked to the death-cell. Public hangings had been abolished in 1868. Journalists could report, but the days of the general public having jollies and watching the felons being strung up had gone. The officials reached the death cell and Dutton stood on the trapdoor. The final prayer was said, and Binns took a close look at his man, who was pinioned. The trap opened and Dutton dropped to his doom.

Then came the problem. The man dangled on the rope, which spun, and time passed. In fact a lot of time passed, and the doctor looked down to see the victim spinning around, struggling, and not at all dead. 'This is poor work. He is not yet dead' the medical man said. Everyone present must have blushed and felt like looking for somewhere to hide. The drop for that hanging was seven and a half feet, so Dutton was not a distant prospect. They would all have heard the choking and grunting, as death came along most agonisingly.

As for Binns, he left the gaol (Kirkdale) speedily. The coroner had questions to ask and he asked where Binns was. He wanted him there, to explain things. The explanation is plain to see: the knot was in the wrong place and so the jolt had not snapped the bone in the spot where death would have been a rapid consequence. All kinds of commentaries were burning to ask if the hangman had been sober. There was no such thing as a sober hangman back in those days.

We also have the author's namesake, Stephen Wade, a Doncaster businessman, who at first assisted Albert Pierrepoint of the famous dynasty of hangmen. Wade kept some pencil records in a notebook now in an archive, and one experience he and Albert had was horrible in the extreme. This was the hanging of a German paratrooper who had been captured in a field after parachuting down. The Nazi was Karl Richter, 29: a large, very strong man. The events in that cell and on the way to the trapdoor were horrendous. Wade wrote in his notebook:

> On entering cell to take prisoner over and pinion him he made a bolt for the door. I warded him off and then he charged the wall with a terrific force with his head. This made him most violent. We seized him and strapped his arms at rear... The belt was faulty. Not enough eyelid holes, and he broke away from them. I shouted to Albert 'He is loose!' and he was held by warders until we made him secure. He could not take it and charged again for the wall, screaming 'Help me'.

Finally, he was ready for the drop. Wade wrote simply: 'neck broken immediately'.

It comes as no surprise to learn that Steve Wade liked a drink and smoked heavily. Syd Dernley, also a hangman, said that Wade was a quiet man. No doubt, when he was running his Doncaster transport firm, he was happy never to speak of his part-time job.

One of the very strangest tales recorded from the death cell was given by a condemned man called Jeans who asked his lawyer, when the noose was waiting for him, to let him have some fresh eggs for his last breakfast. Jeans had callously walked towards the sea and thrown a child in to be drowned. He had since said nothing whatsoever until that request for eggs. On his last morning, the prisoner created a stir and did plenty of shouting and complaining. The lawyer found out that this was because the eggs had been forgotten, and so they were hastily provided.

Jeans spoke at last, simply to say thanks. Then he ate heartily, and walked to the scaffold.

Hangwomen

The annals of crime regarding execution are dominated by male hangmen, but across the world there have been instances of women sorting out the noose. Sometimes it is a case of such a thing almost happening, as John Rowe recalled. Referring to a state in America, he wrote: '... there happened to be a woman sheriff... no hangman was at first forthcoming, and the woman sheriff declared that she was prepared to do her duty in that respect. But no doubt to her own great relief, she was not called upon... a hangman being obtained at the eleventh hour.'

However, in Ireland we have a case of a successful woman executioner: Lady Betty Sugrue. In Roscommon she awaited her own death at the end of the rope, after being convicted of the murder of a man who called at her home in 1789, and the story goes that the man was her own son, Padraig, who had left to join the army years before. There may well be some stretches of the truth in her story (one source is from Sir William Wilde, father of Oscar) but there is no doubt that, waiting for her death, learning of there being no hangman present, she offered to fulfil the role, was given the job, and was most adept at it. Such events had happened before, notably in York in the case of William Curry who did the same thing.

Sugrue was successful, and her tale has gathered some myths and exaggerations, but she had a room in the gaol and she did the flogging when required – a traditional role of the hangman. She acquired the name of 'The woman from hell.'

Hanratty (A6 Murder)

In August 1961, Michael Gregston was shot and killed in what became known as the A6 Murder. A woman who was in the car with Gregston, Valerie Storie, was raped, shot five times and left paralysed. James Hanratty stood trial for the murder and on 17 February 1962, the decision was announced that he was 'guilty' and events progressed in the usual manner towards the death cell and the rope.

But there is nothing decided or final about that verdict. In 1971 Paul Foot wrote a very cogent analysis of the developments in investigation after the execution, and a mystery unfurled. Much of the interest stirred up concerns a man called Peter Alphon. He was an initial suspect but had an alibi, saying that at the time of the murder he was staying at a hotel called the Vienna, in Maida Vale. But there had been a development involving another man in temporary accommodation. This was a reported attempted rape at a house where there were rental vacancies. The would-be attacker had run off, and then events led to the eventual submission of Alphon to the law. There was an identity parade but Alphon was not identified. That seemed to be the end of that line of enquiry, but back at the Vienna, bullets were found and ballistics experts linked them to the A6 murder weapon.

Yet the trial of Hanratty went on, and his attempts at giving an alibi failed. After the hanging, Alphon admitted that he did commit the A6 murder. He died in 2009. It is virtually certain that there was a grievous miscarriage of justice in the case of Hanratty. In 2002 there was an appeal and DNA evidence appraisal initiative. Nevertheless, it is still asked: where is the pardon for James Hanratty?

Heath, Neville (1917–1946)

Neville Heath, referred to in one study as a 'handsome brute', surely deserved that name. Not only was he the quintessential charmer and seducer of women; he was also a brutal killer who murdered two women in 1946. He was born in Ilford and brought up a Catholic, then joined the RAF just before war broke out, but he was always making trouble and pain for someone, even in his spell of training in South Africa, where he was such a handful and rebel that he was court-martialled.

Back in civvy street he started his life of crime, and he went in search of women in clubland; being a playboy who liked a good time led him into the kinds of circles in which women could easily be encountered, and smoothly seduced. The killer in him first appeared when he stayed at a hotel with Margery Gardner, and her body was found the next morning, when Heath was nowhere to be seen. But he had the bare-faced cheek to write to the law and explain a connection to the hotel where the body was found. Then he moved on. He arrived at a Bournemouth hotel and there he met his second victim: Doreen Marshall. He was using an alias, of course, with his knowledge of the RAF he posed as Group-Captain Rupert Brooke (using the name of the famous poet as some kind of joke). Doreen disappeared, and the police caught up with Heath.

When it came to his trial, the issue of his sanity was raised; Heath's counsel chose not to let him give evidence and to plead the defence of insanity. Witnesses said that although he was a psychopath and sexual sadist, he was not insane. In the summing up of the judge (which is always a powerful influence on a jury) his thinking was that Heath was not insane and had planned the murders. He was found guilty. There was no appeal, and he was hanged at Pentonville in October 1946.

His life and criminal career certainly attracted commentators, and one of the first was written by Gerald Byrne: *Borstal Boy: the uncensored story of Neville Heath*, which appeared in a short time after the execution. Byrne wrote a rare volume, containing as it did some letters and plenty of information regarding Borstal and also the medical considerations about Heath's mind. Byrne wrote in his preface: 'It is a moot point whether stiff handling, the birch and a prison sentence might not have made all the difference to Heath.' He had written an indictment of the use of repressive violence against young offenders, and that was a hot topic then, with birching still in use, and physical punishment used across the school system, even being maintained in the reorganisation of secondary schooling in the 1944 Education Act which gave Britain the tripartite system of grammar/ secondary modern/ secondary technical schools.

Byrne incorporated into his book one of the most stark and expressive accounts of a hanging available at the time (when a campaign to abolish the practice was not far off): 'On either side of him are warders, experienced in this task. They are standing on planks stretched across the gallows drop and steady themselves by holding on to ropes that drop to them from the cross-beam that also carries the execution rope They are pressing close to Heath... The chaplain has led the sombre service of the dead. There is a crack as the lever goes over and Heath disappears from sight...'

Highwaymen

The *Newgate Calendar* relished collecting tales of the robbers on the King's Highway. Their profession was a perilous and risky one, as firearms were involved, and even if bullets were not ripping into flesh, the very act of robbing the King's subjects on the general highway was a capital offence. The reports and ballad narratives were often heightened into romantic and glorifying assaults, and even gentlemanly behaviour by some robbers, but this offence was theft with threats and often bloody murder accompanied the act.

Dick Turpin may be the name most associated with the crime, but there were many other notable villains on the roads. Claude Duval attracted the most romantic tales; he was supposed to be the man who was considerate and polite to the ladies in the coaches he stopped and robbed. Others were alleged to have done unbelievable deeds, such as Nevison.

William Nevison is as much a mythic figure as Dick Turpin, and is perhaps Yorkshire's second most notorious highwayman. Most areas in Yorkshire like to claim him as their own, notably in the burgeoning heritage industry, but what is not widely known is that there is a strong oral tradition that he was active around Gomersal and Hartshead, and his most well-known deed here was a murder, when he shot the landlord of a public house near Batley. Nevison's dark fame across stretches of the West Riding and South Yorkshire made him the subject of ballads and apocryphal tales; there is a cutting at Castleford called Nevison's Leap and an inn was given his name. The song Bold Nevison has some patently untrue statements such as:

I have never robbed no man of tuppence
And I've never done murder nor killed.
Though guilty I've been all my lifetime,
So gentlemen do as you please.

The main story on his life is supposedly the feat that won him the nickname 'Swift Nick': a ride north from Gad's Hill in Kent to York. He reputedly robbed a man in Kent and then made his escape on a bay mare, riding north at an incredibly fast pace, going from Kent to York in a day.

We know that Nevison's father was a steward at Wortley Hall and that his brother was a schoolmaster, and we know that the robber himself was married and had a daughter. His wife lived on to be 109 years old, dying in 1732. The oral tales pass on a complimentary view of Nevison, and a diary entry for 1727 records that 'at the same time there lived with this family Nevison, who afterwards was an exciseman, but being out of his place, became a highwayman.' This notes that he was with a family called Skelton who were Wortley gamekeepers. That detail makes sense: that an exciseman would find an attraction in the wealth attainable and turn tables to the wrong side of the law. Further investigation reveals that he began his criminal career when eh started stealing at the age of fourteen. James Sharpe, in his book on Dick Turpin, says about Nevison: 'After being punished for stealing a silver spoon from his father, he stole ten pounds from his father and also his horse, and set off for London, cutting his horse and slitting its throat in case he be suspected...'

It is hard to believe that the robber who haunted the Leeds to Manchester road around what is now Hartshead and the northern fringe of Mirfield was also once in the service of the Duke of York and was at the siege of Dunkirk, but that is the tradition. Everything about him fits the description given him in the Victorian period when the myths were fully generated. One main piece of local tradition is that he used to visit one of his women at Royd Nook and would visit an old inn called the King's Head north of Mirfield; he would most likely make his way from that base onto the Manchester road. The story is that he stopped at an inn in Batley and the landlord recognised him. The man raised the alarm and came to tackle the robber, but Nevison shot him and rode away. Acccording to Victorian antiquarians, there was once a stone in a field near Howley Hall with the inscription, 'Here Nevison killed Fletcher, 1684.'

This was his last caper into the lawless valleys of West Yorkshire. He was pursued and was finally tracked down and cornered at The Three Houses Inn at Sandal. He was taken to York and hanged. He was captured by William Hardcastle.

Someone of equal media attention was John Rann, known as 'Sixteen String Jack.' He only lived to be twenty-four, but he made an impression to compare with the most colourful of the criminal characters of Georgian England. His nickname came from the fact that he wore sixteen coloured strings on his silk trousers. He started out in his life of crime as a pickpocket, and then moved from pockets and purses to the full-blown villain known as a highway robber.

He appears to have been difficult to convict, and he added charm and chutzpah to his villainy. One story recounts how he faced the blind magistrate John Fielding (brother of Henry, the novelist) and when he was asked if he wished to say anything he said, 'I know no more of the matter than you do... or half as much!' In those days, a man in gaol could have visitors and he could arrange entertainments for them, and so, after being thrown into Newgate and then being tried for robbing a servant of royalty, he had a grand dinner just before he was to visit the scaffold and swing for his crimes. On record is the account of his wearing a pea-green suit as he waited to hang, and then dancing a jig. After all, the mob demanded and expected some entertainment.

Then we have Claude Duval, the French robber, from an earlier time. He died in 1670, and figures in the classical collection of highwayman tales, *A General History of the Lives of the Highwaymen* by Captain Johnson. Johnson wrote that Duval, who had been a footman, joined in the refreshing milieu of dissipation and pleasure following the restoration of the monarchy in 1660. Johnson adds that, 'His funds, however, being soon exhausted, he deemed it no great crime to extract contributions from the English.'

Johnson also adds that one of his notorious crimes was robbing a man called Hooper, who was master of hounds for Charles II. When Hooper was questioned about this, he said, 'I have had sport enough for a villain who bound me neck and heel, contrary to my desire, and then took fifty guineas from me to pay him for his labour...'

Duval was hanged at Tyburn. He was only 27, and had been arrested when drunk in a London street.

Humphreys, Sir Travers (1867–1956)

Travers Humphreys was one of the most successful and impressive High Court judges on record. The cases before him included those of Oscar Wilde, Dr. Crippen, Horatio Bottomley and the Brides in the Bath murders. He was prosecuting counsel in the Bywaters and Thompson trial. Humphreys was called to the bar in 1889, and was Judge of the King's Bench in 1928.

In his memoirs he recalls the trials of several high-profile offenders, and he made some strong and opinionated remarks in the course of his writings, often finding a paradox to explore, such as his pronouncement on how the criminal justice system had changed since the mid-Victorian times, as we see in this comment on prisons: 'We hear... that prisons are so full that cells built and intended for a single individual have to accommodate two prisoners, so that by the irony of fate prisoners who were delivered by the philanthropic efforts of reformers from what was called the cruel practice of solitary confinement are today protesting that there is no longer any privacy for a gentleman who is an enforced guest of Her Majesty for a time.'

I

Ilchester Gaol Scandal

In 1821, Henry 'Orator' Hunt published an account of his horrendous stretch in Ilchester gaol, Somerset. He had experienced and seen regular abuse of inmates, from violence to extreme neglect. Finally, after strenuous attempts to make the authorities aware of the abuses there, the Commissioners heard the reports, and Hunt spoke for everyone on that occasion. This was a man who had been at Peterloo at the time of the infamous massacre in 1819. He was one of the foremost radicals of his time, struggling for the liberties and rights of Britons at a time when repressive laws were eating away at individual freedom and any hint of sedition was ruthlessly suppressed. This was the time – the Regency – when a group of 'Luddites' (machine wreckers) up in the West Riding had been speedily tried and hanged at York, with no valid trial of individuals.

Hunt was destined for prison and he had the misfortune to be sent to Ilchester. His work covers what he had to endure in his two and a half year stretch. He explained 'cruel and inhuman practices' applied by the gaoler, William Bridle, with the knowledge of the local magistrates.

Richard Whittington-Egan, doyen of true crime writers. He died in 2016 after completing a possibly definite account of Jack the Ripper.

Master criminal Charlie Peace was hanged here. (*Laura Carter*)

Left: A poster recounting one of many attempts on Victoria's life. (*Author*)

Below: The Rowland Case: Olive Balchin's body. (*Author*)

One of the more colourful Messengers. (*Author*)

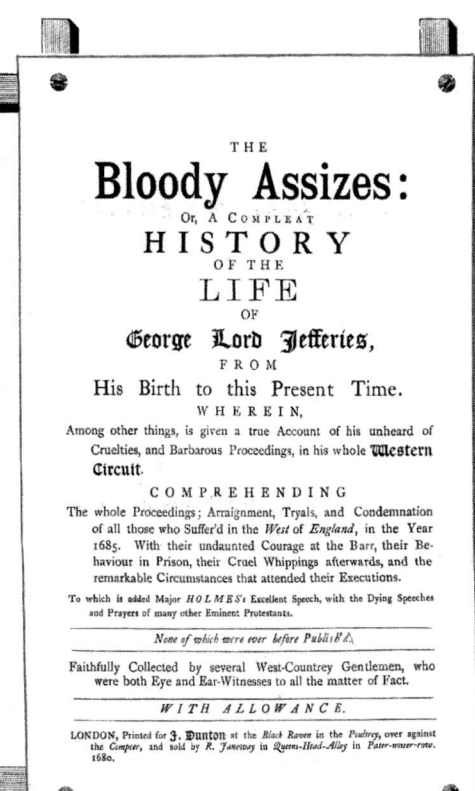

Cover of The Bloody Assizes, 1685. (*Author*)

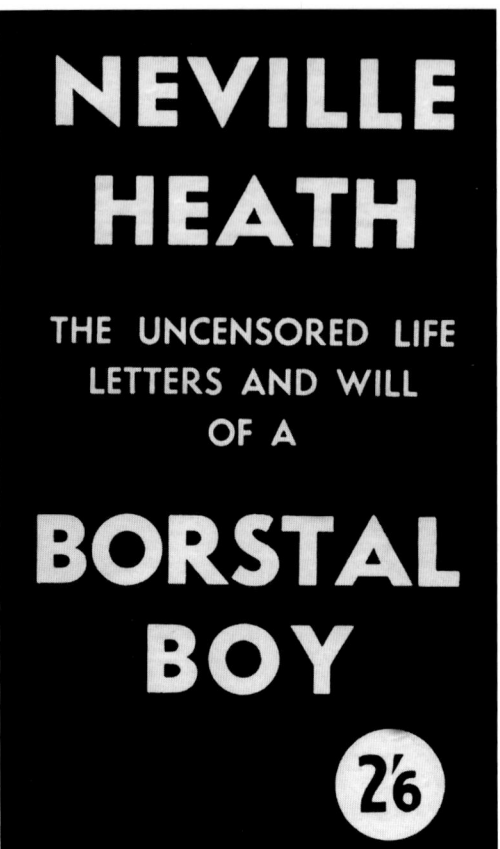

Cover of The Uncensored Life, Letters and Will of a Bostal Boy, published about the life of Neville Heath. (*Author*)

Cover of Bottomley's poems from gaol. (*Author*)

Right: Image from 1950s booklet, The Brides in the Bath. (*New Sensations Series*)

Below: Chief Superintendent Hannam (centre) and family! Hannam led the investigations against Bodkin Adams. (*Author*)

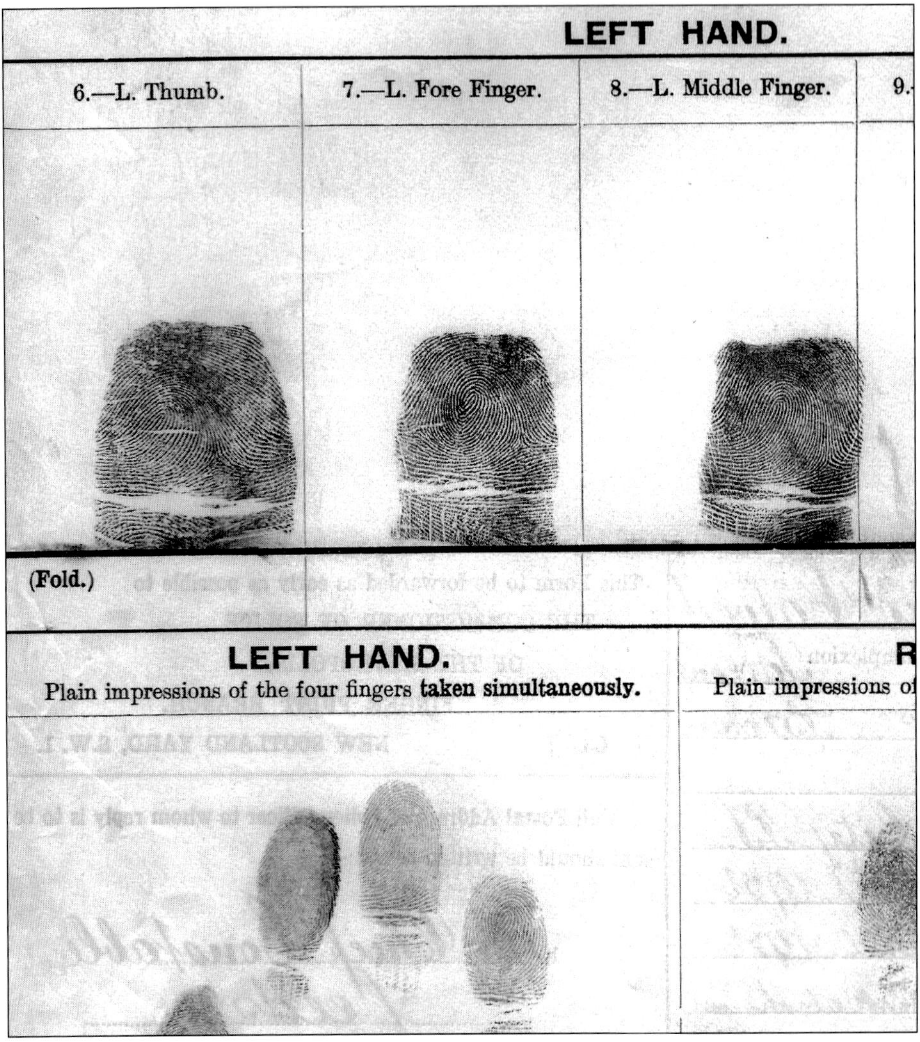

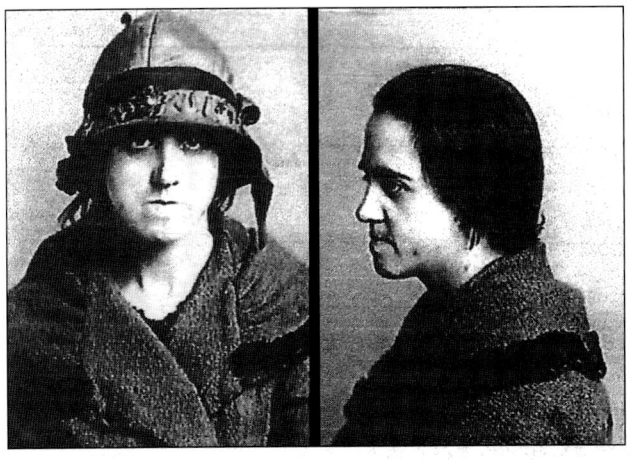

Above: Louie Calvert's fingerprints. (*Author*)

Left: Mugshots of Louie Calvert. (*Author*)

An eighteenth century popular narrative. (*Author*)

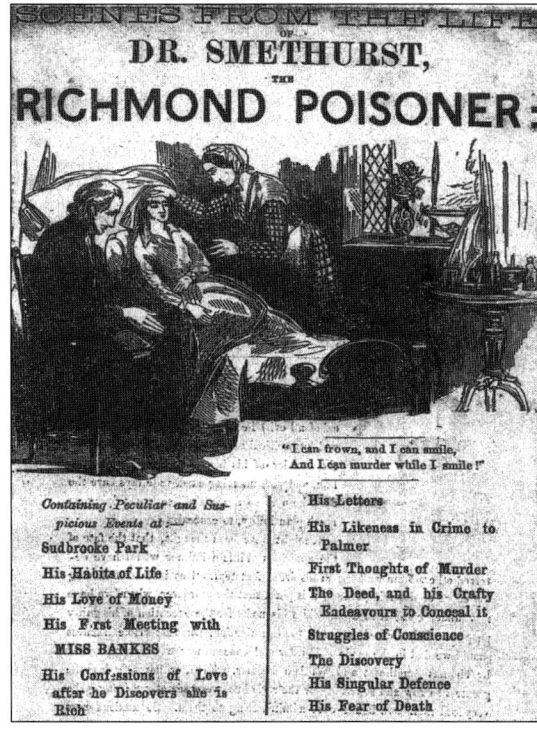

The story of Dr Smethurst c.1859. (*Chapbook*)

Hannah Dobbs, anonymous booklet c.1870s. (*Unknown*)

Master escaper Jack Sheppard. (*The New Wonderful Magazine*)

A Regency print of the Old Bailey. (*Author*)

The Ordinary of Newgate from a penny paper, c.1732.

Palmer, the Rugeley Poisoner.
(*Anonymous booklet, c.1912*)

A penny dreadful cover c.1870s.
(*Author*)

Right: A wing entry of a penitentiary in Port Arthur. (*Author*)

Below: A circular issued in Northallerton gaol. (*Author*)

DESCRIPTION OF

PRISONER JUST ESCAPED

From H.M. Prison,⎯⎯⎯⎯⎯⎯⎯⎯⎯⎯⎯⎯⎯

Date and Hour of Escape	Name and Alias, Offence, Place of Conviction and Sentence	Born at	Age	Complexion	Hair	Eyes and Eyebrows	Build	Height Ft. Ins.	Trade	Dress Worn at Time of Escape	Distinctive Marks and Peculiarities, with Localities to which Prisoner may Proceed

Any persons who apprehend, and deliver up the Prisoner, may receive such reward as the Prison Department or Directors of Prisons may consider their services severally justify ⎯⎯ not exceeding FIVE POUNDS in the whole.

The Tichborne Claimant. (*R. Storry Dean:* Romances of The Law Courts *(1890)*)

Mrs Van der Elst protests on an execution day. (*Author*)

A classic work on York trials. (*Leman Rede, York Castle (1829)*)

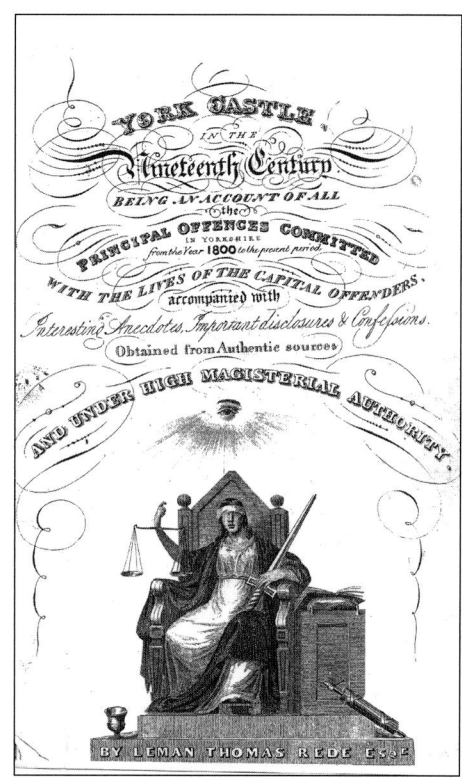

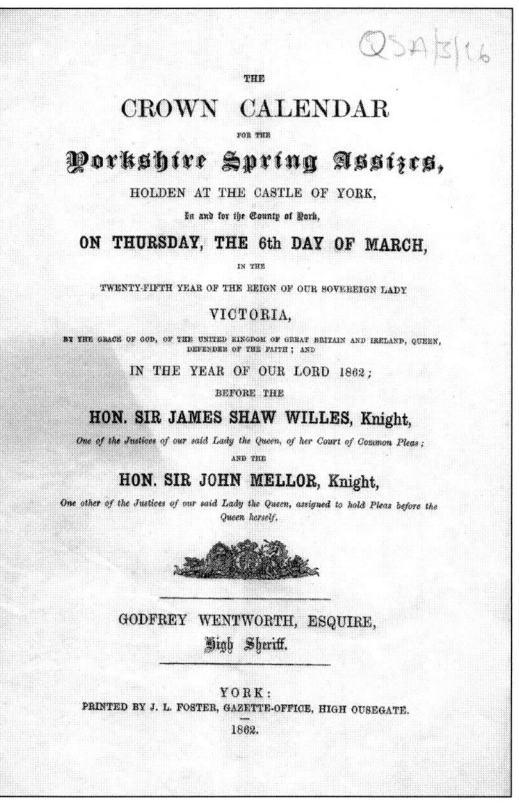

A typical crown calendar of trials. (*Author*)

Above: The prison within the castle at Lincoln. (*Author*)

Left: Mary Bateman, the so-called 'Yorkshire Witch'. (*York Castle*)

A documentary frontispiece to a popular crime collection c. 1890s: *The New Newgate Calendar* (A Ritchie). (*Anonymous booklet, 1890*)

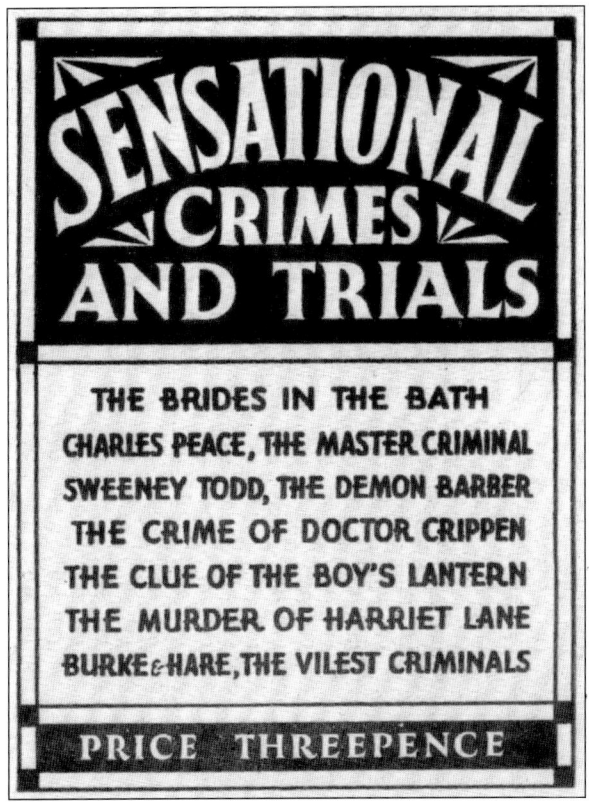

Sensational Crimes and Trials publication, a twentieth century derivative of the 'Penny Dreadful' – when true crime was bordering on fiction and myth.

Image of Dick Turpin from a cigarette box.

J

Jack the Ripper

In January 2023 the news across the headlines was that the face of Jack the Ripper was now known. Of course this immediately invited all true crime fans to investigate themselves. It emerged that in a police museum, a walking-stick had been found that had been a retirement gift presentation to Inspector Abberline, who had been prominent in the investigations into the Jack the Ripper murders back in 1888. The face etched into the top of the cane was thought to be that of the Ripper. Of course, evidence for this was lacking.

The story of Jack the Ripper, who did his heinous work of mutilation and murder in Whitechapel in 1888 over the course of a few months is now one of the grandest, most discussed serial killer narratives in the history of true crime. His identity has been surmised or hinted at on multiple occasions. Even in 1888, the writer George Sims (author of *Christmas Day in the Workhouse*) wrote in his autobiography that, stopping at a drinks stall in London, the seller had thought that Sims' face was the exact likeness of the Ripper. Over the years there have been countless theories of the killer's identity, from tales of alleged uncles and various relatives being the man, to celebrity theories, such as Patricia Cornwell's insistence that the painter Walter Sickert was Jack; more than that, theories of royalty being involved have emerged. Arguably, one of the most impressive and persuasive accounts came from Bruce Robinson, who spent fifteen years of his life researching and writing *They All Love Jack*, a massive 828-page book, arguing that songwriter Michael Maybrick was the killer.

It seems that any person who was moving around Whitechapel in the 1880s is a likely candidate if they had medical and local knowledge. Robinson was aware of the media frenzy around any new theory; he wrote, 'Middle-aged men with disturbing expressions lean over the safety-rail, clutching files. These are the Ripperologists. They are waiting for the Rippers to come out.' That may be so, but then, he has joined their ranks.

At Ripper conferences, criminologists, historians, local experts, medico-legal professors and plain ordinary citizens with a passion for historical truth all come together to show how hard everyone is working to lever out the mystery man from the mass of suspects. But as the years pass, all kinds of 'established' facts are questioned, perhaps most powerfully in recent years by Hallie Rubenhold in her book, *The Five*. In this account, she revisits the 'canonical five' victims: Mary Ann Nichols, Ann Chapman, Elizabeth Stride, Catherine Eddowes and Marie Kelly. She set about questioning the given label of 'prostitutes' applied to them, and finds evidence more of want, indigency and desperation than purposeful 'lady of the night' sex selling.

The facts remain that between 7 August and 9 November 1888 there were vicious, bestial and remorseless slaughterings of women in Whitechapel by a killer who had serious defects of mind, such was the extreme ferocity of the attacks and the methods of murder involved. One writer, contributing to an anthology edited by Richard Glyn Jones, summarises eight commentary positions for the creation of dominant theories, and these are still around: The Foreigner, the Policeman, the Woman, the Mad Surgeon, a Father's Vengeance, the American Sailor, George Chapman, and the Man with the White Eyes.

To this there have been new ones added, but as time goes by, there is more and more research accumulating steadily, and for every new claim or theory, there are experts to respond. Ripperologists have also had to cope with the alleged 'Ripper Diaries' and the line of thought insisting that these texts were written by the Ripper himself. Strong claims have been made for James Maybrick, Francis Tumblety and Montague Druitt in particular. Then, in 2013, the late Richard Whittington-Egan produced *Jack the Ripper, the Definitive Casebook*, and so we have a real compendium of candidates and theories. The author gives labels to the six dominant approaches as he sees them, making room for very modern social science based lines of thought.

As a separate corpus of work, we have the Ripper copycat murders and the cases of murders committed outside London which may actually have been committed by the Ripper. A notable instance of this, which has been examined and most often given as a very likely Ripper murder, occurred in Bradford, and seems to fit in neatly with the theory that the Ripper followed the tours of Sir Henry Irving in the provinces. But nothing really substantial has come from these copycat cases.

Justice Godfrey: Slain

So many nasty murders inhabit the chronicles of crime in Britain, and many of them are concerned either with domestic conflicts or with violent crimes, but some of the most infamous are in that rare category that relates to great national issues and events. Such a murder happened in 1678, when a magistrate called Sir Edmund Berry Godfrey was slaughtered in London.

Godfrey went for a walk in the morning of 12 October and was seen by witnesses. He often went out and was busy all day but, as Stephen Knight, who wrote a magisterial narrative on the murder confirms, an early panic was expressed on that fateful day. The day after his walk, his servants went in search of him, and he was not found. It took another five days before his corpse was discovered at Primrose Hill. The magistrate had been severely beaten up and a sword had been run through him.

Knight produced one of the finest examples of a true crime book that links to multiple themes, and explains that the atmosphere in London not long after the Great Plague and of wars with the Netherlands was one of a nation that 'went mad with fear and hatred'. This 'lunacy' he explained, went on for three years, and in this period, Roman Catholics were vulnerable – more so than usual.

A biographer writing in 1961 called this milieu 'the Angry World' and explained that what lay behind the Godfrey case was the horrendous figure of Titus Oates, known as the instigator of the Popish Plot. Basically, he and a man called Tonge exploited the atmosphere of anti-Catholic feeling around town. The biographer is Charles Ward, and he explains the consequences of their invented plot against crown and land: ' Almost beyond belief, it was at first not taken seriously... but on September 28, Oates and Tonge made their legal depositions before ... Godfrey. On the same day, two conspirators were examined by King and Council.'

It was spread around the city that Godfrey's murder was linked to this terrifying plot against decent Protestant folk.

The whole business grew into a murder mystery. Thomas De Quincey, in the essay on murder (see *De Quincey)* wrote: 'The finest work of the seventeenth century is unquestionably the murder of Dir Edmund Berry Godfrey, which has my entire approbation. In the grand feature of mystery, which in some shape or other ought to colour every judicious attempt at murder, it is excellent...'

Knight's book is an excellent example of how theories on a mystery should be built up and explained. The links are made from a street murder to some major issues of espionage and political extremism, and the story grows and grows in significance at the hands of Knight, a masterly storyteller.

K

Kiszco, Stefan: Error and Innocence

In 1975, above a lay-by near the road from Rochdale towards Yorkshire, a schoolgirl called Lesley Molseed was sexually attacked and murdered; the ensuing police investigation took a wrong turn, based largely on false statements, and they thought they had their man in the person of Stefan Kiszo, a tax office clerk living in Rochdale. Various sightings and statements led to his being arrested and convicted, and what happened next was reported after the man had spent sixteen years in prison.

One report, with a picture showing Stefan kissing his mother, noted that back during the investigation, 'the investigating officer read it to him and gave him a chance to read it himself. "I just signed it in any old way. I was under the impression these officers were going to hit me or do something violent" he said.' What lay ahead was a custodial sentence and plenty of bullying and victimization. After all, the papers had made it clear that Stefan was a child-killer.

In 1977 when he first arrived at Wakefield prison he was kept apart, for his own safety; in prison he had a mental breakdown. The fact is that Stefan was not a well man; he had a disease which had a range of repercussions on his physical well-being. When he was freed, it was then understood, after medical evidence, that Stefan could not possibly be guilty of the crime, and the reasons were medical and physiological. There had been semen found on the clothing of Lesley, and now, just before the release of Stefan, a doctor made it clear to investigators that at the time of the murder, Stefan had been given drugs for his sexually located illness, and it was asserted that it would not have been possible for him to have produced semen until after ten weeks past the drugs being given. The murder had taken place three weeks after the treatment.

A full account of the case is given by Jonathan Rose and two ex-detectives, and this puts light on a sad train of mistakes and lack of understanding, as well as assumptions and prejudice. Stefan Kiszko was a gentle, kind son, whose one real pleasure after his working week was to take his mother and aunty to the garden centre. The statements made about him were marked by narrow-minded prejudice and narrow-minded bias.

In many ways this case has become a template model for so many miscarriages of justice and the police learned a great deal from it.

Kray Brothers

There is a library of works dedicated to the Kray brothers, of course. What can be added when so much has been said? A survey may take the reader from Fred Dineage's book, *The Krays*, on them, which reads as if the 'horse's mouth' is giving us direction information, to the memoirs of family and friends. Much influence has been accrued from the writings of Frankie Fraser, whose gangland stories have played a major role in perpetuating the Kray myth, somewhere between glamour and awesome disbelief.

As well as the library of works in print, Ronald and Reginald Kray, born in 1933, have also been portrayed in feature films in a number of ways, always with a current of enquiry regarding the complexity of their personalities. The basic facts are simple and straightforward: born in London's East End and brought up to box and to wheel and deal in the underworld of deviance, they attained iconic status in the world of true crime as they established their 'firm' and their influence grew. Ronnie's mental illness became more apparent as time went on, but their empire progressed.

In a world of gang rivalry, they learned how to survive, and their criminal acts were pushed to the limit as time went on, reaching acts of extreme violence and murder. In 1967, Jack 'The Hat' McVitie was killed very brutally, after a gun had jammed and a knife had to be used to finish him. Another murder victim was George Cornell. It was going to take something special on the part of the detectives to nail the twins, and in May 1968, a huge force of police barged into the Kray's nest in Shoreditch, finally finding them after more than 100 officers had raided homes and offices all over London. The next step was a trial, and the law had been forced to create a tranche of people to testify. The twins were sentenced to thirty years inside.

We might gain some impression of the status of the Krays in popular culture when we consider their presence in the more colourful and sensational publications such as the handbook of the Crime Museum, which shows a briefcase with a spring loaded syringe and a bottle of hydrogen cyanide, with the information that this 'was supposed to kill and enemy of the Krays.' It never did.

L

*Lags and the Library

Some prisoners cope very well with jail and they need the time inside. Once in a prison library book I found these words scrawled inside: '*Browny, C Wing. Doing three and luvvin' it.*' Others dread each sunrise and wake to find that their dreams of home are just dreams, and they are actually still in their pad, with the smells and the often unwelcome company of their pad mate and their bad habits and noise. But there is no doubt that prison librarians do everything they can to stop their stock disappearing, being chewed up or torn in strips to be used in the 'burn' and for fags. In my own archive of materials, I have a note written on a form requesting the return of some prison library books from a con. He wrote, 'I have not got these books. I was taken down the block and got twistered [sic] up by the screws and so the books got lost in this mess, Miss'.

I am most sorry.' So defaced books and stolen books have been the basis of a number of felonies over the years, and the literary lags (at least some of them) were not always trustworthy as library assistants.

Being notorious is very difficult; being just another con is easy. So we have the literature of prison and the tales of bold and dangerous crime. As John McVicar memorably said, 'Being a thief is a terrific life, but the trouble is, they put you in the nick for it.' In the cases of a number of literary men who were despatched to the Scrubs over the years, their fame was of no consequence. They put their heads down, did the time and came back, paradoxically full of ideas for their creative work.

As with my quote above, it must be said that books in a prison library have a hard time: they provide plain paper for notes, threats, details of arranged rendezvous times, and of course, simply outlets for anger and frustration. For two particular inmates of the Scrubs, the prison library and its contents would have been ironically familiar. The men in question are Joe Orton and John Hampson. Joe Orton, author of the plays *Loot* and *Entertaining Mr Sloane*, was given a six-month sentence in 1962 for stealing 72 library books and committing wilful damage on them; he and his lover Kenneth Halliwell also removed 1,653 illustration plates from library books. Orton told the press that he remained unrepentant: 'I objected to public money going on dull, badly written books' he said, adding, ' I removed books and substituted pictures of my own choosing for the photos of the authors on the back.. then I'd smuggle them back onto the shelves again. I once pasted a picture of a naked tattooed man over a photo of John Betjeman.'

Some of these transmuted books and cover pictures may be seen on the internet today, and in John Lahr's edition of Orton's letters, he includes examples: on *The Three Faces of Eve* by Corbet Thigpen and Hervey Cleckley he pasted two rather Gothic faces and the head of a cat. On the cover of Phyllis Hambledon's *Queen's Favourite* he pasted an image of two half-naked men in an improper and offensive embrace.

The two men were sent to the Scrubs and then transferred on to different jails, Orton to HMP East Church at Sheerness, and Halliwell to HMP Ford at Arundel. Amazingly, prison was good for Orton in a fundamental, personal sense, as he told the papers after release: 'Before, I had been vaguely conscious of something rotten somewhere; prison crystallised this. The old whore society really lifted up her skirts and the stench was pretty foul.' He also said that 'Being in the nick brought detachment' to his writing. John Lahr, his biographer, makes a strong case for the argument that the main experience prison offered was a period away from the oppressive relationship with Halliwell.

Lahr makes it clear that Halliwell, who eventually murdered Orton on 9 August 1967 at their London flat, was the self-defined 'failure' of the pair.

They were very close, and acted as a duo, Orton wanting Halliwell with him after his success in seeing his plays performed with the help of his agent, Peggy Ramsay. Halliwell saw himself as a pathetic failure who never found his voice as a writer, and so he was jealous and possessive. In 1963, Orton sold *The Ruffian on the Stair* to the BBC. It was the beginning of a meteoric rise in which he was to move around with the rich and famous in the theatrical world. Such was his impact on people that actors' memoirs are copious in their attention given to this young rebel from Leicester who was as challenging and aggressive in his writing as he was in his dress and demeanour. He set out to offend in his work, and for a man who experienced jail, his literary content is unsurprisingly radical and restless.

In contrast, Halliwell inside was depressed – so much so that on coming out, he tried to take his own life. Not long after, Orton wrote in his diary that he was going 'up and up.' This was guaranteed to affect his friend very deeply. But his prison life did have a profound influence on him, despite the short stretch. Peggy Ramsay recalled, 'he went on to tell me that he had been six months in Wormwood Scrubs [untrue!] for a series of minor thefts and that it had been remarkably good for him. When I asked if he intended going back to crime, he said certainly not, if it was possible to earn a living by any other way.'

On 9 August 1967, the bodies of Orton and Halliwell were found in their flat: Halliwell had bludgeoned Orton to death, and then taken his own life with an overdose of sleeping tablets. I was nineteen years old on that day, and so I'll never forget reading the reports the next day; in his thirty-four years, Joe Orton had a massive impact on myself and my writing friends. John Lahr summed up the nature of the impact of this provincial iconoclast: ' he believed there was no sense in being a rebel without applause.'

Comedian Kenneth Williams, who knew both Orton and Halliwell very well, made a note in his diary for 10 August 1964 which gives a telling insight into the stormy relationship: 'I though he [Orton] was a really delightful personality. Obviously wanting to shock though. The friend called Ken comes in on cue and most of the time, before cue. It is v. annoying One of the most irritating things in the world is when people correct each other.' Later, after Orton's death, Williams made an even more perceptive comment: ' I think the motive was Halliwell loved Joe. Halliwell felt that something v. big and important threatened that love.'

In contrast, John Hampson, a writer who was emerging in the 1930s to accolades and respect from his peers, was sent to Wormwood Scrubs for stealing library books. He wanted simply to possess them not deface them.

Hampson was born in 1901 in Birmingham, from a large family who ran a brewing business. His real name was John Frederick Hampson Simpson, and he was educated as a writer in the school of the street and factory rather than in a classroom. He did a variety of jobs in places across the Midlands until, in 1925 he was taken on as a nurse to a disabled son of a family in Solihull. At that point he seems to have found the time and space to start writing.

He made an impact with his first book, from the Hogarth Press in 1931: *Saturday Night at the Greyhound*. This was something of a best-seller, having the stunning achievement of two reprints in the first six months of publication. He was then to do what writers Isherwood, Auden and Spender had done – go to Berlin on a research trip for what was to be his next book, *Foreign English*, but his publishers didn't like the resulting manuscript. In spite of this, he made progress, and published several other works. By the 1940s he was writing for John Lehmann's influential anthologies in the series called *New Writing*. Such was his standing by 1946 that the issue for that year not only had a long survey he wrote called Movements in the Underground, but it carried a picture of a sculpture of his head by an artist whose name is a challenge to all in a spelling –bee, Gordon Herickx, who was also from Birmingham. In his literary surveys, Hampson made statements which hint at his interest in radical and subversive writing, and in the dark side of things: 'The underworld serves man as a symbol of his own dual nature. We seek in it pleasure and pain, it nourishes our guilt and recalls our innocence.'

Andy Croft, writing for the *Dictionary of National Biography*, points out that Hampson, in the 1930s '… briefly pioneered a form of intense autobiographical fiction, combining a 'hard-boiled' prose style with experiments in narrative technique.' In that, he sits alongside such writers as Isherwood and James Hanley. He died on Boxing Day 1955 in Solihull. The only aspect of his life we feel confident in providing a glass is that inside the walls, he would have been tempted by the books in the library, and although today it is not so difficult to appropriate books from the prison library, one feels that in 1931 it was more of a challenge.

On the other side of things we have the writer and poet, Reginald Blyth, who was a conscientious objector in the Scrubs in 1916, and then, as if prison life had a certain twisted appeal, he went to Dartmoor where he worked at the Princetown Work Centre. Paradoxically, Blyth did not steal or deface books: he had the tragic experience, later in life in the next World War, of having his library destroyed. At the time he was living in Japan, where he had moved, and where he had become an expert on the culture; he was interned as an enemy alien at the time of the raid.

After the second world war his influence on the study of Japanese literature and on the popularity of Japanese verse forms such as the haiku was immense, and his name is given as one of the major influences on the American Beat writers, such as Jack Kerouac and Gary Snyder. He died in 1964.

In the First World War, arguably the most celebrated and highly-rated conscientious objector to enter the gate of the Scrubs was Northumbrian poet,

Basil Bunting, whose poem, *Briggflats*, has become one of the most widely read and studied modernist works in English. His life has not been widely known until recently, when Richard Burton's biography, *A Strong Song Tows Us*, was published. Burton has unearthed material relating to Bunting's prison experience, which began in Newcastle after he had faced the military tribunal as a 'conchie' and refused to be a combatant or even take a supportive, non-combatant role in the war. He had been educated at a Quaker school and so had sound reasons for this attitude- reasons which were actually stipulated with regard to exemption in the 1916 Military Service Act, but that meant nothing to the Newcastle tribunal. The press report on the hearing said, boldly: ' He would sooner see Germans over-running his country than kill a man.'

The first prison experience would have been at Fenham barracks, before he was shipped down to Wormwood Scrubs, and Burton has found an account by Denis Goacher which describes what Bunting's first experience would have been: 'What they did was put you in a darkened cell and no furniture, no clothes whatever… You just had to lie, when you could sleep, on the floor naked, and you were allowed, once a day, a bowl of water and a crust of bread. This lasted for three days. Then you were examined by a doctor to see what condition you were in.'

In the Scrubs, Bunting said that he was assigned to making mailbags and twisting ships' fenders. Later he recalled that he forfeited his remission 'because for some while before the armistice I refused to do prison work, so I was not released until the end of January.' Much later in his life, in 1982, he said in an interview, .In 1918 all the writing even the most privileged were allowed was confined to a slate. When you had filled the slate you rubbed it off and started again… you were allowed to receive one letter and write one…'

All nicks get their fair share of writers and other creative types, and coping with them is always a special problem. The writers inside Wormwood Scrubs did not generally stay for long, but their time there left a mark on their work, especially in the case of Bunting, who said that when inside he read a book by Ford Madox Ford called *Romance*, and also became aware of that great prisoner-poet from French history, Francois Villon, and in the latter case, Villon became a major figure in Bunting's writing.

It has not often been remarked on, but there is something about doing a stretch that relates to the silence, contemplation and soul-searching which is often an integral part of creative writing. Joe Orton found that, for sure. As to the conscientious objector-writers, they were more deprived in their time, when the production of words was seen more as a potential threat to general stability. One common consequence of writers' stays inside the walls is the tendency for much of their future writing to use prison as a metaphor in various ways. In the case of many who have made the most of the 'material' gathered from a cell, the metaphor has always been there in their lives.

Lee, John: 'The Man They Could Not Hang'

In late 1884 a large house in Babbacombe, Devon, was on fire. In the flames a body was discovered, that of the owner, Miss Keyse. However, it was not the fire that killed her, because her throat was cut. Miss Keyse employed four servants, with the only male being John Lee, who was being given a second chance in life, as he had previously (when very young) stolen and sold goods from the place. He had been punished and then failed to make a career for himself in the navy. Now he was back in the Keyse house, and this time he was in serious trouble, as he was the main murder suspect due to circumstantial evidence. He was tried in Exeter and condemned to die after being found guilty,

In his autobiography, published in 1907 in instalments and then in a book, by a local newspaper, he describes prison life and the trail, but most of all, he explains what happened in the most sensational phase of his life: three attempts to hang him. The facts are that the platform of wood was supposed to flap open and leave the condemned person to fall down into an open space, the 'drop', and so die of a broken neck. On this occasion, the trapdoor would not budge. Lee explains what he thought and felt after standing at the very edge of a violent death and then finding that he still stood, alive, in the gaol, waiting for a third attempt to hang him:

> But death had not come yet. I sank two inches as before, and there I remained. The horrible stampings and hammerings were repeated, but all to no purpose. I heard them saying, 'Stamp on it... Now see if it will work.' But the trap refused to move. 'Take him off,' commanded someone, and I was made to step back two paces off.

The sentence was commuted to prison time, and he was incarcerated until 1907. He always claimed that he had a vision that he would not die in prison, and he insisted that he was innocent of the murder. In the death cell, the hangman, James Berry, had come to him and said 'Sorry old fellow... I don't know what I'm doing.'

What happened to this man who had lived through repeated unimaginable terror was summed up by Paul Sieveking: 'Lee became a barman in London but abandoned his wife... and went to America. What became of him is unknown. The mystery of the reluctant trapdoor was solved in 1897, when engineer Cyril Penny found that the pit below the gallows was subject to flooding... and the damp had rotted the trapdoor.'

Lord Haw Haw (William Joyce, 1906–1946)

For many years after the end of the Second World War, British folk remembered the phrase 'Germany calling' and the name 'Lord Haw Haw.' This was William Joyce, who played a major role in the promotion of Nazi Germany's propaganda in that conflict. Joyce was born in New York and this proved to be an important fact when his trial for treason came along.

He was in the ranks of Oswald Moseley's British Fascists, but that was not enough for him; there was a split and he led a breakaway party of his own. This was the British National Socialist League. Germany would clearly be the place he would run to when the going got tough, and he did just that. The Germans saw that Joyce's clipped, upper class voice would be a useful propaganda tool. Broadcasting was in its infancy really, but Germany's Nazi party had some excellent 'information arms' in its structures, and Joyce soon became 'Lord Haw Haw' as he broadcast from Hamburg and Bremen, mostly. But the war ended in a defeat for Germany, of course, and he had to run somewhere. His actions had been treasonous. The 1351 Treason Act has these words: 'When a man compasses or imagines the death of our lord the king, or our lady his queen, or his eldest son and heir...' that was a treasonable act. Joyce was also, in other wording in the Act, ' adherent to the king's enemies.' If he were to be captured, then he was certain to die.

If he were to be captured, then he was certain to die. Joyce went to Holland; there he was caught and brought home for trial at the Old Bailey. Was he a British citizen? That was important. He was an American citizen so he might have thought at first that he could avoid the treason charge. But then the prosecution reasoned that Joyce had a British passport at the time of his first broadcast from Germany. He was sentenced to death; two appeals followed, but he had a date with the executioner. He was hanged at Wandsworth in January 1946. He had even appealed to the House of Lords, and there was a majority against him of four to one.

An interesting footnote to Joyce's story is that the hangman, Albert Pierrepoint, is silent about his hanging of Joyce in his memoirs. Around that time he was busy at Nuremberg as the Nazi culprits of wartime atrocities were in his tender hands en route to death. Maybe he was too disgusted that an Englishman would do such things in wartime.

Lord Jowitt, the Lord Chancellor, made a statement on behalf of the government to make their position clear regarding the passport and citizenship: 'In these circumstances, I am clearly of the opinion that so long as he holds the passport he is within the meaning of the statute a man, who, if he is adherent to the King's enemies in the realm or elsewhere, commits an act of treason.'

M

*Macaroni Parson (Dr. Dodd)

One of the most dissonant and repugnant sights the public ever witnessed when they went to enjoy executions was surely on 27 June 1777, a clergyman, Dr William Dodd, was hanged, along with a teenage boy whose offence was the theft of two-and-a-half guineas. A learned churchman was a rare sight on the scaffold, and was memorable, but not with the same impact as that shuddering sight.

Dodd was the son of the Vicar of Bourne, in Lincolnshire, and had excelled as a scholar, starting out as a poor sizar, a scholar receiving funds from the college for his study but had to wait on the more wealthy scholars as a servant. In spite of this lowly position, Dodd did very well at Clare Hall, Cambridge, where he impressed in his studies. He also earned income from his writing and from public speaking, being a first-class communicator and also a man of fashion and wit. He graduated in 1749 and went to London, spending two years living by his pen, as so many had done before. Then strangely, he married someone who brought no wealth: Mary Perkins, who was, in the language of the time, 'Of no family.'

From that point, he became a man who lived beyond his means, obviously with high ambitions and plenty of talent for sale. Yet, as with so many in his age, his extravagance led to debtors' prison, and he was only rescued from that when friends told his father. In that situation was the germ of his future career, because the church was the natural social move to try to establish himself back in society. He was ordained in Cambridge by the Bishop of Ely and took a curacy at West Ham.

His writing helped to make a name in the right kind of society, particularly when he published his book on Shakespeare, *The Beauties of Shakespeare*, and mixed in literary circles as well as in religious ones, as his sermons were also successful; this was a time in which volumes of sermons sold well. It was the era of the rise of Methodism and there was a readership for religious writings. He was made a lecturer at St James, Garlick Hill in London and then at St Olave's where Pepys had worshipped. Still his reputation grew and he also had the position of chaplain at a new refuge for fallen women at Magdalen House. Dodd was a rare spirit, indulging in both selfish attempts at preferment in an age of nepotism and 'jobs for the boys' but also in charitable works, founding a society for the relief of poor debtors, for instance, and he was also part of the initiative which established what later became the Royal Humane Society.

Yet he was always an unstable personality, clearly with an addiction to risk. The society he lived in was one of notable extremes of rich and poor, and when a man fell, his descent was to the lower depths of Hell, even though he had known the heights of power and influence. Dodd knew the right moves to take in order to at least try to stay solvent and successful, but there was always a chance that he would over-reach himself. For example, he had extra income from tutoring and housing boys of good backgrounds at his West Ham home; but also fortune was on his side at first, because he was noted by George III, who made him chaplain-in-ordinary- one of 36 such who work in a rotation at St James's. However, as social preferment often works by recommendation, his name was dropped to the Earl of Chesterfield as a potential tutor for his son, Philip Stanhope. That was a foreboding of his future disgrace, and yet paradoxically at this time he also gained his doctorate- a Doctor of Laws from Cambridge.

Then, in the late 1760s, he transformed his lifestyle from that of a preacher and tutor who wrote as a hobby, into that of 'a life of ostentation and luxury' as Lord Birkenhead puts it in his account of Dodd's life. At that time, he won a lottery prize of £1,000 pounds, and that probably encouraged his tendency to risk and speculation; he should have progressed well, because he also had two benefices, in an age of clerical pluralism, when a man could have these ecclesiastical incomes for doing no or very little parish work. He made a house at Ealing his main abode, and kept his young men for tutoring work when he could spare the time. He even bought a share of the Charlotte Street chapel in Bloomsbury, from which a later incumbent, according to a writer in *Notes & Queries* in 1896, made 'a thousand pounds a year in pew rents.'

The ominous event of 1773 then happened: his employer, Philip, became Earl of Chesterfield- the man he was destined to attempt to swindle. But before that he indulged in some other activities which made enemies and increased his negative image around town. One of these was his publication of a novel called *The Sisters*, in which there are elements which would scandalise the more conventionally moral in the higher circles of society.

This was followed by a scandal of a much higher level, such that it made Dodd leave London for the country for several months. What happened was that a vacancy arose: a very lucrative living in London became available, and the Lord Chancellor had the power to place the new man in the position. This was Lord Apsley, so Dodd did what many in the eighteenth century did – he approached Lady Apsley with the offer of £3,000 if she could arrange for him to be the chosen man. Lady Apsley showed this to her husband, and then the King was told. The result was that Dodd lost his royal chaplaincy; it was the beginning of the end for him, because the attempt at bribery went public. There was even a satirical drama on stage on the affair; the papers went to town attacking him. He was corrupt and had been found out- the worst sin in an age of corruption and bribery. Dodd had been a very busy writer in the ten years before this faux pas, writing all kinds of material, and some of this had been to win favour, such as the *Ode to the Marchioness of Granby* (1759) and *An Epistle to a Lady Concerning Truths in Religion* (1753). The Georgian years worked by the sale of offices and sinecures were common; there was even a printed guide called *The Red Book* which listed the sinecures and their emoluments. Maybe Dodd thought he was doing something totally normal, but he was wrong. He had stepped too far over the line, being too extreme even for a society that functioned on a 'jobs for the boys' system.

He gave a last sumptuous dinner for special guests and a farewell sermon, then retreated into rural banishment. But when he returned he was ruined. In desperation, this man of chance and risk made his fatal move into criminality. He approached a broker called Robertson, with the intention of using his association with Chesterfield to gain a huge profit on a bond. He told Robertson that he was raising a sum for the coming of age of 'a nobleman.' Robertson's task was to find a person or firm who would give a loan based on the bond and eventually he found Fletcher and Peach, who gave the £4,200 of the bond with the forged signature. Robertson earned £100 for that negotiation.

But it appears that the firm noticed a blot or mark on the bond and they became suspicious. When they showed this to Chesterfield to check, he was sure that it was forged. Robertson and Dodd were traced and arrested. All varieties of forgery, uttering and counterfeiting were dealt with severely and they were capital felonies; in the monumental legal work of Blackstone, he wrote that 'There is now hardly a case possible to be conceived wherein forgery, that tends to defraud, whether in the name of a real or fictitious person, is not made a capital crime.' It was extremely unusual for penalties of pillory, fines or imprisonment to replace death by hanging. At this point, Dodd was taken to the Wood Street Compter to await trial at the Old Bailey.

One has to ask why he was not saved from that awful fate? Dr Johnson was asked, and his reply is on record: 'If the King could have saved any man it would have been Ryland whom he personally loved, but having tried his interests for that man, "Now" said he, "if I am every solicited to pardon for forgery, you shall be made to remember these arguments.' Ryland was an engraver who was hanged for forgery in 1783, and being engraver to the King did not mean that he would be saved.

Martin, Jonathan: Arsonist (1782–1838)

Until the introduction of the M'Naghten Rule in 1843, there was no concept of those deeemed to b 'criminally insane' but these strictures explained the legal view of insanity.. In Victorian times, Broadmoor had been the destination of many criminal lunatics, having opened as a special facility in 1863, but before that, various asylums had been in use to hold dangerous citizens. We have to look at individual cases in order to understand the thinking concerning mental illness and criminality before the advent of abnormal and clinical psychology and psychiatric treatment.

One classic example of a serious criminal act which shows the importance of psychology in this context was that of the man who committed arson at York Minster in 1829. This was Jonathan Martin (1782-1838). He was born in Hexham, and he had a number of physiological ailments from childhood, including being subject to a speech impediment and was 'tongue-tied.' His brother was the famous landscape artist, John Martin. Jonathan was brought up by his uncle, after suffering the horrendous sight of his sister being murdered. Life was harsh to the boy, as he was later press-ganged into the navy.

However, he managed to return home to Durham, marry and start a family. The man was always trouble, and he caused trouble. His manic tendencies first became extreme when he said he was to kill the Bishop of Oxford in 1817. His fate was to be taken to a lunatic asylum, and then moved to another. He escaped in 1821. His sorrows went on: his wife died of cancer and he was rebuffed by church congregations. Jonathan was often on the move, and always living a turbulent and disordered life. Hence he arrived at York Minster in February 1829, after marrying again and now living in York, and started the fire.

First he hid in the Minster, and then waited for his chance to set fire to the woodwork in the choir, before running away. The fire had raged for some time and a large section of the roof was destroyed. Other items such as the pulpit and choir stalls were ruined. The Annals of Yorkshire record in more detail what he did inside the building: 'He went to the belfry where he struck a light. He then cut about ninety feet from the rope of the fire bell, which he converted into a ladder which he did by tying knots at certain distances, and made use of it to obtain access to the interior of the choir.' He said later that he had had a two dreams, telling him to cause the fire. The damage done was estimated to be around £70,000 (around £6 million today), and this was paid for by public subscription.

He was caught back in his home town and then taken to York for his trial. He was sent to the famous Bethlem Hospital, where he would receive the usual harsh treatment given to such people. Ironically, it was in York at the time that one of the most humane developments in the care of the insane occurred. This was the York Retreat, where Allen, the future owner of High Beech Asylum in Essex, was to treat Tennyson's brother, and also the poet John Clare. Unfortunately, Martin had no such luck. He had nine years in Bethlem, where the artistic talent in his family came through, as he produced a number of drawings. The fact that the term 'bedlam' comes from the name of the hospital says all one needs to know about the regime there.

Maybrick, Florence

Such was the furore around the trial of Florence Maybrick in 1895 that the popular press were very quick to make a dollar or two. As well as special features and popular street literature, there was printed, in 1895, an illustrated *Police Budget* print of Florence kneeling by her bed in her prison cell, and the caption is: 'Will the Home Secretary answer the prayers of an innocent though misguided woman?' An angel stands by her, holding out an Order of Release. This came from one of the most controversial trials in late Victorian criminal history.

Florence was indicted for the murder of her husband, James, who had died after a long regime of arsenic being administered to him. What complicated this was that Maybrick had been in the habit of taking very small doses of the poison in order to increase his potency and sexual pleasure. In addition to this, he was constantly taking drugs of all kinds, fearful of his health to such an extent that he was surely a hypochondriac. He was also a philanderer, and had several bastard children by mistresses. This was not rare in Victorian culture, but of course, when he died in suspicious circumstances, there were criticisms growing that would be seen as motives by a jury.

When his death was investigated, a massive amount of poison was found in Maybrick's body. She was arrested and charged, and at the trial at St George's Hall in Liverpool, the real drama was in the summing up by the judge, Mr Justice Stephen. Unfortunately, in an age when the public had a bias when it came to applying their morality against women and in favour of men. Florence had been conducting an affair with a man called Bierley, and that was a reason to condemn her. Stephen was condemnatory and biased in the respect of showing his opinions, with the jury intently listening and open to influence. Florence was sentenced to death, but there was an appeal. As there was a document with 100,000 signatures in support of staying the execution, a commutation was announced and she went to gaol.

Florence, after serving fifteen years inside, went to live in the United States and she died there in 1941.

*Messengers (Kings' and Queens')

Some of the most compelling historical stories come from the footnotes: the intriguing little small-print sentence at the bottom of the page that invites some further enquiry. When that note is combined with something puzzling and entirely new to the writer, then something opens out – an invitation to dig a little more deeply into the archives perhaps. That is exactly what happened when the idea for this book began. I have written widely in criminal history, and in the course of researching material for *Criminal River*, a history of the Thames River Police, I came across a paragraph recording an arrest made by 'two of the King's Messengers.' In 1810 two Messengers had arrested a man suspected of committing treason. They were not police officers.

In the course of dredging the archives of law and order in Regency England, when the River Police were being formed, I tended to encounter glimpses of these puzzling officers, in such snippets as these:

> On Friday, between six and seven o'clock, Mr Staley, a King's Messenger, was stopped by a single highwayman between Butcher's Grove and Granford bridge on the Hounslow Road, but on presenting a blunderbuss the highwayman rode off as he was going out of the road his horse stumbled and threw him, upon which the post-boy pursued him...
>
> Mr Ellys, one of the King's oldest Messengers, on his return home from Minto, the seat of Sir Gilbert Elliot, had nearly lost his life by the carelessness of the driver; the chaise overturned and dragged but by the presence of mind of the old gentleman, he received only a few bruises.
>
> Sunday night Mr Flint, one of the King's Messengers, arrived at the Duke of Leeds's office with dispatches from Mr Whitworth, His Majesty's Minister at the court of Petersburg. He was also charged with dispatches from Mr Ewart, the British Minister at Berlin...

Who were these men who, in 1810, when there was no national police force, made an arrest in London? They were not Bow Street Runners, that elite force stemming from Henry and John Fielding's mid-eighteenth century police court and network of thief-catchers. They were not military personnel. In an age in which proper professional police forces were being discussed and theorized, here were some men who were acting as officers with a power of arrest.

The year was important. In 1810, the paranoia created here in Britain by events across the Channel was at its height. In 1799–1800 the Combination Acts had been passed, and these made it clear that fear was in the streets; gatherings of more than a few folk on street corners were seditious; printers, writers and journalists were likely to be prosecuted and tried sometimes without a trail being guilty *in absentia* as the writ of Habeas Corpus was suspended. Only a year after these strange arrests, the Luddite violence was to erupt in Yorkshire, as machine-wreckers set to work on mills; the Bow Street Runners had been sent up to Huddersfield to help investigate workers' militancy. The special constables were called out. The militia were cleaning their guns.

In the midst of this, two King's Messengers made an arrest. I investigated the case a little, and sure enough, they were part of a very well-established corps of special government officials, and among other things, they had powers of arrest. But as their job title implies, they were essentially people who carried messages for the sovereign, and indeed that is what they are today, though much reduced in number.

But the sense of these men being engaged in something highly dangerous was increased when I learned that they are individuals who work alone, trusted with diplomatic baggage, and who travel almost anywhere. Today of course, there will be many technological developments that make the work more manageable and less risky, but I imagined a man in say 1850 travelling by rail from London to Turkey, with a briefcase strapped to his arm, with no military escort. He was the James Bond of Victoria's state.

Inevitably, as a historian, I gathered many more questions about these people. The popular media would have us believe that the job began with Richard III, but in fact, they were probably around in Saxon times, working for Alfred and Ethelred. In their role as considered today, though, the tale of their real professional existence, in the reign of Charles II, is probably a valid line of thought. The story is that when Charles was living in exile, he arranged for four trustworthy men to work for him, maintaining contact with home. He supposedly took a silver bowl which had four greyhound figures as part of its design, broke them off, and gave one to each man. They were from that moment, 'silver greyhounds.'

In *The Strand Magazine* in 1896, for instance, we have some profiles of the men: Harry Taylor is pictured muffled in a massive fur coat and fez; Conway Seymour is huge, dignified and reflective; Captain Philip Wynter is every inch the officer, with his slid moustache, immaculately cut and combed sideburns and fixed glare of command. One picture in the feature shows 'the late Major H. Byng Hall, Queen's Messenger, surrounded by the fruits of his many travels.' He sits in a splendid study, so full that it rivals a room of Sir John Soane's, with urns, sketches, statuettes and curios cramming the study as Byng Hall himself writes on a map.

I wanted to know more about these Messengers of course. They were mostly army men, the types of retired officers who continuously returned to civvy street and took up responsible posts such as prison governors or administrators in th4e civil service. Their work has always been a mystery it seems. The writer of *The Strand* feature, J.Holt Schooling, expressed this curious situation in just the way we might do so now: 'The silver greyhound has been from time immemorial the badge set apart for the Queen's (or King's) Foreign Service Messengers. Most of us know that such persons exist, but there is only a very hazy notion of who Queen's Messengers are, and beyond the fact that they "carry the despatches" very little is known about these gentlemen and their duties.'

Their story moves from obscure beginnings through to the Messengers in diplomatic work, and along the way, there are a few candidates for the James Bond role. In Chaucer's time, as J.J. Jusserand explained, they were more Basildon Bond than James Bond: 'The king kept twelve messengers with a fixed salary; they followed him everywhere, in constant readiness to start; they received three pence a day and eight pence a year to buy shoes.' But by 1890 they were very special officials, men of the highest probity and trust. Fortunately for the modern reader in search of a dramatic narrative, their lives and adventures were not without incident and adventure.

Moat Farm Mystery, The

This is a murder tale immersed in mud, ditches and determined searches for evidence. As usual with so many alleged murders, the investigation was in need of a body, after suspicions were confirmed. The killer was Samuel Dougal, who met a woman called Camille Holland. She was deeply attracted to the ex-soldier, and they set up home at Moat Farm in Essex. Trouble soon disturbed things, in the shape of Dougal's sexual designs on a maid called Florence Havis. Dougal attempted to force his way into Florence's room.

Dougal was told to go. Dougal's campaign of forgery and emotional pressure led to his eventual murder of Camille. Miss Holland would not tolerate his behaviour at all; shortly after that fracas, Camille completely disappeared, and if anything was bound to arouse suspicion on Dougal, it was the discovery of forged cheques, taken from her funds. The police had their man, but no body. Some photos exist of police – both detectives and 'uniform' – doing the searching and digging. It took four years for a body to be found, and sure enough, it was the remains of Camille Holland. This was after working on a drainage ditch. In the skull of the remains was found a bullet, and that matched Dougal's gun.

The killer met his doom after trying to state that he had shot Camille by accident; the trial took only two days, and he was executed by William Billington at Chelmsford on 14 July 1903

Moll Cutpurse (Mary Frith, c.1584 – 1659)

Moll Cutpurse was known as both Frith and Markham, and her life in the lower depths of criminal life during the reign of the early Stuarts makes her the epitome of the enigmatic underworld Madame. She was bisexual, and she also laid claim to being the first professional actress in England. She began as a 'cut purse' (a pick-pocket) – this was at a time when the fashion for men was to carry a purse or 'pocket' on a belt or strap. What the Victorians called a 'fingersmith' would apply to her also. It was all a matter of swift and skilful art. So renowned was Moll that a successful drama called *The Roaring Girle* by Middleton and Dekker was made about her.

Her big mistake was in robbing General Fairfax in Hounslow, after which she was arrested at Turnham Green, and only cash would buy her freedom then. She made it to her 70s, and that was a rare achievement then when life expectancy was around 35. There is no doubt that the epithet 'Moll' connotes a certain type of women, and Daniel Defoe made much of this in his classic tale of the woman on the make in the London underclass, *Moll Flanders*.

Moors Murders, The

This has to be one of the major murder cases of the twentieth century, and the two perpetrators, Myra Hindley and Ian Brady, reached the dimensions of major monsters in popular culture, particularly after Brady spent many years in jail refusing to give the police any idea of where one of the bodies of the children the pair had killed was to be found. Little Keith Bennett became the focus of much media attention as time went on.

Brady was working at a chemical supply company, and in his spare time he read about the Nazis and other unsavoury topics of cruelty and fascism. He met Hindley, and their first date was to watch the film of the Nuremberg trial of Nazi leaders. Their deviant concerns led eventually to torture and cruelty, and to the murder of five children. But they were arrested after the killing of Edward Evans in 1965; David Smith, Hindley's brother-in-law who had been made to watch this, reported them, and the arrest was effected, followed by the search for more bodies.

At Chester Assizes in 1966 they were both convicted – Brady of three murders and Hindley of two. There has been a veritable industry in the media about these two, and Brady's refusal to inform the law about where bodies of victims were buried increased the public hatred and criticism of him, up to his death in 2017. Information that Hindley had also refused to disclose up to her death in 2002.

Murder That Never Was: Beverley Nichols

In 1972 a truly original and unusual memoir was published. It was called *Father Figure*, written by Beverley Nichols, a well respected writer who, though he had written several murder mysteries, was widely known as a humorous writer who was at home with writing about gardens and cats, but Father Figure was very different. A statement by the author on the back cover reads: 'To say that this is a shocking book is an understatement. But the shock is neither deliberate nor contrived; it emerges inevitably from the record of the facts – a record that stretches from my early boyhood.'

Of course the book was shocking: one sentence says it all: 'The occasion of my third attempt to murder my father can be precisely dated, and it is not a date that I am likely to forget.' The father in question was John Nichols. Nichols had already written a play called *Shadow of the Vine*, which dealt with a drunken and violent father. As a prologue to the new book in 1972, Nichols quoted an anonymous letter concerning such violence and terror within the family: 'Who told you about my husband and what he did to me and my children? When did you learn what we had to go through... How did you find out about the sickening little details – like standing on a chair to reach the bottles he had hidden...'

This and other letters sent to Nichols lay behind his own confessional story – something perhaps referred to now as a 'misery memoir' – and it is clear that he thought the book would be a work of universal importance. Nichols is depicted as a monster and a mystery. One aspect of the style is sheer hyperbole: 'When my mother spoke her wedding vows she was sealing her death warrant.' The book offers a steady, relentless build-up of fear and outrageous behaviour, so that an appearance from the father is expected like a scene from a horror film.

The progression to murderer is staged and inevitable, and the reader eventually confronts this: 'I dragged this seventeen stone of flesh through the french window, into the night. His close-cropped head bumped on the kerb of the porch, and as it did so, the octopus eye opened again for a moment. There was life in the old boy yet... A few last heaves and tugs and seventeen stone of paternity was deposited in a prickly shrub, with the snow coming down. No octopus eye this time. Not a sound. Not a movement.' He recovered. Then we have this: 'I shall kill you' I repeated, 'I want you to be quite clear about that... I shall kill you...'

The reader of this strange tome closes the book with the question: did this really happen? Then they might ask, is this a novel or a memoir? Where is the truth?

In his biography of Nichols, Bryan Connon gives an explanation. Someone had to answer the issues expressed in print. *The Sunday People* put the tale of the attempted murder on their front page; Cyril Connolly, the famous critic, wrote: 'Homicidal ruthlessness must be added to my estimate of Mr Nichols' character.' Now, it must be asked, where were the officers of the law? There had been a demand in parliament that Nichols should be prosecuted by the Attorney-General.

Connon explains that really it is a work of fiction: 'The theatrical drive of the narrative takes the reader from climax to climax, with the evil spirit of John soaking into every page.' It is not openly stated, but the fact is that the book's uneasy situation regarding a genre classification is as flexible as many works of postmodernism. Whatever Nichols's real intention, the result is almost a spoof of a misery memoir.

Through his long career as a writer, Nichols had always used every scrap of travel and life experience; this strange work is yet another variation on themes of 'docufiction' or perhaps of a 'dramadoc.'

Musical Milkman, The

This epithet refers to George Arthur Bailey, who poisoned his wife with prussic acid in 1920, and was tried and convicted of murder in 1921. He was executed in Oxford in February of that year. Bailey was a career criminal and a notably eccentric individual. He had committed a number of minor crimes, working under several *noms de plumes*, before elevating his misdeeds to rape and murder. He had an interest in musical notation, and had developed a new system of that convention, as he claimed. It was not successful.

But this trial became famous and notable for another reason: it was the first murder trial at which women were included in the jury. The 1919 Sex Disqualification (Removal) Act had opened up opportunities for women to take roles in the functions of the criminal justice system. There were three woman present, and the occasion was something of an ordeal, as they had to be locked in to be kept away from media and the public. On the humorous side, the public were entertained by the judge's extra care of them, asking if they needed a tea-break and generally showing concern for their welfare in the face of accounts of a corpse and of sexual offences. The press took extreme interest, as in this account: 'The three women jurors attracted considerable attention as they walked across the square to the church. They expressed some alarm when told that a kinema [sic] operator proposed to take a picture of their march to church.'

The women were Miss Maude Sophia Stevenson, Miss Annie Andersen White and Miss Matilda Tack. They may be seen on the internet, dressed in thick coats and solid hats, rather enjoying being the centre of attention.

N

Naked on a Ladder: R. V Collins, 1973

Some crime stories attain the level of iconic status in law studies; these are landmark cases of fine distinctions and legal definition. One such case arose from a young man called Collins who visited a woman he had known previously, though not very well, and stripped himself naked, apart from his socks, and found a ladder; thus he could climb up to the woman's bedroom. He made it to the window ledge, and there he was seen by the woman, who was in her bed; she thought the figure on the ledge was her young man, and so she admitted him. They had sex, but the woman began to realise that the man in bed with her was not her boyfriend. The situation *vis a vis* the law was very difficult. This was because the woman had admitted the man into her room: that could not be interpreted as rape as she had seemingly given him permission. On the other hand, did Collins have an intention to rape?

The police considered that Section 9 of the Burglary Act could lead to a prosecution. They were wrong. The point at issue was the detail that being on the ledge, the intruder was not within the property. Therefore he was invited in. There was no violent entry. The attempted application of the 1969 Theft Act had failed to convict. The whole affair, nonetheless, provides a fascinating legal discussion.

Newgate

In British prisons, Newgate stands out as a place related to writers and poets; not only has it housed hundreds of scribblers, but it has also spawned the famous *Newgate Calendar*: stories of criminals issued at various times between the late eighteenth and early nineteenth century. This compendium of tales from the gaol includes biographies covering the whole spectrum of criminals from pirates to fraudsters and from robbers to killers. Many of the inmates of Newgate over the years have been writers, going back to the fifteenth century, when Sir Thomas Malory was locked up in there, no doubt working on his *Morte D'Arthur*. The prison reached mythic status in John Gay's hugely successful *Beggar's Opera* of 1728. But in more recent years, other prisons across the land have had their writers, from Jeffrey Archer in Belmarsh and Lincoln to Charles Bronson, in virtually every prison within the system. In 1873, the four Americans went through its dismal walls, but one of them – George – was to become a writer. His autobiography, *Forging His Chains*, is one of the best prison memoirs in the canon of that genre, by any standard.

In the Georgian period, Newgate was in a horrendous state, and in 1818 the Grand Jury of the City of London, following other reformers who had been busy trying to improve the penal system for the previous fifty years, wrote to *The Times* and had this to say about the prison: 'The deplorable situation of the male prisoners, with respect to clothing, particularly the juvenile part, made a melancholy impression on our minds. Many were without shoes or stockings, others without shirts, and one almost in a state of nakedness… we are of the opinion that the general health of the prisoners of both sexes would be improved if an allowance of soap was granted…' Matters had improved somewhat by 1870; at least criminals were not hanged outside its doors any longer, as they had been up to 1802.

When Daniel Defoe's Moll Flanders enters Newgate, she describes it in this way:

> I was now fixed indeed; 'tis impossible to describe the terror of my mind, when I was first brought in, and when I looked around upon all the horrors of that dismal place I looked upon myself as lost, and that I had nothing to think of, but of going out to the world, and that with the utmost infamy; the hellish noise, the roaring, swearing and clamour, the stench and nastiness, and all the dreadful crowd of afflicted things that I saw there, joined together to make the place seem an emblem of Hell itself, and a kind of entrance into it.

For the poor prisoners and the habitual criminals, it was mostly a regime of repression and solitary confinement. We have several accounts of visits there, and one of the most detailed is from an anonymous writer who produced a work in 1818 called *Old Bailey Experience*. In that work he writes at length on the treatment of prisoners in that prison, and he makes a special point about the use of solitary confinement: 'But if a mind, totally void of sources of reflection, be shut up in a cell for years, or even for months, what can be expected but that every day will stultify its powers and at last render it callous and unimpressionable…' At the time of this publication, the penal laws were such that the prisons were crammed with all kinds of offenders, and he lists the most common crimes, including the slang names for them, as in the example of pickpockets, known as 'buzzmen', or coiners, known as 'bit-makers'.

Newgate was a place where the underclass were dumped out of sight then, but it was also for white collar offenders as well as the violent killers and robbers, and yet the prison experience was the same for everyone. It was a gaunt, high-walled place, standing where today the Old Bailey law courts stand. In 1870 it was unchanged since its rebuilding after the Gordon Riots of 1780 had wrecked a large part of the site. There were rows of cells on different levels, and men were separated from women; there were also areas for healthcare and for the treadwheel, a punishment involving long hours walking up wooden revolving steps to power a mill-wheel for industrial production.

Newgate Calendar

This publication – known initially as *The Malefactors' Register* – which featured stories of Newgate's prisoners, really took off as a massive cultural narrative collection in the late Regency years, alongside many other similar collections of scaffold and trial tales, mostly all produced with an aim of moral lecturing and the establishment of a trajectory of crime following the classic template of offence/ investigation/ pursuit/ trial/ punishment/ closure. The last phase boiled down to death, transportation, the madhouse or, of course, some kind of release, or simply a prison sentence. But the masses wanted hangings in their reading material. They tended to get the moral lecture and the scaffold. One similar work, *York Castle* by Leman Reid (1829) included a longish moral sermon and reflection with every case. A typical example is this, on the robber, William Johnson:

> Over a case like this the moralist must shudder. It does not contain one mitigatory trait; it is a coarse detail of the worst barbarity, in its most obdurate shape; yet it contains and awful lesson to the guilty, for it shows by what minute and apparently trifling circumstances guilt may be traced home to a criminal...Sentence of death was passed, and the delinquent executed on the following Monday. He behaved with great levity during the trial, shook hands with all the prisoners on leaving the dock, and died unimpressed with his awful situation.

Along with these publications were the 'Ordinaries' narratives' in which gaolers made some profit from having their memories of working with notorious felons published in cheap collections.

In his edition of the *Newgate Calendar* of 1991, historian Christopher Hibbert explains the immediate context: 'In the days of the early publication nearly all the crimes which the Calendars promised to describe, from bigamy, burglary and buggery to felony, forgery and false pretences, were punishable by death. There were no fewer than 160 capital offences in the 1760s, and by 1819 according to one learned authority, 63 further offences had been added to the list.'

P

Palmer, William, Prince of Poisoners (1824–1856)

Such was the hatred and contempt for William Palmer in Rugeley, where he poisoned his victims for gain that, after his campaign of terror and awaiting trial, an act was passed called the Palmer Act which enabled a case to be tried in London if there was such local violence threatened that a trial taking place in the assizes close to the crimes' location would endanger public safety. His victims totalled eleven, including friends and family.

Palmer, a medical doctor, had befriended a man called John Cook, who had inherited a vast fortune, in order to exploit him and take his cash; largely on horse-racing. When Cook died, it was easily ascertained that suspicion had to fall on Palmer, who performed Cook's autopsy and issued. This was the beginning of a media feast on the doctor's name, and he became notorious across the land.

Palmer owned racehorses and was well known around Rugeley as a man of the turf and something of a wild blade; of course, he could exercise the power available to a doctor, so he could issue death certificates and give a cause of death that suited him. In the case of Cook, which spelt the end for Palmer, the doctor had actually collected some winnings for the dying man, and then he stated that 'apoplexy' was the cause of death. At the time, this was a term which could cover all kinds of illness.

The result of this was suspicion; Cook's father wanted a professional autopsy done, and he got his way. No less a person than Dr Alfred Taylor did this work, and he found enough antimony in the victim's stomach to arouse suspicion. Taylor was a respected authority on what we would now call forensic medicine, although at that time it had very limited armoury in its opposition to foul play. Douglas Wynn explains antimony and its effects in a guide to poisons: 'In Victorian times, the most popular antimony compound met with was antimony potassium nitrate, called tartar emetic... most poisoners have used it in small doses over a period... when they hoped the symptoms would be confused with gastric fever.' (see *Graham Young*).

Palmer was tried at the Old Bailey, after the passing of the Palmer Act, and later hanged by Stafford prison on June 14 1856.

Peace, Charles (1832–1879)

The history of crime is swimming with characters – people who would be notorious and even charismatic even if they had never broken the law. Such a one is Charles Peace, who practised his trade of burglary in both the north and south of England. He came from Sheffield, but lived and worked in Hull and elsewhere. Had it not been for the fact that he committed two murders, he would have entered the records of crime as rather an eccentric genius: he was rated a first-class violinist though one arm was badly maimed in a factory accident. His physical appearance was repugnant and he appears to have moved around when robbing or assessing places for burglary in a very fit and agile way.

He was not exactly careful in the trade though, as he served a number of gaol stretches up to c.1872. But then, in 1876, he killed the owner of a house he was robbing in Sheffield, Arthur Dyson. Charlie fled to London, and there he did well for a while until someone shopped him and there was a fight, involving him shooting at the police, resulting in him wounding a constable. The game was up. He had been using false names, but now, under arrest, his real identity was found and he was traced to the murder of a police officer elsewhere.

He was to be tried for murder in Sheffield, and Charlie's last dash of reckless courage was on the train journey to the trial, as he tried to jump off the train, and being severely injured in the attempt. He was hanged at Armley prison in Leeds in February 1879.

Penny Dreadfuls

This is the name given to the cheap popular magazines printed in the Victorian age, dealing with notorious crimes and villains. The stories were usually in small print, on poor paper, and were sold in the streets along with broadsheets. Before these there were woodcuts and pamphlets of various kinds, dominated by such rogues as killers, pirates and highwaymen. Compared to the *Newgate Calendar* these were shoddy materials.

*Phonetics (Forensic)

Use the word 'phonetics' in conversation with the ordinary person and the word will not mean or suggest very much. He or she mighty possibly link it to something such as speech therapy or to the ever-expanding world of teaching English to speakers of other languages. These are quite valid reasons for understanding the word and its applications, but phonetics also has a fascinating place in crime detection. The science is about far more than 'The rain in Spain falls mainly on the plain' and people might be forgiven for relating it to the traditionally very important business of elocution.

The world knew all about the famous 'Ripper Tape' back in the days when the Yorkshire Ripper instilled fear into every woman in West Yorkshire. The taunting recording, goading the police chiefs into believing that they were near to catching their man. What they wanted to know was where did the speaker come from? Not just that he was vaguely a 'Geordie' – but where *exactly*. That is, almost to the street corner of the village, not just the city or the district. Who would be able to know such things?

The answer was the dialectologists and, at the University of Leeds, slap in the middle of the Ripper's hunting ground, academics Stanley Ellis and Jack Windsor Davies got to work on the voice of Wearside Jack. Ellis had worked on the Survey of English Dialects back in the 1950s and he was my tutor, telling me that he used to travel around his allotted shires of England on a motorbike, using questionnaires to elicit exactly what man from the land south of Lincoln would call the weakest pig in the litter. This was a way of working out linguistic boundaries.

This might seem like useless knowledge, but it was quite the opposite, because Ellis could tell police where a speaker came from, very accurately. Yes, he pinpointed the speaker who tormented George Oldfield to the former pit village of Castletown, Sunderland. We have to recall that Ellis was aware that this did not mean that the voice was the voice of the Ripper – it was just information for the police to use.

Today, the analysis of speech is much more sophisticated than in the 1970s, as computer technology has enhanced analytical methods. The basis of this thinking is that we each have an *idiolect*: a very specific voice print, unique to us. It is merely a case of knowing how to study and log that voice print. Anyone who has used sound recordings, such as the Adobe programme, will know what the visual representation of the spoken voice looks like. Phoneticians work in several ways, but at the basis of the work is the minutely different ways we make sounds, from our vocal chords, through to our tongue, pallet, teeth and lips. We even use our nose. Of courseost of us would recognise a

Liverpool or a South Country accent – but an accent is just a general feature. Person A and person B speaking the same sentence, 'How are you today, Phil?' would have immense differences if studied closely. Our intonation patterns vary considerably and within a rising or falling intonation there are a number of other features which lend themselves to close study.

When PC Ian Broadhurst was shot and killed near Dib Lane in Leeds in December 2003, the accused was brought to trial and the jury heard recordings of a certain 'Nathan Coleman' placing bets on the phone. Dr John French was able to show that 'Coleman' and the man in the dock, David Bieber, were one and the same. Bieber is a Canadian, but he had been some time in West Yorkshire. The phonetic mix of those two components gave him distinctive features. Dr French studied the tiny speech utterances such as allophones – particular variants of each sound made – and concluded that the chances of the two voices being different to be 'very remote.' Fingerprint evidence backed this up too, and Bieber was convicted of murder.

The TV show, *Who Wants to be a Millionaire?* provided its own very special challenge to the phonetics professional: the accused, Tecwen Whittock, had allegedly produced coughs while in the audience to give aid to Major Charles Ingram, helping him reach the top prize. Dr French was called in once again, and his investigation was summed up in his explanation: 'We have two ears which help us to determine directionality so a person receiving sound would have a very sharp indication where that sound comes from.'

That was one side of the problem, answering the question about whether Ingram could have heard the coughing guidance. As for the coughs themselves, even a short production of a sharp rush of air through the larynx will have certain characteristics, and these may be studied very closely. Though Dr French did say that 'the analysis of coughing is still in its infancy.'

The same precision attained in the study of the spoken word extends to the written word. The classic example is the suicide note. In the case of the death of Mrs Sandra Weddell in 2008, there was an alleged suicide note, and the forensic linguists had to conduct an authorship study: this is now a very sophisticated area of their work, and they were able to show that the real author of the note was the husband, Garry Weddell, who had taken his own life after killing others. Psychologists had previously had a lot to say about the authenticity of supposed suicide notes, relating language to the reasons for wanting to take one's own life in the subject's mental profile. But modern linguistics offers something more precise. It can be something as simple as a use of an ungrammatical past tense ('he scored - he *done* it with a banana shot') and that may related to other writings by the person in question. More general features help too, such as repetitions, particular vocabulary or use of pronouns.

In contrast, the case of Eddie Gilfoyle offers a more complex study of how experts can get it wrong: a tale of wrongful imprisonment. Mr Gilfoyle, who had been jailed for life after being convicted for murder in 1993, partly on the view that the suicide letter his wife had left was written by him, was released in January 2010 and a gagging order imposed. In *The Times* on 25 February 2008, David Canter, famous for the development of crime mapping and a psychology professor, confessed that his previous opinion of Mr Gilfoyle's wife's suicide letter (that it was a fake) had changed. We can all get it wrong, and linguistic analysis of the written word is a truly complex challenge for the most expert scholar. The complexity of the case was summed up in the fact that the jury had been asked to believe that the pregnant Mrs Gilfoyle had had the note dictated by her husband, and had then hanged herself – with her husband present. This has been a terrible miscarriage of justice, but as the police spokesperson pointed out in 2010, there was a lot of evidence presented at the trial, and the linguistic analysis was just one element in that material.

The forensic linguist has to be able to tackle any kind of language use in context. One of the latest is, of course, the language used in writing. The basis of study is the simple notion that we all write or speak differently in different situations and over different mediums. This is called a *register*, and from that simple basis all kinds of individual features may be isolated. But above the register there is the totally individual use of words in sequences and in units. These may be studied very closely across a text, and the more text there is, the more chance of patterns and features emerging.

In the case of *R v. Bailey* (2007) at Lincoln Crown Court, the issue was whether or not text in a diary was written at the time of the alleged offences, or whether it was written after the actions in question. The linguist used a range of other varieties of text to find out what language structures were used to express particular reference to present time as opposed to time in retrospect: the academic words being whether or not Bailey's words had 'contemporaneity' or 'historicity.' The diary was stated to have been written at the time of the events – and those events were those of arson, criminal damage and disconnecting an electricity supply to a residential home for elderly people.

Knowledge of a human voice played a part in a conviction as long ago as the execution of King Charles I. When his executors were later being charged and tried, a man was identified by the report of the nature of his voice (the axeman had worn a mask) and so charged.

But today the specialists are being more prominent as every day passes. The Forensic Linguistic Institute offers courses in all aspects of forensic linguistics, and universities such as Aston and Cardiff have established similar degrees. People may now specialise in a very specific area of this work and make a business out of it, of course, coaching other professionals. At the base of all this is the skill of transcription – being able to reproduce and construct a notation of the words uttered or written.

Stanley Ellis had recording equipment the size of a tank, and he was very familiar with a cassette player and its pause button. He had a very good 'ear'. Today, sound editing and recording can quickly identify and monitor a voice profile, and the exactness is perhaps beginning to rival the triumphs of DNA profiling. As a forensic tool in support of police investigations, phonetics and linguistics may still have their best work to come.

The science of forensics is now burgeoning in universities, and young people are clearly attracted to the study, being inspired by the many crime television series so popular now, with their slick and wealthy protagonists. The voice and speech utterances play only a small part in that, but some high-profile cases have made the area of forensics one of the newest elements in the degree pathways in college. It is to be hoped, though, that students entering this academic discipline will widen their horizons, learning something about criminality itself, as well as the specialist pleasures of analysing discourse and studying the human voice on recordings. There is a particular delight and satisfaction in being able to transcribe every utterance from a Zulu click to a glottal stop in the speech production of a Yorkshireman. But Stanley Ellis, a quiet man with a fascinating ability, was far more than the man on the radio who could tell where the caller was born: he was a trailblazer in a new science with an exciting career trajectory. He and other analysts studied the Ripper tapes.

That foundation work was done long before the computer revolution. Today, lawbreakers have to watch every word and be very careful when they write anything down.

Pirates

'Sailing the seas for private ends without authorization from any government with the object of committing depredations upon property or acts of violence against persons' covers the definition of piracy. The crime was explained very clearly by Sir Harold Scott in the 1950s. Popular culture has ensured that most people think of the 'black flag' and Long John Silver or Captain Jack Sparrow when piracy is mentioned; a maritime activity absolutely soaked through with myth and derring-do. In reality, it was a horrendous profession, being highly threatening to everyday mercantile trade, and in its heyday during the seventeenth and eighteenth centuries, was so detrimental to all trading across the burgeoning empires and new trade routes that Execution Dock by the

Thames was used to hang the bodies of hanged pirates to instil fear into any aspiring wrong-doers.

There is more than enough material available on the major figures in this crime such as Blackbeard and Bartholomew Roberts, but a tale from the 1690s will provide a more typical case study. This is the story of the adventurous pirate captain called Every, who took possession of the *Charles the Second* by Corunna in 1694. The captain, Gibson, was gravely ill and Every took his chance. He gathered plenty of allies and then went on a trail of attacks and robberies across the globe. He was active in the Gulf of Guinea, which was a centre for slave-trading, and at one point he attacked a Danish ship and his men had to prove their mettle in a scrap. They also confronted a fleet of merchantmen at Mocha, and they gathered in a considerable quantity of gold and silver.

As Storry Deans explained, writing in 1906: 'All the pirate ships were fast sailers; and the men who manned them were seamen of the utmost skill. Indeed a speedy ship and skilful seamanship were as necessary for the piratical profession as were an entire absence of conscientious scruples and a plenitude of physical courage.'

However, roving across the oceans tends to be a finite pleasure. The crew longed for home in England. After they were tricked into entering harbour by the Governor of Providence, Every slipped away into obscurity, and most of his crew were arrested and eventually tried. Chief Justice Holt headed the trial, and they were sentenced to death. Their bodies were hung in chains. Storry Deans sums up the attitudes towards the end of the golden age of pirate raids: '... ere long the British people and government realised that the Sovereignty of the Seas involved the co-relative obligation of keeping the seas clear of the robbers who had formerly infested them.'

*Poaching

In a day of revenge in the little township of Bingley, between Leeds and Bradford, in 1862, the endless war between keeper and poacher ended in a terrible murder. James Waller, persistent poacher, approached his victim in the evening with a double-barrelled shotgun. He turned, being seen, and let the gamekeeper give chase, then stopped, turned and fired. Smith put his hand to his chest and said that he was done for. Then Waller shot him in the chest again. This was a most uncomplicated crime, with no attempt to cover things up or be in any way subtle. Several people were around and they came to where they heard the shots. It took Smith (who was known locally as Davey) a long time to die. There was soon a police chase in action, searching for Waller. There were no other suspects.

Inquests back then were often held in public houses, and this one was held at the Angel Inn, Baildon, and the jury were taken to see the corpse of the victim. An officer from Otley, Sergeant Inman, said he had heard Waller say he would blow Smith's brains out. Waller had always been rash, reckless and outspoken. Surely the most interesting witness was Ann Wilkinson, because she had experienced Waller simply walking into her home, openly saying he wanted a good place from which to see and shoot his victim. It was just a case of when they would track him down – not if they would. They found him in a barn and he was said to be 'pale and haggard and much reduced.'

He pleaded not guilty at the trial at York but that meant nothing. The facts were clear; the motive was well known and the evidence was substantial. There were several reliable witnesses. He was condemned to hang and a large crowd turned out to watch him die. When his neck was stretched almost ten thousand people were there. It took him ten minutes to die – a horribly inhumane statistic in the history of York executions. His last words were that he hoped there was no bad feeling between him and Smith, when they met in the next world.

What this shows is that the enmity between the two occupations may fester for years, and there is always a grudge somewhere in the story. The keeper stands in the way of a meal for a man's family, perhaps, or maybe he has always been too smart for the transgressor. When I first researched this story, I missed its significance in the long and sorry chronicle of poaching and homicide: that one incident in a long and very rocky relationship may linger and then emerge one day in a raging violent encounter. Poaching has always had that incipient aggression.

As so often with a great scholar, Dr Samuel Johnson goes to the heart of the matter when it comes to poaching and where its fascination lies. In his great dictionary of 1755 he quotes 'You poachers have such a way with you that all at once it is done.' This is from an old volume from Tudor times, and it pinpoints the continuing appeal of a poaching story. The fact is that poaching is a *mystery* in the old sense of a special skill, a word used of skilled artificers who had a mystery in their occupation (hence mystery plays). The very idea that a man may step onto private land, in the dangerous night, and snatch creatures for his kitchen and table is one of derring-do, effrontery, courage – and often foolhardy risk.

The popular literature of crime shows that there has always been a profound fascination with crime in England, and for many centuries that crime was largely rural. There were few very large towns throughout the years before say the late Tudor times; the songs and ballads of our history before modernity are placed in the kinds of transgression that was often thought of as 'social crime' but more deeply, the theme was freedom and escape from the daily grind of work.

In the famous Lincolnshire song, *The Lincolnshire Poacher*, the first line has 'When I was bound apprentice.' The speaker was 'bound' – fastened to the terms of his apprenticeship, in restraint. By the second verse we have, regarding the gamekeeper, 'for him we did not care.' Now we have a definite aversion, if not a hatred. The song ends with 'bad luck to every magistrate...' What emerges is a song that comments on the central, persistent confrontation of keeper and poacher, and it is a story that is embedded in the very heart of our social history.

Then there is the continuing human story of the poacher that is packed with dramatic interest. In 1819, Sarah Dunhill was convicted of stealing two geese, and she was sentenced to seven years transportation. At her trial she threw her hands up and shouted that she wished the whole bench would be sunk into perdition by the Almighty.

Back in early medieval times, when there were massive stretches of common land, for a man to take a rabbit or two to feed his family was nothing with any serious consequences. There was common land and there was waste land, and animals were abundant, easily killed and bagged, and so the society survived, with those on the edge of real work or social position managing to survive. Later came parishes, demesne land of Norman barons, and of course, the royal land, which existed as huge areas of forbidden territory for the common man and his family.

There was plenty of forest in those centuries after the Romans left in 410 A.D. up to the Tudor years when vast numbers of trees were needed to forge the Henrician navy. Neil Oliver, in his book *A History of Ancient Britain*, imagines the land re-forested if humans died out: 'Within decades, or a few centuries at most, towns and neighbourhoods are swallowed up by trees.'

As the commercial imperative drove social change in Britain, most markedly from the last years of the sixteenth century when the East India Company was founded and the new American colonies were about to be opened out, the centrality of property and ownership of material wealth became universal. The inevitable development of the haves and have-nots was to bring with it all the legal and criminal issues associated with such a situation. The early eighteenth century consolidated this, as the British Empire took shape more prominently and the wealth at home gathered by investors led to building of country houses, estates, landscaping, deer parks and the culture of hunting, shooting and fishing.

There was then the Industrial Revolution and the more widespread creation of enclosure, with more and more common land being enclosed; in the war period of 1792-1815, Parliament assented to 956 bills of enclosure. The poor suffered terribly; as historians have often pointed out, the damage done to rural communities was both material and moral. Of course, crime and deprivation go hand in hand.

In such extreme circumstances, the notion of common land and food sources being open to all, there was a certain credence given to what was later the campaign ideology of Proudhon the French socialist: 'property is theft.' In other words, if there were game birds and rabbits both accessible and plentiful, surely a poor family man could feed his family with their flesh? At the centre of this was the ancient craft of poaching and it attendant culture. This gave rise to the trade of gamekeeper, and thus began the land wars, going on all the time like a cat and mouse game, with its own rituals and rules. When that code was broken, and a poacher shot dead a keeper, the punishment was extreme and merciless.

A succession of repressive 'murder acts' in the century after the 1688 rebellion gradually assembled hundreds of capital crimes. The Game Laws were prominent in this; the game laws of 1684 made the taking of game by anyone other than persons who owned a freehold estate of at least £100 per annum, or who were the son and heir apparent of a person of a higher degree. In 1723 the 'Black Act' made many kinds of poaching into felonies, and there were others such repressive acts, up to 1816. An indication of the severity of the regime in the first fifty years of the eighteenth century is that between 1700 and 1750 in London and Middlesex, there were just over 3,000 capital convictions and 1,714 executions. There was also the hiatus between the loss of America and the new use of Australia as a destination for felons: this period meant that it was perhaps easier to hang than to fill the gaols to a point of crisis.

The spirit behind such famous folk songs as *The Lincolnshire Poacher* expresses much of the popular mediation of what was for some a sport and for others the only activity that kept away starvation in the family. As poaching offences were tried largely at a magistrates' court in the first instance, there would be local knowledge and a certain degree of leniency and human understanding, as with sheep-stealing also, but in the statutes such offences as robbing warrens, being armed and disguised in a forest, stealing any fish from a river or pond, and breaking down the head or mound of a fish pond were capital offences.

Sheep stealing is an interesting case. In many English counties, a desperate mad could easily steal a sheep and feed his whole family. But there are numerous cases in which people were clearly making a large-scale business out of stealing sheep, so repression was severe. James Huntingdon stole three sheep in 1784 and was hanged for it. William Teer stole three fleeces of hog wool and a hempen sack and was transported for seven years in 1795. William Crow, in the same year, stole a milk cow and was hanged.

Horse-stealing was common throughout the seventeenth and eighteenth centuries (it was Dick Turpin's main trade). The theft of a mare could easily mean fourteen years in Van Dieman's Land; it was common practice to hang for most animal thefts in the years c. 1790-1830.

The following chapters trace the story of poaching, from the early laws of the forest and the lives of outlaws, to the tales from the great estates and from the shires when enclosure had robbed the ordinary working folk of a major part of their livelihood.

The escalation in poaching offences went hand-in-hand with the steady increase in land and property that had to be preserved and protected. In the so-called Age of Enlightenment, more wealth was in the hands of the nouveaux riches who wanted large estates and grand homes which they could pack with material wealth – and the animals on the land were just as much in need of preserving and protecting as the ornaments in the sitting-room and the treasures from home from the young aristocrats' Grand Tours in Europe.

This entry tells the story both locally and in the grand sweep of what the historians call 'metahistory' – the overarching narrative that makes the mainstream development of a society. There is no doubt that poaching played a significant part in that greater story. After all, it had far greater significance than the statistics of how many thousand game birds had been shot dead over a regular shooting weekend at some magnificent country house.

In the core of every story is the attraction of some lines from the rural poet George Crabbe on the poacher:

With greedy eye he looked on all he saw.
He knew not justice and he laughed at law.
On all he marked he stretched his ready hand,
He fished by water and he filched by land

Arguably, our most persistent images of poachers and poaching from film and popular literature are of Robin Hood emerging from Sherwood Forest with a deer over his shoulders, and a shady-looking gunman walking out of dense vegetation with a few birds or hares in his clutches. The first one is a clue as to where we begin with the chronicle of poaching in our culture.

This is because the forest and the laws relating to it are centrally important to the subject. In pre-Norman England, and in the country throughout the Middle Ages, there were vast tracts of forest across the land, and if we look at first towards the Saxon years, when there was widespread outlawry, the fruits of the forest, both flora and fauna, play a prominent part in the lives of those poor individuals who were outside the law and on the loose, existing in groups living on their wits and on hunting, in the wilds of the waste lands.

Even before William the Conqueror, the kings had massive forests and we only have to note that there were officers known as verderers to see how important it was for the monarchs to protect what they had. The verderers date from the early years of the eleventh century, and there were four of these men to every defined forest. They were in that position for life, and they were elected by the county freeholders. They had power, and this was to be seen in the Court of Attachment, which was held every forty days. Clearly, they were a kind of constable, and had a considerable responsibility. The Court of Attachment was a vehicle for obtaining goods and possessions for a designated creditor.

In other words, as with the crowner or the magistrate and also with the travelling justices of the King, the verderers were just one more part of the powerful legal mechanism of grabbing back what was the property of the Crown.

The kings back then really did want their forests to be patrolled, protected and regulated. Poaching the royal deer was really risking your neck. It was not simply a matter of keeping the deer off the poacher's back. It was a notable logistical problem keeping these areas overseen. After all, the royal forests covered very extensive land masses. For instance, the clay soils of Oxford across to Northamptonshire, striding across what is now the A43, were all forest. If one travels on the A42 today from Nottingham to Birmingham, the sign saying 'The National Forest' is a laughable concept and very much a piece of wishful thinking when we compare it to the forests across that stretch of middle England as it would have been c. 1300.

Forest law became what might be termed a system under William the Conqueror. The concept of a royal forest lay outside the idea of the common law. It was a special creation, much as the later Tudor Court of Star Chamber was to become. That is, the forests existing for the King's pleasure was a very different concept to that of the earlier Saxon counterpart. For the Saxon monarchs, there was no thought regarding any land that was set aside as in any way special or outside established legal definitions and applications.

The Normans had the ideas of 'the vert' and the 'venison' and these forests were reserved for the monarch, who had exclusive use and access. By the time Shakespeare arrived and started to use notions of life in the forest as retreats or places of banishment, a forest could be an almost paradisal image, as Shakespeare conveys in *As You Like It*, but this has a lot to do with myth and nothing to do with the forest as a place where transgression was so easy to do. These words, by Duke Senior, express a common image of forest:

> *Are not these woods*
> *More free from peril than the envious court?*
> *Here feel we not the penalty of Adam,*
> *The season's difference, as the icy fang*
> *And churlish chiding of the winter's wind...*

This was far from the horrendous truth of the life of a medieval outlaw who had to exist in the forests. The forest law – established by William The Conqueror – embraced trespass against the *vert* (the vegetation) and the venison. There were five animals protected: hart, hind, boar, hare and wolf. There were also the beasts of chase and warren, but these were outside the forest law itself.

It was not difficult to break the forest laws, as they also covered such things as felling trees and bringing dogs into the forest. It is when we look at courts and punishments that the plight of the poacher is highlighted. At the heart was the aforementioned Court of Attachment, but that court passed cases on rather than deciding on them. The alleged offenders went to the *swainmote*. Punishments could include blinding, mutilation or even death. The swainmote was held three times a year, and the Warden and the verderers presided.

It is in the assize of the forest of 1184 that the hard truth of the forest protections may be seen, and clarifications were sorted out by 1225, and the fine detail is seen in such passages as this: 'No forester.... shall gather corn, lamb or pig nor shall make any gathering, but by the sight and upon the view of the twelve rangers...'

Who was in trouble, then, if he poached in such forests? In most cases, the answer is the outlaw. To be an outlaw in medieval times was a life-endangering status. He was termed 'a wolf's head' and could be killed lawfully by anyone. The forest law had created a separate, inviolate domain, and one passage in The Anglo-Saxon Chronicle has this, referring to William and his forests: 'He made many deer-parks... so that whoever slew a hart or a hind should be deprived of his eyesight. As he forbad men to kill the harts, so also the boars... he decreed respecting the hares that they should go free. His rich men bemoaned it, and the poor men shuddered at it.'

The wealthy nobles then, were to be the only hunters and stalkers in great swathes of forested land. Efforts to preserve and protect continued to be made, and more and more draconian legal measures were made. Poachers had to be confronted, taken on and dealt with. In 1293, foresters, parkers and warreners were protected from prosecution if they killed poachers, by the old ambiguous words of 'if they resisted arrest.'

Cases where this protection could be carried out were of course common, and there would have been rankling resentment in the ranks of ordinary folk about that increased danger to their lives if they ventured out to take a hart in the woods, and also, in the years before the tightening of the law, there had been escalating animosity between poachers and crown. At Rockingham in 1272 a gang of poachers killed no less than eight deer, and one animal had its head sliced off and then in its mouth was placed a strip of wood so that its dead face would face the sun. The record states, 'in great contempt of the lord king and his foresters.'

More legislation over the years before the Tudors reduced the number and nature of those who could venture into the forest. By 1500 the restrictions were for freeholders having forty shilling in property value and to clergymen who earned over £10 per annum.

It was during the reign of Henry VII (in 1485) that the death penalty for poaching in royal forests was established as standard statutory practice. It has to be said that there had been so much hunting and poaching in those vast forests that something had to be done, from the standpoint of the rich and titled, to preserve the status quo. If we need a story to illustrate the possibilities in big business poaching, then we need the tale of Richard Stafford and 'Frere Tuk.'

Richard Stafford led an outfit of reckless rebels and outlaws around Surrey and Sussex; he had created a name for himself, much as the figure of Ned Lud appeared in the early nineteenth century, and that was 'Frere Tuk.' A contemporary record gives the essential facts:

> May 22 1417 Commission to William Lasyngby and Robert Hull to enquire into the report that a certain person assuming the unusual name of Frere Tuk and other evildoers have entered parks, warrens and chases of divers lieges of the king in the counties of Surrey and Sussex at divers times, hunted therein and carried off deer, hares, rabbits, pheasants and partridges, burned the houses and lodges for the keeping of the parks, warrens and chases, and threatened the keepers.

It took a while for it to be known that Stafford really was Tuk, but the truth came out after a later indictment, and it was then known that Stafford was in fact a chaplain from Lindfield. Clearly he was in need of some adventure and a lot of money. He had not appeared in court to answer a plea of trespass and enquiries revealed the truth about him. He was known to be alive in 1429.

This raises the question of where the Friar Tuck of popular Robin Hood tales came from. Was it from this story? Tuk was a May Games figure in the fifteenth century, and investigations into earlier Tucks have not been entirely successful. But maybe one theory that St Robert of Knaresborough's family name, while being Flores, does have a 'Touk' in his father's genealogy.

The royal forests then, were dangerous places to venture for the ordinary churl or man on the run. The centuries after the first Normans and their forests were to bring the extreme and relentless game laws and ever more repressive statutes against poaching. Of course, it was in the work of the magistrates that the local and small-scale poachers were to be dealt with. Here, the notion of social crime comes into the discussion. A man had to feed his family and times were hard when there was no social security; a pension was a concept only for those who had a sinecure or who found favour with the wealthy.

The greater national history also plays a part in how we understand the necessity for poaching. The classic example is the period of the first half of the fourteenth century. These years included almost constant wars in France and elsewhere, famine, economic depression, and finally the Great Black Death of 1348 that wiped out around a third of the population. In such a time is there any need to speculate as to why the labouring man or the member of the parish poor would have no choice but to go out with a bag and a weapon to find the day's food? One thinks not. Magistrates had to learn discretion, have a human angle on matters, and act pragmatically. Unfortunately, many on the local benches were aristocrats or in the pay of the local manor.

It is often suggested that the richest, deepest art and literature comes from hard times, and that harsh realities mix with societies in the process of revolution. This certainly applies if we look at the works of Geoffrey Chaucer, who makes food, dining and cooking a theme at the very heart of his Canterbury Tales. There is plenty of fun there about over-eating and hunting food, but a history of poaching and hunting has to make note of what could happen in these hard times: things such as cannibalism. Where there were localized famines, there was always the potential for cannibalism.

Such a fact makes us think again about the need to go poaching. Property, to communists, might be theft, but to the poor, it staves off suffering and death, and in this case, it is the dinner on the table.

Poison Everywhere: Thomas Overbury

At the court of James I, there were favourites. People jostled for prominence, and strategies for getting close to the king were always being concocted. If your face fitted somehow, you were likely to do well and find favour. Such was the case of Robert Carr with King James I. One of Robert's close friends was

Sir Thomas Overbury, but when Carr became involved with Lady Frances Howard, trouble began to brew.

Otherwise known as Lady Essex, as she had married the Earl of Essex, and so was in a position of power, when Sir Thomas advised against their marriage, this dangerous mix of emotions and power was destined to lead to Overbury being dragged to the Tower, from where he would not return into the daylight again.

One historian noted that Lady Essex was 'an unchaste lady with manifestly criminal instincts' and when she took against Overbury, his fate was sealed. A charge against Overbury was created: 'acting contrary to the orders of the Sovereign Lord the King' as he had refused a post offered to him by the king. Overbury was taken to the Bloody Tower, where Richard Weston, a friend of Carr's, was placed as warder to that dark place. Overbury had no chance.

Poison was to be the instrument of his death, and to that end, Carr, Lady Essex and Weston had a master plan, something nefarious that would be assisted in the execution by one Lobel, a Frenchman who had chemical knowledge. There were others involved, and the whole outfit was referred to as a 'gang' by an early historian of the Tower, Sir George Younghusband, who explained what came from all this: 'Sir Thomas Overbury was kept strictly secluded from his friends. Even his doctor was committed to the Fleet for making an attempt to see him professionally... Overbury was, according to their amateur calculation, induced to swallow enough poison to kill twenty ordinary men.'

However, the poor man struggled on and survived this onslaught. The result was that every possible item in the victim's life was poisoned with arsenic: wine, salt, pepper and everything else. Then, in September 1613, the gang did the ultimate in determined bloody murder: they 'applied a clyster' – in other words, poison was forced up his rectum. Overbury died, and he must have felt some relief as death eclipsed his pain.

But the killers met their apt reward: they were taken to the Tower a few years later. They were then the Earl and Countess of Somerset, and their eventual fate was to be not quartering, but as Younghusband explains, 'the little house in seclusion where the Somersets ended their days was their St. Helena.' That is, they were totally obscure and unable to walk out into society, to be visible and valued; quite the opposite, they were erased from view, and that was after several years in the Tower, languishing and falling ill.

The story has long gone down as a classic instance of death by poison, long before the period we perhaps most associate with that method of killing – the Victorian years.

*Police Murders: The very first, and a typical death

An officer of the law on the beat has always faced violence and even death. The Police Roll of Honour Trust refers to 'some 5,000 police officers' killed in the course of doing their duty or as a result of doing duty. But who was the first metropolitan police officer to be killed? The unfortunate man was Joseph Grantham.

This was in 1830, within the first year of the new professionals. Grantham did what so many well-meaning folk would do – he intervened in a fight. Two drunken men were fighting in Somerstown and Grantham was set about and beaten to death. It is the verdict that fills the modern reader with disgust, as it was *justifiable homicide*. Was this due to a dislike of the new police force?

History records far too many everyday deaths of police officers, and if one has to find a typical example it might be one from the North East.

The Hiring Fair was a very old institution in English history, dating back over the centuries to the reign of Edward III, and later, in the Tudor period when affairs concerning masters and servants were regulated more forcefully, days were named on which labour could be hired, and the High Constable of the shire would define terms of pay and working conditions.

The annual fair then became a major event: we know from social history and from literature that the hiring fair, or mop fair as it was sometimes known, became an occasion when labour was hired for a year from Michaelmas to Michaelmas. Men and women would stand in line, set to show off their trades and skills, so that, as L.W. Cowie described, 'cowmen had a tuft of cowhair, carters a piece of whipcord, shepherds a tuft of sheep's wool and thatchers a fragment of yellow straw, while servant-girls carried a mop or wore a white apron.'

The token was taken when the individual was given work, but of course that description suggests a smooth, organised system. In fact, the fairs were occasions at which drink might flow too freely, competition might become too heated, and old jealousies and resentments might explode. No doubt the hired men and women, when the fast-penny was pressed into their hand to seal the bargain, felt in need of something to wet their whistle. All around them were the amusements of the fair, and fun was in the air. Pleasure could easily transmute into aggression.

At Alnwick in Northumberland at the March Fair in 1875, the jollification changed into a riot, and in the midst of the violence and unrest was the constable. As one account has it: '… the said [Sergeant] John Hately came to his death whilst in the execution of his duty in endeavouring to quiet a disturbance which took place… on the hiring day of the 6th of March.' He left a widow and eight children.

What was given least consideration was the safety of an officer. Hately was hit by a stone, flung at him from the crowd, and he died of the injuries sustained. Here was a brave man, standing out and being counted, as it were, in the struggle to maintain order and reason. He paid for that bravery with his life. What had the law done to organise and streamline the force around him?

The most significant legislation came in 1856 with the County and Borough Police Act. After the report of a Select Committee on Police in 1853, it was made compulsory for county forces to be created and for some amalgamations to be effected. To supervise this, special offices were created to be called Her Majesty's Inspectors of Constabulary. The report of 1853 had stressed the vagrancy problem, as that was considered to be a major cause of crime, and in the larger rural counties we can see the implementations of his Act taking that into consideration. In Lincolnshire, for example, the reports on the Lincolnshire Constabulary by the Chief Constable in 1857 given to the Joint Police Committee lists the strength of the force: Lindsey had seven superintendents and 43 constables; Kesteven had one superintendent and 20 constables, and Holland had one superintendent and 16 constables. The magistrates met in 1856 'convened by the Lord Lieutenant and held in the castle of Lincoln in October 1856 for the proper taking into consideration the Act 19 and 20 Vic. Cap. 69 to render more effectual the police in county boroughs of England and Wales.'

As to the important features such as ratio of police officers to population in the counties, these varied greatly. In Norfolk, for instance, there were 196 officers in 1856, a ratio to population of 1/ 3451. In Dorset there were only twelve men at the time. Essentially, the police officer at the time of Hately's death, had no hope of assistance in times of trouble: later in the century, there were death and burial clubs of most constabularies, and superannuation came in. Some forces, such as Hull for instance, had superannuation funds as early as the 1860s, but for many, if the worst happened, it was a case of charity and humane responses to personal tragedy. Hately's force did have a superannuation fund, but with eight children that was hardly adequate. Still, as a deed of 2 May in 1875 states, £81 was given 'as a gratuity' from the police superannuation fund 'after providing for the immediate wants of the widow and family.'

The constable was a vulnerable figure. Hately tried to stop a riot. The result was that the reputation of the hiring fair for trouble and disorder was confirmed, and the community was left with a widow and eight orphans to somehow help and supervise. Documentation shows that there was, in fact, the most stunning and impressive response to the sergeant's violent death. Notices were posted across a number of parishes. The aim was to 'raise a fund for their immediate and future benefit.' Subscriptions were called for at banks and stationers' shops. The response was massive and overwhelming.

By 21 June 1875, when the trustees of the Hately Fund arranged to meet, a sum of £743-1-4 had been raised. A list of subscribers between 15 May and 27 May that year has no less than 39 people, and they had given sums as small as one guinea, up to large amounts such as £5 from C.W Orde. By June a huge list was issued, properly in print, listing several hundred donations of sums between 2s 6d down to one shilling. His Grace the Duke of Northumberland, at Alnwick Castle, gave £25 – a four-figure sum in today's values.

The records of the work undertaken on behalf of Mrs Mary Hately by the trustees shows what could be achieved, in those dangerous days before proper social welfare and support, by sheer energy and commitment, done in recognition of a deed of courage. In fact, what the trustees did was what every right-thinking person of wealth did at the time: invest in railways and in the government. Everyone was doing it, from the Rothschilds downwards. A letter from the trustees describes the matter:

> It is also declared that the said trustees shall have full power to invest the trust funds in government or real securities or in Railway Stock, where the whole capital has been called up... and that all indemnity clauses under the statute (22nd and 23 Victoria Chapter 35) to save trustees from risk, shall be considered as incorporated... into this deed.

It was decided that the Trust should last '19 and a half years at least' and in the formal agreement concerning the fund's investment, there was a remarkable degree of attention given to Mary's welfare, separate from a long list of trust sums held for all the children. The deed says that all sums not apportioned for the children are 'for the benefit of the said Mary Hately for her life for her sole and separate use only and not to be subject to the debts or control of any husband she might have...'

Mary Hately was forty years old when her husband died. She must have been astonished at the local response to the sad death of her husband of course: the result of that flying chunk of rock at the hiring fair highlights two important and fascinating mid-Victorian elements of social history: the fragile nature of every community in tough times, when hard farming work ground down the working population to seek consolation in drink and in high-jinks, and naturally, the dangerous nature of those guardians of law who faced the trouble head-on. There was solidarity when tragedy followed, and Mary Hately would have noticed that, aside from the huge sums given to her by tradesmen and professional people in her community, there was a very large sum of over £27 raised by the men at the Northumberland Constabulary, and what stands out, apart from the £7 paid by his superintendent, is the £7.12.5 from a simple constable – P.C. Spence. We have to speculate that this man was a close friend indeed, maybe the man who grew up with him in the force.

Pressing

In the history of our criminal law, there are serious issues relating to offences and penalties when an accused would not plead. In Tudor times, a person not offering a plea could be 'pressed' which means that heavy stones would be placed over a board, under which the accused lay, until their death. Perhaps the most widely known case of this barbaric method of torture (and usually of execution) is that of Margaret Clitherow in York in 1586. Visitors to the Shambles shopping street today will see the tiny room of prayer devoted to her in her former home. She was a Catholic and was arrested for harbouring Catholic priests, a crime punishable by death. Margaret refused to plead, preventing a trial, and was therefore sentenced to death by pressing..

*Prison: Escapes

There have been numerous escapes from British prisons, but one that has to be told is from Lincoln gaol at the time of the Irish rebellion around Easter 1916 and afterwards.

Visitors to the city of Lincoln would never be aware, unless they were suddenly taken very ill, that there was a grand and formidable Victorian prison close to the centre; it stands opposite the County Hospital, dominating Greetwell Road with its long, rounded-topped walls and castellar gatehouse. Opened in 1872, it replaced the old Georgian prison which was inside the castle grounds. In that long history, there have been very few escapes from Lincoln. George Brewer escaped in March 1943, only to be recaptured within twenty-four hours, and in 1966 a man escaped using knotted bedclothes. But by far the most notorious escape was that of the future Taoiseach of the Irish republic, Eamon de Valera.

It was an amazing story, hitting the national headlines, and *The Times* reported the bare facts the day after – 5 February 1919: 'Hue and cry at Lincoln – Eamon de Valera, he Sinn Fein M.P, for East Clare, with two other Irish prisoners, escaped from Lincoln gaol some time between half past four o'clock yesterday afternoon and nine o'clock in the evening.' Tall and distinguished de Valera had been a key player in the Dublin Easter Rising, being captured and imprisoned afterwards, and after spells at other prisons, was sent to Lincoln with other Sinn Fein men.

De Valera was a scholarly type, a mathematician. One of his friends at college was Charles Walker, and I have been told of a time much later in de Valera's life when Walker's text books were given to 'Dev' on a day when the famous politician invited Walker's daughter and grandchildren to tea. It says a lot about the man that he was so welcoming, but of course, his life was full of contradictions and puzzles (what politician doesn't have such complexities?). He was born in New York but raised in County Limerick by his grandmother; he was later educated at University College, Dublin, joining the Gaelic League in 1904 and the Irish Volunteers in 1913. He was involved in gun-running at Howth the year after, and commanded the third battalion of the Dublin Brigade in the Easter Rising of 1916.

Before ending up in Lincoln, he had been put in Kilmainham jail after the Rising and there he expected to be shot, writing this note to Mother Gonzaga at Carysfort Convent in Blackrock, where he was a maths teacher: 'I have just been told that I will be shot for my part in the Rebellion. Just a parting line to thank you and all the sisters... for your unvarying kindness to me in the past...' But he was reprieved and lived to see the inside of several other jails in his long career.

He escaped from Lincoln with two other men, John Milroy and John McGarry. The description given of de Valera says a lot about him: 'aged 35, a professor, standing 6ft. 3 ins and dressed in civilian clothes.' The report neatly summarised the fact that tracing the men was going to be virtually impossible, 'A close search has been made all over the city, but so far as was known at a late hour last evening the escaped prisoners had not been found.' They were not the only escapees from the Sinn Fein ranks: four men escaped from Usk prison the week before.

De Valera had been arrested in the 'round up' of May that year, stopped by detectives as he went home to Greystones in County Wicklow. He was then taken across the Irish Sea to Holyhead. The forecast by journalists at the time that he would make his way back to Dublin and 'arrange for a dramatic reappearance in Irish politics' was quite right.

How did they manage to escape? Lincoln prison fronts Greetwell Road, but behind at that time was merely open ground, beyond the rear exercise yards, and to the left, along the road heading out of Lincoln, there were merely limekiln areas then. The escape was arranged so that full use could be made of the vulnerability at the rear. But having said that, there was constant supervision, and of course, they needed a master key.

A committee of Irishmen was set up to arrange the escape, and they selected a number of men to do the job. The focus was the small patch of ground used as the exercise yard; it was surrounded by barbed wire, armed warders watched in the daylight hours, and an army unit came to patrol at sunset. Sensibly, the first decision was to decide not to try a direct assault – a rush – as there would have been a gun fight. The next plan was to start by finding a way to communicate with de Valera. The answer was to use the Irish language. An Irish prisoner who was working on a garden plot in the jail sang a song, and the words gave de Valera of the planned breakout. The second time a song was sung it was to direct de Valera to have an impression made of the key that would open the back gate. Today such methods would not be possible, but then there was more work outside and so there was a degree of vulnerability with regard to the system. According to one report, the key impression was made with the snatching of a key from a warder to press it into soap, but this seems very unlikely, given the fact that the key would be on a chain and always snapped into a belt-purse when not in use. Far more likely is the theory that a prison chaplain made the impression in soap or in a bread paste. The first two keys made did not fit anyway, and then the third model worked well.

The impression was wrapped in brown paper and thrown over the wall. Then came the hard part. De Valera would be able to walk through from the main prison building, but there were the sentries to consider. They would have to be distracted, and the way to do that was to use female allure. Two girls from Ireland were used, as the local girls may well have split on them. *The Lincolnshire Echo* reported that they were 'attractive, vivacious Irish girls, both university graduates, and they were directed to flirt with the guards.' On 3 February, four cars were sent around the country around Lincoln, to create decoys and keep the police occupied, then at dusk, the Irish girls began to work on the guards. They lured them away from the prison recreation area and the Sinn Feiners then cut through the barbed wire and waited for de Valera to appear: he did, after some initial trouble. The key broke in the lock from the outside, as Michael Collins, who had come to lead the attack, tried to force it, but luckily de Valera, from the inside, managed to force it out.

They had to move very quickly, because Collins and Boland drove straight to the city railway station and caught a train to London. But de Valera and the others split and drove to Manchester.

The conclusion given by the prison authorities about the escape was that it was facilitated by the fact that the internees were allowed to associate much more closely than ordinary prisoners, and were not subject to such close supervision. Shortly afterwards, Terence MacSweeney was released on parole from Lincoln as his wife was seriously ill.

In their time in Lincoln, the Sinn Fein prisoners were treated very well. The journal of the prison doctor records his examinations of them, and there are regular entries in that book. For a long period, several were on hunger strike, and the doctor records his comments about each one, as well as noting their weight. Paradoxically, one of the prisoners put on weight during the hunger strike – a footnote to history perhaps not widely known, and a fact that adds a humorous dimension to those troubled times.

Much more mundane, and typical of such deeds, is the case of John Jackson, who escaped from Strangeways in Manchester in 1888. He killed a warder while doing a building repair job, for which he had been given tools, which soon became murder weapons in his hands. Escape stories cause local sensations, and sometimes national ones, and the Sporting News published a booklet on the story, which has been reprinted by the enterprising bookseller and true crime specialist, Clifford Elmer Books (see bibliography).

Jackson was eventually caught and hanged. But before that he went on a spree of burglary and robbery, and the story has its highlights, and also a lively sense of humour, as the booklet recalls:

> This is the second time that Wood's house has been entered, and Jackson is believed to have been the burglar in the first case. He is a glazier by trade, and obtained an entrance by taking a window out. After ransacking the house, both above stairs and below, he smoked some cigars and then left a note on the table 'Goodbye captain, though lost to sight, to memory dear – Yours truly, Shakespeare.'

*Prison: Mutinies

Today, we need to understand what our prisons were like in the 1940s. One way to understand this is to have an insight into the crises they faced. The regime was a mess. Not only was part of Wormwood Scrubs taken over by MI5, but all kinds of misfits and proto-Nazis were locked up, along with the career criminals and black marketers. There had been some attempts to bring about some minor reforms since the Edwardian years, when Borstals were established, but then all the wars did when they came along was complicate the whole business, because now not only were there German parachutists landing in the fields, in order to engage in spying, but there were assumed and suspected traitors everywhere and of course 'walls have ears.'

In the years following the end of the First World War in 1918, some prisons were closed, and in 1922 Northallerton ceased operations, though the buildings were left standing by. In the old British tradition of utilising existing establishments when new necessities arise, when war came along in 1939 the place was in use again, this time as a training depot for the military police.

The cells provided accommodation for the trainees, and from a mere store it was transforming into a busy military location.

In the early days of the Second World War the military police comprised all kinds of personnel, from the Auxiliary Territorials in the service to the elite such as the 150 Provost Company, whose men took part in the 'Phoney War' with the British Expeditionary Force in 1939 in France; in that action, there were numerous thefts of stores and equipment and a Special Investigation Branch was formed. But for most officers in the military police at the time, routine duties were such things as the enforcement of order and discipline, instructor work, record office clerical work or security duties. But there were different kinds of military police: the red Caps are of the Provost Wing; the Traffic Control Wing work by particular areas; then the Vulnerable Points Wing guarded important sites and installations. Clearly, the latter group were the Northallerton deployment.

For a few years at the outbreak of war, then, these men had special training for those duties; though destined to become the Royal Military Police in 1946, in those first years they had an important but routine set of duties on their agenda.

In 1943 it was needed as a prison once again and became a military detention centre. There was to be a radical transformation in the next few years, as the prison changed from a place where soldiers would be trained for such things as the prevention of sabotage at important sites to a military detention centre. By 1946, Northallerton became national news, though not for good reasons. It was the location of a mutiny. To tell the full story of what became known as 'The Glass-House Mutiny' it is necessary to place the events in the context of that year.

In the House of Commons on 26 March 1946, Mr Lawson, Secretary of State, responded to Tom Driberg with regard to an enquiry into conditions at Stakehill Detention Centre near Bolton. This was the report in *The Times*:

> [Lawson] said that he had recently received the final report of the Court of Inquiry into conditions at Stakehill detention barracks. The general conclusion was that the allegations which had been made in the public press and in letters to the Rev. Urien Evans, or to members of Parliament, were either unfounded or grossly exaggerated. The Court of Inquiry, which which included among the members a KC and a psychiatrist, examined every aspect of the problem in great detail. Every effort was made to call as witnesses all those who had made allegations about the treatment of prisoners at Stakehill, and also all soldiers under sentence who had any complaint to make. They examined in all 195 witnesses including 47 members or ex-members of staff....

It was all very thorough, but his conclusion that 'there is no need to make any further enquiry into conditions at Stakehill' is very much at odds with personal testimony from some sources, and this evidence enables us to take a less than sanguine view of the kind of prison conditions which were to affect Northallerton severely.

If we set beside Lawson's words this extract from a memoir, *I Couldn't Paint Golden Angels* by Albert Meltzer, we are led to re-think these matters. Meltzer was an anarchist who had already done a stretch in Brixton before he was sent north to Stakehill:

> Stakehill had hit the news because a prisoner had been found dead. The Church of England chaplain is usually in such circumstances a minor administration official but in this particular case an enthusiastic young parson objected to the guards declining to take their hats off when escorting prisoners in church. He protested but to no avail. Then one day he was down in the detention cells and heard cries. He rushed in to find that two warders had just hit a man who was lying on the floor. One of them was saying to the other, 'Kick him staff, he's still breathing.' When the horrified padre asked what had happened, the other staff sergeant said, with an equal heavy attempt at jocularity, 'Don't mind him, Sir, he's always lying on the floor, crying.'

Meltzer wrote that he found the place 'seething with mutiny.' He saw that something was deeply wrong, and he noted that many of those being abused were 'a credit to the nation.' He pointed out that the cruelty was often extreme: 'Yet for some minor infraction of absurdly imposed regulations or breach of discipline... we were kept in cages. It was Brixton gaol all over again but more so.'

At the same time, Aldershot military prison experienced severe problems on 23 and 24 February, when a detainee managed to smash his way out of his cell and release others in the hall where he was kept; they overpowered the N.C.O. and gathered more men as they went on the rampage. The Commandant addressed them with a loud-speaker and used threats of severe reprisals but this had no effect. Troops surrounded the block where the men were, and the mutineers took to the roof. There were around forty men involved and their rage of destruction lasted well into the next day.

Some of the men involved there were recently arrived from Northallerton, as it was reported at the time: 'There seems no doubt that the disturbances were a development from a frustrated attempt by six soldiers under sentence recently transferred from Northallerton, and were not a generally concerted act of mutiny.'

In fact, Northallerton was to see the same thing, just a week later. On 1 March rioters there forced their way into one of the prison stores and set fire to it. Some of the men climbed onto the roof and began throwing bricks. The local fire brigade arrived and put out the fire. The rioting took place in a hall holding seventy men, and exactly how many men were involved is a matter of conjecture. They were long-sentence prisoners and things were in a condition of extreme danger: armed soldiers from Catterick camp were called in and a cordon was placed around the block. There had been two earlier incidents and the first was the one in which the men sent to Aldershot were involved: in the first riot there was considerable damage done to buildings. Sixteen men had escaped after morning church parade on that occasion. A week later another sixteen men broke down the gate through which the earlier escape had been attempted. The use of a hosepipe put paid to the latter trouble.

In the main mutiny, what happened was that the outbreak was confined to the one barrack; officers and managers acted quickly and efficiently; the rioters could not get near the armoury. Of course, there were some serious repercussions. An officer was hit by flying slate. But there were no escapes. The War Office official announcement said:

> The trouble appears to have been started by nine prisoners transferred from overseas on February 26. The mutiny was confined to some of the men in one block only. Men under custody in the other block and in Nissen huts were not involved. Fifty troops from Catterick have arrived to reinforce the barracks staff, but the situation is now under control except that about nine men were still on the roof at 5 p.m.

The leading lights in the insurrection were from the British Army of the Rhine. The main source seems to be a unit which had served in Italy and the disaffection that began there was carried with them back to England. The Secretary of State made a speech in which he hedged around the whole area of what underlying grievances might have been. The main one was that sentences for quite minor offences were very long, as Meltzer had claimed in his memoir. The Secretary bluffed and spoke vaguely, saying, '...it is clear that some of the soldiers under sentence, some of whom have criminal records, were in a mood to take full advantage of the opportunity to join in this act of mass indiscipline.'

In Northallerton, the papers created a narrative of high drama and dramatic incidents. The *Daily Mail* photographer managed to take a flight over the prison and to take a shot showing all the events: he labelled the picture to show the hose being used against a man on the roof; he showed the positions of all the fire brigade installation, and made sure that his readers would be reassured by seeing the armed guards placed around the gaol. The same paper later printed a shot of the destruction, with the caption: 'Two pictures from a Daily Mail cameraman who visited Northallerton (North Yorkshire) military prison during yesterday's riots, when long-sentence prisoners seized the main block of the gaol, smashed everything they could, and set fire to the Army stores.'

The Mail main headline said it all: 'National Glasshouse Plot Suspected.' It was a case of hype on a grand scale; unfortunately, in the years since then, there have been exaggerations and distortions. One account states that 'two regiments' were needed to quell the riot.

The end of the mutiny was described in the *Daily Express* on 2 March, in these words from Reginald Butler 'inside Northallerton prison':

> 'Seven long-term prisoners, bedraggled and shivering – they had been drenched by hose-water for hours – climbed down from the rafters of this of this military prison at 7.45 tonight after a roof-top siege which lasted eight and a half hours. So ended an all-day riot involving nearly 300 soldiers – less than a week after the disturbance at Aldershot, Glasshouse No.1.' Butler went on to say that 'most of Northallerton's century-old prison was wrecked' – which was clearly grossly inaccurate.

Naturally, there was a trial of the mutineers. The evidence suggested in their defence was that their commanding officers in Europe had indicated that the men would only receive a short sentence, and that was very wrong. The men had originally gone AWOL after serving well in the theatre of war; their sense of injustice is not difficult to imagine. On 27 April it was reported that eleven of the soldiers were charged with mutiny and faced court-martials at Catterick camp. The men were from the Pioneer Corps, The Royal Scots, The Royal Northumberland Fusiliers, the General Service Corps, The Seaforth Highlanders, and (most ironically) from The Loyal Regiment. The men were named and shamed in the national press.

The story from Stakehill/Northallerton highlights something rotten at the core in the prison establishment and in the army's handling of offenders. With this in mind, there is no surprise when we consider that, when it came to the criminal process of dealing with American servicemen, who were here in vast numbers during the war, the British government was happy to leave the judicial process, and the penal element in punishment, to the American allies. HMP Shepton Mallet was the dark hole for offenders. There was quite enough to worry about in the management of our own military troublemakers, whether they were simply restless and feckless characters or whether they were mutineers. The entire subject is run through with odd narratives, such as the paradox that Fred Copeman, who led a mutiny in Scotland, later supervised the whole London underground air-raid shelter organisation and was awarded an OBE.

Q

Queen Victoria: Edward Oxford, Would-be Assassin

In Victoria's long reign (1838-1901) there were eight attempts on her life. Barrie Charles has written a special study of these, and there is plenty to say about them, but arguably, the young Edward Oxford presents the most intriguing instance of the would-be killer. As Charles puts it, 'The two guns bulging from his trouser pockets, Edward Oxford left the house with a feeling of purpose and determination.' He pulled a gun as the Queen's carriage went down Constitution Hill; Victoria saw Oxford and ducked down, with Albert making sure that she stayed down. Oxford fired again.

Oxford was overpowered and dragged away; the story and the consequent trial were to provide a media sensation. On first reading this, a modern reader might assume, on learning that Oxford had some problems of mental derangement, that perhaps he might still hang, as this was high treason as well as attempted murder. The distinction between treason and high treason was distinct. Only an argument for the lad's insanity would save his neck, and it did.

Oxford was later set free and his future lay in Australia. He was in his forties when he arrived in Melbourne, and he found work as a painter. He died in 1900

R

Rillington Place

Some addresses related to crimes became weirdly debased and sick: Cromwell Street, Hilltop Crescent, and perhaps worst of all, 10 Rillington Place. The latter address was the home of serial killer Reginald Christie. Christie, working as a part-time copper, should have been beyond reproach, but he sued that 'front' to engage in his persona of helpful medical expert, there to help women in trouble. The result was a gradual accumulation of corpses at the address, from bodies in the back yard to cadavers in cupboards.

With an intricate method of applying gas infusions, he sent many women to their graves; he even let Timothy Evans go to the gallows for murder. Reginald Christie was, whichever way we try to understand it, a twisted and dangerous personality with a penchant for applying deaths of extreme suffering.

Christie (1898-1953) was born in Halifax, and his life in employment began when he served in the local police; he moved to London and there he became more familiar with the interior of prison cells than the domestic premises he shared with his wife Ethel. They were living in Rillington Place by 1938. Ethel became one of his many victims, and he was tried for her murder, along with other women, in 1953. With such a horrendous and heinous track record of murder, it is interesting to see what the hangman, Albert Pierrepoint, had to say when he officiated at Pentonville in July 1953. Steve Fielding, in his account of the Pierrepoint dynasty of hangmen, explains what happened in the death cell: 'Smith lifted Christie's skinny wrist and Albert secured it before removing his spectacles... Christie blinked his eyes as he focused on the side door... Albert recalled later that his face seemed to melt. 'It was more than terror... at that moment I know Christie would have given anything in his power to postpone his own death.'

*Riots: Politics and Dripping

Throughout human history, whenever people have lived in communities, there have been riots. Often these are about serious concerns, such as political issues, but they may be over such basics as food prices or scarcity. Here are some examples of each variety:

> The first is about three days in a hot summer of 1911 when citizens of Lincoln must have thought they were living in a war zone. That August, a huge, raging crowd set about a campaign of destruction in the city streets between the railway crossing gates and the Stonebow. What started as a show of support for the railway workers' strike by the Boilermakers' Union gradually developed into a perilous situation, made worse by the fact that most of the major figures of authority in the city were away on holiday. By the time trouble reached its peak, there was a search for a suitable dignitary to read the Riot Act.

As so often with riots of this magnitude, there are festering resentments and grudges swelling beneath the surface, and on many occasions when industrial problems have become antagonistic, these feelings emerge to find a savage expression. In the case of Lincoln, there was a man at the centre of the drama who could be either hero or villain, depending on the perspective. This was Chief Constable John Coleman.

Coleman was deeply unpopular. He had taken a very hard line, and done something very rash just three days before this trouble. On 14 August, he had ordered the banner of the Boilermakers' Union to be torn down during a peaceful demonstration. Now, on 18 August, as a crowd stopped the crossing gates from being opened, he once again made a poor decision, ordering his officers to clear the crowd using their truncheons. This was the first uneasy confrontation in these days of riots: as the police roughly attacked the crowd on one barrier and cleared a space, the people on the other barrier forced it into immobility. Coleman was roused to more aggression: this time a few brave officers advanced with truncheons, but mayhem was breaking out now. The crowd started smashing the signal box. As the normal running of the railway was now halted, and missiles were showered at the box, a teenage employee of the railways managed to get inside and pulled the levers. But even this did nothing to restore normal service: in fact it caused an escalation of violence, as a large number of men forced a gate shut and the oncoming locomotive smashed through.

This acted like a fuse to ignite the whole area, and objects were thrown at police, buildings were attacked and damaged, and Chief Constable Coleman knew he had a major incident on his hands. This was ten at night and it was dark. The thugs leading the crowd knew they could not be seen and recognised. One constable was knocked unconscious, and Coleman himself was struck in the back. By midnight, Coleman left and it was a communication of defeat. With his senior officers, Coleman had to walk about half a mile from the centre to the Sessions House with a crowd behind him, booing and hurling bricks.

It was the end of the first phase, and gradually the crowd faded into the dark streets and went back to their homes. But it was only the beginning. It is not difficult to imagine the feelings of Coleman as he licked his wounds and tried to understand how his 'patch' had exploded in that way. There had been serious riots in Tonypandy just nine months before, and that had ended with the home secretary, Winston Churchill, actually agreeing to talk to the union leaders in London. Coleman must have feared for his reputation if things escalated in that way. He must also have known that he had made tactical errors. He did what every police chief would have done at that time: contact the military commander in the city.

Up the hill at the barracks on Burton Road, Major Fitzgerald Cox was asked to have his men ready to assist. Captain Mitchell-Innes had troops ready also. This was at 7am the next day, and Coleman personally went to look around the city later on, after things had been quiet all the evening. He made another misjudgement: he sensed nothing to worry about and told the major that 'there was no fear of a riot' and that the troops could be stood down. Coleman apparently had nothing to go on when making this decision, other than the apparent calm.

It was nothing of the kind. There was, in fact, a highly-charged atmosphere, as huge numbers of men were inside or in quiet groups, just waiting for a reason to create hell again, and the cue came when two lads throwing stones were arrested. It was a challenge to the rabble and also a desperate assertion of authority when two officers grabbed one of the youths and marched him towards the police station, but a crowd gathered and the constables were engulfed by people who were rabid for revenge. When other police officers came it caused the worst and most intense trouble of the riot period, and a voice cried out in the night, 'Now lads, we've got 'em!'

The battle that ensued was nasty and violent in the extreme; constables were cracking skulls with truncheons, and it seemed as though the whole populace was out looking for a fight; even women joined in, throwing various missiles at the constables. Rioters gathered and advanced in pulses, being driven back for a while and then moving en masse again. County police officers had now arrived and stood in a double line. For two hours, one record noted, law officers were striking people with truncheons. The wounded were taken out as in a war zone and carried to St Benedict's Square. In St Mark's Street, the station was the focus of assault, and a gang of thugs smashed doors and windows there, then started a fire. The Great Eastern Railway offices were gutted and destroyed.

A normally quiet, businesslike city in a rural county well away from any of the industrial towns with their huge ethnic mixes of workforce people was now as furiously raging with anarchy and disorder as any town involved in the Chartist troubles or bread riots of the previous century.

Where was Chief Inspector Coleman? He was also head of the Fire Brigade and he made his reappearance in that capacity. The fire was intended to flush him out; the general feeling was now that he was a coward and that the first encounter had shaken him badly. A cry went up: 'Bring the bugger out – we'll murder him!' To his credit, Coleman did walk out to face the crowd, not with a large force behind him, but with a respected, solidly moral officer, PC Clay, a lay preacher well known to the Lincoln people. This was a sensible, politic move on Coleman's part. It showed courage, but also indicated that he stood in the same camp as the morally upright and law-abiding Lincoln people, who still existed, even in that anarchy.

At this point, Coleman's toughness came through. He was assailed with stones and insults but stood firm in the tumult. He may have done thoughtless and extreme things to enforce the law, but now, terrified but resolved not to flinch, he faced the mob. His men pulled him out of the fracas and he knew then that the city could only be won back into the King's Peace with the help of the army.

Before the troops could be called in though, the Riot Act had to be read. It took some time to find a magistrate, but Dr Mansell Sympson finally came, and he made his way to the Midland Station. As he did so, Major Cox and troops of the Lincolnshire Regiment moved into position. Sympson spoke those words so familiar to the mobs of Britain through the centuries, and ended with, 'If there is not an immediate cessation of disturbances, the soldiers will fire upon you.' Drawn bayonets filled ordinary folk with terror; a slow realisation of the enormity of what had happened in their own city came into their minds, and a dispersal began.

By the early hours of the morning of 21 August, the streets of Lincoln were silent. By four in the morning the troops left. Labour delegates, in the cold light of morning when time had passed and questions were asked about those terrifying nights in the streets, put the blame firmly on Coleman, the bearded disciplinarian who saw violent repression as the natural expression of law. The Labour men said, 'We further protest at the unwarrantable provocative attitude of Chief Constable Coleman which we consider was directly incentive to riot and disorder...'

Twelve men were placed in the dock eventually, mostly labourers, and they stood in a double row. Eventually, after Assize trials in October, most of the leaders were given sentences of between three and nine months, some with hard labour. As for Coleman: it took considerable discussion and debate to decide on the amount of his pension and the nature of his 'ill health.' A judgement had been made, with all the moral force of fear and remorse. Not only had there been a profound disbelief that such ordinary people could act like savages, but it might not be too fanciful to note that several august and respectable Lincoln councillors and magistrates might have begun to question the habit of constables 'cracking heads like walnuts' in such circumstances.

As with all public riots, there had been a mix of larger political issues and a few personal vendettas in the course of the general mayhem. But one thing is certain: the exercise of force, discipline and compulsion was not the way to handle things. It may have been the usual way, and the way that 'won the Empire', but it did not achieve anything in Lincoln that year. Some used the word *war:* the streets had the look of a battlefield after a conflict, that's for sure.

An analysis was written and presented to the council, the local press and therefore to anyone who wanted to know, and it was headed 'Discrepancies.' This was written by Edwin Pratt, an alderman. His questions and comments read like a sergeant-major chastising the troops on parade. Of all his questions, surely the one that hits home most powerfully with regard to the chaos is:

'Who is REALLY responsible for the military being kept at the barracks? Did the magistrates or the Chief Constable expressly request that the military should not appear in the city unless required for positive action?'

※ ※ ※

There were times in the Victorian period when, in spite of the usual demands of the law and the innate sense of the importance of order and peace, the much distressed working class just found it too much to tolerate when an injustice was seen to be done. In some cases it was about the price of corn; other disturbances were in response to the heavy hand of the law being so severe it offended decency and reason. But then there were other causes of terrible acts of rebellion and destruction that stemmed from something very small – like dripping for instance.

Dripping has long had a place in the Yorkshire cooking repertoire and older Leeds people will still talk fondly of their youth, when society was less health conscious and a treat was a dripping sandwich, salty, rich and satisfying. Back in 1865 dripping had dozens of uses for the woman of the house feeding her usually large family, and in the case of domestic servants, taking a little dripping from the cooking done for their employer was common practice and generally accepted. But not so that February in the household of Henry Chorley in Park Square, Leeds. Chorley was a powerful man in the city: a magistrate and also a respected surgeon, but his actions against his cook cost him his reputation.

Eliza, fifty years old, was Chorley's cook and when she roasted a joint for him, she expected the dripping to take home. Chorley saw this as an offence and she was convicted of stealing two pounds of the stuff (which she did take) in January 1865 and given one month's imprisonment in Armley Gaol.

Eliza was quite new to his employment, having been there for only a few months, living in. When challenged about the matter she said that she was allowed it 'as a perquisite though I said nothing about that perquisite when I was first engaged to do the work.'

All hell broke out around Chorley's place. What had happened to make things worse was that her trial had been held in camera (privately), and the Mayor of Leeds himself had been on the bench. The spark was lit, so to speak, by an article in a paper, as a report at the time noted:

> In a few days after the committal of the woman attention was called to the case, in a spirit of indignation, by one of the local papers which is best known for its publication of sensational stories and in its indulgence of caricature sketches of local personages…

The report also noted that newsboys were shouting out scraps of gossip and jokes, and that people were chatting about the affair in disgust; in the street this rhyme was heard:

> *Now all you cooks and servant girls wot's very fond of tipping*
> *Don't take your master's scraps of fat and boil 'em down for dripping:*

For if you do bear this in mind, the magistrates won't fail
To try you in a private court and send you off to gaol.

Time passed and graffiti appeared on the walls of the Chorley home and on plenty of other walls, with such words as ' A month's imprisonment for 2lbs of dripping.' Then things escalated so that Chorley was vilified in the street and indeed harassed and bullied. He received threatening letters, and then placards began to appear expressing the view that Leeds people should assemble for a large celebration when Mrs Stafford came out of prison.

But before that, pressure mounted. A large and aggressive crowd gathered outside Chorley's house. At first they shouted insults, and then they threw missiles at the house, including snowballs and stones. Chorley had the courage to come out and face them; he tried to talk to them and explain his position on the matter but to no avail. They threw dirt at him. When the police arrived they gradually dispersed, but there was worse to come.

Late in the evening on 22 February, a huge crowd assembled outside Armley Gaol expecting Mrs Stafford to appear, but she did not. The mob expected celebration but instead found that their friend was still locked up, or so they thought. In fact she had been let out earlier. After that the crowd were determined to go again to Chorley's house and this time they contrived to hang a bottle and an old dripping-pan to the end of a long pole. The police who stood by took a very long time to move the mob away.

Still the Leeds populace were not satisfied. The next day stones were thrown at the Chorleys' windows and the mob were pressing heavily on the forces of the law. To make matters worse, Chief Constable Bell, while trying to help move the crowd, fell heavily and dislocated a shoulder. The crowd mentality took over and when people fell they were crushed and trampled. One man was under the feet of the mob and was so seriously injured he had to be taken to the infirmary. The police could not cope.

The army at York were called for by telegraph, so by the evening men from the 8th Hussars were in Leeds, having travelled by train from York, and extra police from Bradford were called for as well. There was a feeling of the riot being calmed by the time that the local journalists posted their reports but late that night a crowd of about 2,000 gathered outside the town hall and shouted out insults. The police took the brunt of the anger as usual and as this mob was moved away, a stone cut deeply into the temple of one officer. There were several arrests, which was inevitable given the scale of destruction and lawlessness that had filled the city like a rising tide of rage.

All this time, Mrs Stafford had been elsewhere. She had left Leeds much earlier, going to Scarborough where her daughter lived. *The Times* man reflected that she showed good sense 'preferring to avoid the questionable honours the crowd intended to confer upon her.' In other words, her appearance before her supporters would either have intensified the anger or made her a local hero. The politic action smacks of a reaction to sound advice from the police and prison governor. In the end, it was decided that the five men arrested should not be dealt with seriously. There was perhaps a feeling of regret for the mean and thoughtless use of power by a bench of three influential men of high status, with one woman in front of them and the Chorleys and other witnesses trailing into the town hall to condemn her. The newspapers had imagined and recreated that scene in the eyes of the public, and the formula was one for extreme disorder on the streets of Leeds.

We have to remember that the workers were one thing but the so-called 'underclass' were another matter. Usually when disorder hit the streets it was the lowest social order who were involved, desperate and pushed to the end of their tether by economic pressures such as the price of bread or the lack of jobs. The Leeds dripping riots were, as far as we can gather, events in which decent people were goaded into militancy and sheer rage because of a terrible injustice against a decent working woman. In simple terms, it was a case of a confrontation betweenthe practice of goodwill and convention ('perks of the job') and the letter of the law.

There was an element of absolute disgust at the immorality and injustice being shown by a man in high position. With hindsight, it is possible to say that the results of the street violence were partly a continuation of the old social convention of 'rough music' when a local wrongdoer was subject to torment and bullying for a moral 'crime' and also it was a case of total callousness on the part of a man who should have known better.

His main contribution to true crime literature was his involvement with the Notable Scottish Trials and Notable British Trials series, published by Hodge in Edinburgh. Roughead edited several of these meticulous and detailed accounts of trials, and so produced solid volumes of inestimable use to criminologists and legal professionals.

Road Hill House Murder, The

This remarkable and enthralling child murder is as much the story of detective Jonathan Whicher as it is about the victim and his family at this notorious address. In 1860 at this Wiltshire home, young Frances Savile Kent (only four years old) was found horribly murdered on the property, after being reported missing from his bed. The family and the domestic servants were tucked up in bed, and police could not find evidence of any entry by robbers or burglars, so who within the house committed the crime? The first line of thought was focused on the nanny, but nothing came of that.

When local police's efforts led nowhere, Scotland Yard were asked to help and Inspector Jonathan Whicher was sent to Wiltshire. He found that, at the time of the murder, sixteen-year-old Constance Kent's bloodstained nightdress had been found in the scullery before it strangely went missing. Based on this, Whicher wanted Frances' sister Constance to be arrested and tried in court. But, as Judith Flanders puts it, this was to the horror of the middle class world – 'arrest the daughter of a middle-class house purely on suspicion?'

Constance did appear before the bench at this time, but the result was merely a release on a recognizance of £200. The press enjoyed all this, but nothing was resolved and finally everything was left as it was before the killing and Whicher exited,

That was until much later, in 1865, when Constance Kentconfessed the murder of her little brother to a priest and there was a trial, in which she was found guilty; obviously she was given a death sentence, but this was commuted to life in prison. She was eventually released 20 years later. Even the confession was not certain and a mystery remains.

Roughead, William (1870–1952)

See the *Introduction*

As summarised in the introduction, it may confidently be claimed that Roughead made the writing of true crime cases something that had literary quality to match writers usually defined as from 'high culture' rather than from plot-driven popular cultural texts. One aspect of this is the fact that Henry James became an avid reader and close friend of Roughead, the Scottish lawyer, and they had a correspondence that lasted for years. Roughead's books mark him out as a perfectionist with a defined, judicious style and narrative voice. On top of that, he actually attended many of the murder trials he wrote about.

*Rowland, Walter: Twice Condemned

Walter Rowland was condemned to hang after he killed his daughter, but he was released on commutation and then served in the army; then in 1946 he was convicted of the murder of Olive Balchin in Manchester.

The strange, baffling personality of Walter Rowland has presented writers and legal professionals for over half a century, and although he was hanged for murder in 1947, there has always been a shadow of doubt over that conviction. A few years after his execution, the entire subject of capital punishment was a matter for heated debate in parliament as well as in the pages of the popular newspapers, and after the hanging of Ruth Ellis in 1955 the publications dealing with execution and the law brought all the most contentious aspects of such deaths into focus. Along with the notorious case of Timothy Evans and the Christie story, that of Walter Rowland was the subject of much discussion.

People forgot the actions of the young Rowland, as sensational events arose, related to a prison confession of the murder of Balchin and some complex detective operations around Manchester, which had the involvement of the famous 'Count of Scotland Yard' Bert Hannam, of whom I have written previously. Had Walter Rowland killed Olive Balchin? Who was the prisoner in Walton jail who had confessed?

In 1975 the celebrity legal writer and professional, Henry Cecil, went to work on the case, writing an analysis of the trial. Cecil turned everything on its head and questioned the earlier writings on the case. As usual, every interpretation of the known facts was brought into question as more brains set to work on the case. The result is now that most reference sources state that Rowland was most likely guilty, but that the questions still hang over the case.

In 1961, when Penguin Books produced a rush of paperbacks related to murder casess and the law, reflecting the ongoing debate on hanging, the writer of one of these, Leslie Hale, presented a very concise account of the Balchin murder. He gave lengthy extracts from the prison confession of the Balchin murder written by prisoner David Ware from Walton gaol, and pointed out several points which should have been of interest to the defence counsel. The book Hale wrote was *Hanged in Error*, and the main element he noted was that the enquiry into Ware's prison statement had to be rushed, as a date had been fixed for Rowland's execution, and that could not be changed or held in abeyance.

There was nothing convincing or even materially influential when a new argument of Rowland's innocence was presented to the appeal court; despite doubts cast on the identities of men seen near the scene of the murder, and in spite of anomalies relating to times of events, the verdict of the jury stood.

Reading the study written by Cecil over four decades ago, it is possible to see a bias in the analysis, despite the plentiful good sense and meticulous approach to detail. The key to understanding the issues and the actions taken to follow up alibi narrative, is the heart of the story. Today, there is still a strong argument for the re-examination of the importance of the statements given by police officers at the trial, and there is doubt over the records kept at Rowland's lodgings regarding his alibi.

When the man who made a confession of the Balchin murder from Walton gaol, David Ware, killed a woman after his release, in the same manner as with Balchin, a re-think had to occur, and doubts continue.

Rush, James: Slaughter in Norfolk

James Blomfield Rush was a farm tenant in Norfolk in 1849, his landlord being Isaac Jermy, until Jermy went into action to have Rush evicted, . Rush's response when the fear of being homeless was against him was to slaughter Jermy, along with his son. He almost killed Jermy's daughter-in-law too, but she survived, minus an arm. This became a huge sensation in Victorian Britain.

One interesting sidenote, telling us so much about the case, was recalled by Michael Diamond: '...one of Mayhew's informants described how he saw "one evening after dark, through the uncurtained cottage window, eleven persons gathered around a scanty fire." An old man was reading to the others, by the firelight, a broadsheet on Rush's execution.'

A very early volume on the case was published in Norwich by Bacon and Kinnerbrook, which sold the tale as 'an unparalleled crime.' The crux of the case was that Rush was bankrupt as well as being in debt to Jermy; a further detail was the Jermy's governess, Emily Sandford, was pregnant by Rush.

The actual circumstances of the double murder were dramatic in the extreme, with Rush, in November, coming out of the fog to commit the murder. We must add to this the success of Rush's own supposed poem on his life and situation, which includes the lines:

My cause I did defend alone,
For learned counsel had I none;
I pleaded hard and questions gave,
In hopes my wretched life to save.

As if there would be any sympathy for him as he stood in court; but the public hunger of 'ordinaries' tales' (warders' accounts) and writing from the cell was insatiable at the time.

Rush's 'Sorrowful lamentation' contains enough anguish to compete with the dream of Richard III before Bosworth in Shakespeare's play; Rush provides a fair amount of remorse and lengthy plaintive disgust with himself, before giving the reader no doubt that the killer now longs for death, though hell may be waiting. He leaves forgiveness out of the matter, but still calls on God, just in case such a fallen soul as himself might be redeemed:

> I think I see each murdered form,
> Wrapped in their deadly shroud.
> Remorse now tears my troubled soul,
> When I think on my guilt,
> That through revenge alas! It was,
> My victims' blood I spilt.

His last hours were spent in the prison at Norwich, and he was allowed meals prepared at a hotel. He had the arrogance to send a note to the hotel: 'Pig today and plenty of sauce.'

Ruxton, Dr. Buck (1899–1936)

Bungling incompetence in criminals has always been fodder for popular publications. Journalists and biographers relish a villain who makes so many basic errors that there is a trail leading to him for the police to follow. Such was the case with Cumberland doctor Buck Ruxton. So numerous were the clues he left in his trail of a double murder that even one of the most talented lawyers in the land, Norman Birkett, speaking for him, thought he was destined for the scaffold and the noose.

Ruxton was a doctor, with a practice in Lancaster and, in September 1935, his wife Isabella and their servant, Mary Rogerson, disappeared. The search began, and eventually some human remains were found at Moffat in Dumfriesshire; the investigation started at that scene, in a ravine and stream, and body parts were found scattered. Then, some miles away, a left foot was found at Johnstonebridge. The hunt for the killer was then made much more simple by the fact that the newspaper used to wrap some of the body parts was a special local edition, especially for the Lancaster and Morecambe areas.

A keen sleuth then observed that there was a similarity between a description of one of the bodies and an image of Mrs Ruxton. Matters were beginning to find a focus on a certain place; Buck Ruxton was soon on the police radar. He was born in Bombay into a Parsee family, and after qualifying as a doctor, he worked at the Bombay hospital and was involved in projects done by the Malaria Commission. In 1927 he moved to Edinburgh, and not long after he took the practice at Dalton Square in Lancaster.

The forensics, done meticulously on the body parts, were most impressive. For instance, thumbprints were taken from the hands of Rogerson and matched to prints in the Ruxton residence. Everything fell into place. The forensic expert behind the work was Professor John Glaister, who reconstructed the two bodies. The trial then took place between November 1935 and March the following year. The case for the prosecution was very strong; perhaps most impressive of all the materials gathered as evidence was the superimposition of Mrs Ruxton's head and face on two stages of skeletal pictures. As to Ruxton facing the court and jury, Sir Sydney Smith commented that 'In the witness box Ruxton, insignificant in appearance and pathetically nervous in manner, cut a sorry figure under cross-examination.'

In was a death sentence and, in spite of an appeal, Ruxton was hanged. He had produce a written confession, stating, 'I killed Mrs Ruxton in a fit of temper because I thought she had been with a lover.'

S

Sheppard, Jack (1702–1724)

In traditional classic true crime stories, the media assumption has been that the general public adore a con who defies authority. There is also a certain glamour (hard to believe) in notorious villains, from Turpin to the Krays, if some quarters see them as 'working class celebrities.' In the eighteenth century, Jack Sheppard was such a popular hero. Back then, he was a specialist in prison escapes. A publication of 1840 explains the incredible media impact of this man. It points out that he was just 23 when he was hanged at Tyburn (this was at the space on the edge of Hyde Park, opposite what is now Bayswater Road). After a number of prison escapes and some incredible housebreaking adventures, Sheppard was known in all ranks of society.

As well as pamphlets and books, there was a pantomime produced at Drury Lane called *Harlequin Sheppard*, and also a short play called *The Housebreaker*. Naturally, he figured as one of the glamorous stars of the *Newgate Calendar*: 'No public robber ever obtained more notoriety than the man whose life and adventures are now presented. No violator of the law had more "hairbreadth escapes" than Jack Sheppard. He found employment for the bar, the pulpit and the stage.'

One of his typically inventive escapes figures in the *Calendar*. He was a captive and due to go to the Old Bailey for his trial. The *Calendar* explains: 'About two o'clock in the afternoon of the following day, one of the keepers carried him his dinner, and having carefully examined his irons, and finding them fast, he left him for the day. Some days before this, Jack had found a small nail in the room with which he could...unlock the padlock... He first took off his hand-cuffs and then unfastened the padlock that fastened the chain to the staple.' He was soon on the move, but then he found an iron bar in a chimney, and so he wrenched off a lock in a small room and was free.

Back then, the masses expected entertainment at a hanging, and Jack did not let them down. He was lively and brave, but there was a horrible moment: 'He died with difficulty and was much pitied by the surrounding multitude.'

Slater, Oscar (1872–1948)

Anyone who has worked behind bars will tell you that the gaols are packed with innocent people. Many cons will tell visitors that, and they will all have their stories, but few can compare with this story of mistaken identity.

When it comes to bad luck, and how it applies to a story of crime, the woeful tale of Oscar Slater is surely placed in the premier league of cases. The reason for this is that this Norwegian man was arrested and imprisoned when he was mistaken for the actual perpetrator of the murder of Marian Gilchrist in Glasgow, which took place in 1908.

Arrested in 1909 in New York, Slater voluntarily returned to Scotland to clear his name

He was not short of friends and supporters, one of whom as Sir Arthur Conan Doyle, who published *The Case of Oscar Slater* in 1912, but his suffering was long and miserable as he was incarcerated as an innocent man. Originally condemned to death, this was commuted to life imprisonment. He served 18 years in Peterhead prison. Conan Doyle and William Roughead, amongst others, continued to campaign for his release, and eventually he was set free.

Smethurst, Dr. (1805–Unknown)

This case all began when Isabella Banks, a wealthy woman who chose not to live at home with her family but took lodgings instead, found herself staying at a place in Bayswater. Isabella had a personal fortune of £2,000 – a very large sum indeed in 1859 – and in the lodgings there also lived a married couple, Dr and Mrs Smethurst. The doctor was twenty years younger than his wife; he was fifty years old at the time, and he was attracted to Isabella, who responded to his advances. They became very close and naturally the landlady noticed this. She asked Isabella to leave the place and only a few weeks later, Smethurst followed her, leaving his wife.

Early in 1859 Isabella and Smethurst were married at Battersea Church. Although this was bigamous, the first wife did not act. The barrister writing about the case in 1882, noted that 'Oddly enough, no surprise was expressed by the doctor's wife, and her position in the affair is very difficult to be understood.' The newly married couple moved to a new address in the London suburbs and from that point, as was known afterwards, Isabella became ill. As she was rich, she was seen by a celebrated doctor with a good reputation called Julius, and he confirmed that she was not pregnant, but that there was a problem with her digestion. He was worried, and called in some more advice; the sick woman's sister came, and poor Isabella's condition deteriorated. A second medical expert was called for and he said directly: 'That lady is being poisoned.'

Arsenic was found in Isabella's vomit, and by this time there were three doctors involved, the last being Dr Taylor who was very well known at that time. Together, they agreed that the law must be contacted and they asked for a warrant for Smethurst's arrest. Amazingly, at the magistrate's court, Smethurst spoke about the possible fatal effects of his being away from his wife when she was in such desperate circumstances. The landlady in the lodging house where the poor woman was dying stated that Smethurst was the only person taking care of the patient, as he would not pay a nurse, and she told the press that 'no portions of the food sent up to the room ever returned.' What Smethurst did next is repulsive in the extreme and points the finger of guilt at the man. The barrister, Ballantine, tells the story:

> On Saturday, the 12th April, preceding the death, the accused man went to a solicitor and requested him to call at his lodgings the next day for the purpose of drawing out a will, at the same showing him a draft that a barrister had prepared.. The solicitor objected to doing so on a Sunday but being told that the lady was ill, consented….. The lawyer wished that a medical man could be present but that was denied.. a will was drawn up which left everything to the accused…

Smethurst was arrested. The trial was before Lord Chief Baron Pollock, but before we recall the nature of the court events, we must return to the forensics, such as they were, at the time. The Dr Taylor who was the last medical man to be called in to see the patient was famous and admired for his post-mortem work, but the barrister, Ballantine, was convinced that Smethurst had set up the celebrated doctor to fail. After Smethurst was released from the magistrate's court, he found a way to get into his own rooms, and set a trap that would cancel out Taylor's attempts to prove the act of arsenic poisoning: he left a bottle of colourless liquid along with other materials and instruments that a medical man would have. When Taylor later examined all this, his attention was, of course, drawn to the liquid; the test he would have used was called the Reinsch Test, the standard test for detecting the presence of arsenic.

At the post-mortem there was the undoubted fact that there was arsenic present in the body, but Taylor had to show that it had been given from the equipment in Smethurst's room. The test involved pouring a mixture of the tested liquid and hydrochloric acid onto some copper gauze, which would then attach itself to the liquid if there was arsenic present. But the gauze dissolved. Finally, after several attempts, some attachment became apparent and so the doctor told the court that there was arsenic detected in Smethurst's liquid, but then scientists for the defence reported on the bottle and its contents and stated with confidence that it was chlorate of potash. It was then shown that the only arsenic Taylor had found was in his own gauze – traces being there from the first two experiments.

The result was that there was no credence given to the scientific evidence of the prosecution. In 1859, arsenic was being used by women for cosmetic purposes,, and of course, there could have been antimony from tartar emetic used as a treatment – an effort to make the poor woman vomit out the arsenic.

What Ballantyne did point out was that Dr Taylor, after the event, tried to gather expert advice on the matter but, in the end, the barrister's thoughts are hard to argue with: he said, 'The difficulty that presents itself to my thoughts is, why the presence of the chlorate was not ascertained before the test was applied.'

At the Old Bailey in August 1859 the sentence of death was passed on Thomas Smethurst. Then there began several months of appeals for a reprieve. The Lord Chief Baron passed the death warrant and it was arranged that Smethurst be taken from Newgate to the county gaol of Surrey, Horsemonger Lane. The doctor was incessantly talking of his innocence and he was obsessed with Dr Taylor, who he claimed was so concerned with his good reputation that he would see a man die rather than admit shortcomings.

At that time, executions took place two weeks after sentence and once again, incident and drama were part of this extraordinary man's life: *The Times* reported on 22 August that 'Some doubts appear to be entertained, notwithstanding the conviction of the prisoner, whether the capital sentence will be carried out.' This was based on a report about opinions 'from a high quarter.' The Chief baron, passing sentence, had left out the statements about the prisoner preparing to leave this world. It was said that 'persons well qualified to form a judgement' on the matter thought that there would be a recommendation for clemency. But a week later nothing in that respect had happened. There was still a rumour that the Home Secretary had sent a respite to Smethurst, but all the press could do was keep the public's appetite for news of the prisoner on the boil by documenting the situation.

The condemned man was said to have a calm and indifferent demeanour and even when his usual clothes were removed and he was given prison-issue clothes, there was still mystery and intrigue stated, such as the speculation that it was thought he might have some poison hidden in garments that he might use to forestall the hangman. When the Rev. Jessop went to see Smethurst to confirm the execution date and to advise him spiritually, the reported response was that if he were to become a waxwork at Madame Tussaud's in his prison dress he would look 'a complete guy.' And he added: 'If the sentence is carried out, I am a murdered man.'

The doctor's argument to anyone who would listen is that such were the dimensions of the investments made by Isabella Banks that she would have been the source of greater profits for him if alive rather than dead. He also said that his nursing of the woman in her last days, excluding all others, was done from care, not control of a slow killing. Then by 2 September, the clamouring for a respite by various parties, represented by Henry Sheridan, resulted in a meeting with the Home Secretary in which a petition was presented. The doctor's wife and the landlady from Bayswater were also present, and Sir George Lewis listened to statements and arguments and talked of the prisoner for an hour and a half. Nothing was resolved, and the date with the hangman was very near. He had the reprieve, but he did not know the nature of the commutation of sentence or of any other fate. The supporters of the saved man were still working hard to have a total remission of the sentence given.

But, as he was awaiting trial for bigamy, the end of the murder trial and the complex consequences came in the form of a free pardon from Queen Victoria. In Southwark magistrate's court, a free pardon was read aloud by a Mr Robinson, with the powerful and redeeming words at the head: 'Under the Seal of Our Lady the Queen.' The pardon stated: 'We, in consideration of some circumstances humbly represented to us, are graciously pleased to extend our grace and mercy unto him, the said Thomas Smethurst, and to grant him a free pardon...'

Yet even that is not the end of the story. In December that year a correspondent to *The Times* pointed out that, after the pardon, Smethurst had been given a year's prison sentence for bigamy at the Old Bailey, and so he was a felon, and a felon would forfeit his inheritance. As the writer expressed it: 'The effect of his conviction ... precludes him from obtaining a single farthing under the will.' He went on to point out that the City of London 'under ancient jurisdiction' had the right to claim property of felons in its domain. Smethurst in court was found guilty because the jury presumed his first marriage to be a valid one after Smethurst's counsel had been unable to convince the court of the invalidity of the union with 'Mrs Johnson', as she was sometimes known.

The final irony has to be that Louisa Banks, the sister of Isabella, appeared at the bigamy trial and said, ' I see the name of Isabella Banks to the entry in the book before me – that is the handwriting of my murdered sister.'

Sweet Fanny Adams

This popular phrase stems not from the music hall, as its use might imply, but from a murder of 1867, when the dismembered body of a young girl was found in the Alton hop fields. The dead girl was Fanny Adams, who had gone for a walk to that area with her sister Lizzie. Here, a man called Frederick Baker befriended them, and things came to a head when he carried little Fanny off into a hop field and she wasn't seen again; there was a hunt, and Baker was tried, convicted and hanged. As for the popular phrase, that comes from naval slang, meaning 'nothing whatever', this being a reference to their rations, which they thought might be the remains of Fanny Adams.

T

Teeth Say It All (The Dobkin murder)

Molly Lefebure, known as a writer today, was also involved at close hand with wartime crime during the London Blitz, and in her casebook, published as *Murder on the Home Front*, there is one murder she calls a 'Case of a Lifetime.' There is a good reason for this, as she refers to the murder of Mrs Dobkin by her husband, who had thought that killing her and having her body placed under a considerable weight of Blitz rubble would hide his iniquity. He was wrong, and what pinned him down as her killer were his wife's teeth.

Molly writes, 'Four nights after Mrs Dobkin disappeared... a somewhat mysterious fire broke out in the Baptist Chapel.... Dobkin, the fire-watcher, said the fire started at 1.30 a.m. but he didn't call the fire brigade. That enlarged the police suspicions about the man. When the body was found it went to forensics experts, and as there was not very much body material available, the woman's jaw and teeth were the most promising sources of identification. They had to prove that the bone remains were of that person.'

Molly describes the moment when the dentist, Mr Kopkin, gave his report: 'Dr Simpson politely handing Mr Kopkin Mrs Dobkin's skull, Mr Kopkin taking it in both hands and then saying, without hesitation, in a tone of mingled triumph and amazement, "This is Mrs Dobkin's upper jaw. That is the jaw I attended and those are my fillings".'

It had been a determined effort by police and by the forensics team to find some way of identifying Mrs Dobkin. The team around Molly Lefebure had spent three months guarding the secret of the discovery of the body. Now there was evidence and the police moved in on the husband. Dr Keith Simpson, Molly's boss in the difficult work on forensics, spoke in court, and Molly noticed that Dobkin '... shifted in his seat, gripped his knees with his big hands until the knuckles gleamed. If ever a man was shattered, Dobkin was.'

He was found guilty of murder, and Molly was present, with other professionals, when the dead body of Dobkin was in the mortuary at Wandsworth prison. Molly summarised the effects of that significant case, noting that police were promoted and forensic science had a notable milestone in the list of achievements in that developing profession.

Thompson/Bywaters Murder, The

In February 1923, the writer Beverley Nichols went to pay a call on a Mr Graydon in North London. Nichols is known today more for works on houses, gardens and cats, but at that time he was working for a daily paper, and Mr Graydon was the father of a young woman who had been tried and convicted for the murder of her husband, along with a merchant seaman called Freddie Bywater. The daughter, Mrs Edith Thompson, had been hanged, along with Bywater.

Nichols gives a powerful account of the Old Bailey and the trial; he notes the odd, morally wrong mood of the place, writing, 'The court was already packed to suffocation, and I sat down. Five minutes to ten. In a few moments the curtain would rise on the biggest tragedy of 1922. And yet, what was the mood of the audience? Pleasant, amused expectation apparently.'

The events leading to this sentence of a double hanging have always been especially interesting to crime historians, as so very few women were hanged between c.1900 and that of Ruth Ellis in 1955. Bywaters had lived with the Thompsons. It was the classic ménage á trois, and Bywaters was very young. The relationship had appeared to work well for some time, but Freddie was burning inside with a desire to take Thompson out of the picture. When he went away to sea, Edith wrote passionate romantic letters to him, and extracts were read aloud at the murder trial. Freddie had waited, armed with a knife, on an evening after the Thompsons had been out in London and had to walk part of the way home. Freddie attacked, and Thompson died.

One study of the murder explains: 'The injuries that Percy [Thompson] received consisted of three wounds, each between one and a half and two inches long. One stab had penetrated the spine... another passed upwards into the mouth.' Bywaters tried to argue for self-defence but that failed to impress. As to Edith and her letters, the Lord Chief Justice said that the correspondence was 'of the most mischievous and venomous kind.' There were appeals against the convictions; the one for Edith argued that her letters of love were not to be defined as evidence against her. But the Appeal Court accepted that the judge at the trial had put the case for the letters as evidence of a joint enterprise very fairly and clearly.

The two lovers were hanged. As for Nicholls, he saw Mr Graydon again, and he asked, rhetorically, what was there to say? To which he added, 'Eventually we did speak – or rather I spoke. "Bit knocked up" was all he could say. "Bit knocked up over and over again like a child repeating a lesson...."'

Tichborne Claimant, The

This has to be booked in as a classic case for study by all law students and true crime aficionados. It is the story of a butcher from Australia who was determined that he was the lost and assumed dead aristocrat Sir Roger Tichborne. More than that, he decided to travel to London and tell everyone so. He was generally thought to be an imposter, but then Tichborne's mother said she confirmed he was her son and accepted him. Opinions on the stranger were divided and in the two trials for fraud a national sensation was created. One barrister who was involved commented that 'the rush for seats was much noticed and commented upon in different journals.

Sir Roger Tichborne was born in 1829 and educated at Stonyhurst; he lived in Paris for a while and then returned to England, where he had a commission in the Sixth Dragoon Guards in 1849. A few years later he set sail for Jamaica in the *Bella*, which was wrecked, and it was reported that he had drowned. But the claimant had a different tale to tell: he said that he (Sir Roger) had been saved and eventually went to Australia, where he settled in a village called Wagga Wagga as a member of the Orton family. The lawyer who wrote on the case after being involved in the process had this to say about Orton:

> He was stout and unwieldy, with marked but not coarse features... but his hands and feet were certainly not what I should have expected to

find upon a low-bred person... His manners were not those of a person who had ever moved in good society....What was a noticeable point was that a great likeness was discoverable in him to many members of the Tichborne family.

The issue to hand is obvious to see and understand from any viewpoint. As Lady Tichborne was siding with the man she thought to be her son, this was going to be a challenging trial, and so it was. The lawyers, Hannen and Ballantine, were speaking for Orton and matters began in the Court of Chancery. The second trial was at the Queen's Bench, and the notable judge Henry Hawkins, Lord Bramwell, presided. This began in April 1873, and the claimant lost. There were too many inconsistencies in his story and a charge of perjury was to follow. His sentence was two consecutive terms of imprisonment. The trial had lasted until February 1874.

On his release, Orton was soon in decline; in 1897, the man of letters and amateur criminologist Churton Collins, went to visit him in Bayswater. Orton told him, 'he had drawn up the acknowledgement that he was Orton to get £3000 which was promised to him for the confession for his wife's sake. He added that it was the great mistake of his life, but added that his identity with Sir Roger was so indisputable that no affidavit or recantation on his part could affect it.'

Treason Tales

On Christmas Day 2021, Jaswant Singh Chail was found in Windsor Castle, armed and dangerous and, when faced by an officer, said that he was there to kill the Queen. He was tried under the 1842 Treason Act, which created an offence of having a weapon in the Sovereign's presence, alongside the ancient High Treason offence which was created and defined in 1351. He was convicted for this in February 2022, and that made him the first convicted of the crime since 1981 when Marcus Serjeant was convicted. He was sentenced to 9 years in prison, with a further 5 years on extended licence. The 1842 Act was passed as a reaction to another attempt at a royal assassination, as in May that year a man named John Francis had aimed to shoot Queen Victoria in her carriage on Constitution Hill, pointing a pistol at her, but not firing. Witnesses spotted him and when he tried again, and this time actually fired at the Queen, he was apprehended and sentenced to death under the Act, which was later commuted to transportation for life.

Since c.1800 there has been a long string of murders and attempted murders of royalty and celebrities and legislation, as well as the criminal law process, have had to cope and adapt with this feature of modern history. The reasons and motives have always been of interest. In Chail's case, he claimed that he was carrying the crossbow, with an intent to kill, as an act of revenge for the 1919 Amritsar Massacre. But treason tales are so numerous and so varied that one needs to look at extreme instances, from across the spectrum, to understand the aspect of true crime we look at here (see also *Lord Haw Haw*).

A common instance is that of William Gregg in 1708. Gregg was born in Montrose and then studied at Aberdeen. Going to London, he became a diplomat and attained the post of secretary to the Ambassador to Sweden. Letters from Gregg to the court of France were found and read, and it was discovered that the man was offering his services to the French government. Robert Harley, the great spy-master, had employed Gregg and it appears that he had not done a thorough character check. The man was a turncoat and a slippery customer who was out only for himself.

Repercussions of this affair led to Harley's resignation. In fact, some desperate types were in the employment of someone in the government, and one report declared the following in the *Newgate Calendar*: 'The order that was constantly given to them was that if an English or Dutch vessel came up to them, they should cast their letters into the sea, but that they should not do it when the French ships came up to them...'

Gregg had, as the 1351 Act has it, 'adhered to the King's enemies.' His death was demanded, and he was hanged at Tyburn in April 1708.

In more recent times, the case of Roger Casement illustrates the kind of narrative linked to treason in time of war. In total there had been more than 3,000 arrests in 1916, then many were released, and over 1,500 were interned in England. But one person stood out as an extraordinary case: Sir Roger Casement. He had been liasing with Germany, seeking military aid for the 1916 Easter Rising, which sought to gain Irish independence. Casement was arrested for high treason and his trial took place on 29 June, the prosecution being led by F.E. Smith (later Lord Birkenhead). Casement's situation was bizarre and contradictory: he had taken a knighthood from King George V but insisted that his only country, his own real allegiance, was Ireland.

He had enjoyed an unbelievably interesting and adventurous life previous to his involvement with the 1916 Rising; in 1914 he had tried to create a Liberal party in Ulster, as well as his adventures far afield. But in his trial he claimed that his highest aim was to serve Ireland. He had tried to recruit an Irish Brigade in Germany, and he failed in that. In visiting the PoW camps in Germany, he had been unwelcome, and as was noted at the time, he had to have a guard with him on those visits in his attempts to divert them from their duty.

Casement had gone to Germany, his movements monitored by British spies, and when he returned to Ireland it had been in a U-boat, landing off the coast of Kerry, where he had soon been arrested. His earlier life and career had been extraordinary; he had made the world aware of atrocities in the Congo and in South America, and he was something of a hero, particularly in America. He had made friends and contacts in high places. It seemed outrageous and incredible that such a man should be a traitor.

The basis of his indictment was the Treason Act of 1351 which states that the offence is defined by 'compassing or imagining the King's death' and 'levying war against the King in the realm' but also, and this was the crucially important clause for Casement, 'Adhering to the King's enemies in his realm, giving them aid and comfort, here and elsewhere.' That comma and what followed was his death sentence. 'Elsewhere' was easily defined in a way that included activities at sea, in Germany and in fact in Ireland, so loose was the definition of the word.

His trial has been the subject of a vast literature, including an account by F.E. Smith himself, published soon after the events, along with other famous trials in history. Smith recalled the issue of whether or not Casement had actually committed treason, and he expressed the situation in this way: '... When I closed the case for the prosecution, the legal argument began. It was necessarily long, technical and intricate. It involved the true leaning of the Treason Act, which was originally drawn up in Norman French. It necessitated a minute examination of a number of musty statutes, long since repealed.... It was essential to grasp the details of an antiquated procedure...'

Eventually an agreement was reached; the dates of earlier precedents in treason trials had to be noted and finally the wording used against Casement was 'adhering to the King's enemies.' When the sentence finally came, it was done after much deliberation, as Smith wrote: '... after Counsel's speeches and a judicial summing up by Lord Reading in terms most scrupulously fair and impartial, the jury convicted and Casement was sentenced to death.'

Turpin, Dick (1705–1739)

Was there ever a more universal image of a complete villain than Dick Turpin, alias Richard Palmer? The name is surely known to everyone, and with each generation there appears to be a renewal of his name and myth. His life and dark deeds have been told and examined across the genres of writing, from professorial analysis to popular ballads. Visitors to York, where he was hanged in 1739, are constantly aware of his presence in the productions of the heritage industry. He figured prominently in the criminal experience in Essex, Lincolnshire and East Yorkshire and no doubt was known in most areas alongside the Great North Road.

One of the most concise accounts of Turpin's reported foul deeds and eventual arrest and trial comes from the collection of York Castle tales assembled by William Knipe and published in 1867: *Tyburn Tales: The Criminal Chronology of York Castle*. Knipe recounts Turpin's reign of terror in Essex and London, and then explains Turpin's excursion north, after his gang had been confronted and some of them taken by the law:

> ... a reward of £100 was offered for the apprehension of the offenders, in consequence of which two of them were taken into custody, tried, convicted on the evidence of an accomplice, and hanged in chains; and the whole gang being dispersed, Turpin went into the country to renew his depredations on the public.

In south Lincolnshire he took up horse stealing, a definite capital offence. He had already murdered someone, so the weight of his offences was building; he was caught but escaped, and went hurriedly to a village near Beverley – Welton. Here he started living under the assumed name of John Palmer, and his nemesis was approaching.

The notorious brigand and killer was destined to face the law over the shooting of a cockerel. He gave his name as John Palmer. From the local quarter sessions, he was sent to the bridewell. The local magistrates wanted to know who he was and what connections he had elsewhere and so a man was sent to Lincolnshire., where it was discovered, in Long Sutton, that their petty criminal was a very dangerous wanted man, accused of several capital offences. Turpin was taken from Beverley to the fastness of York Castle where he rotted for months, awaiting the assize trial. A letter written to his brother whilst there became the beginning of the end for the villain. He wrote, asking for help and cash, 'For heaven's sake, dear brother, do not neglect me....' The letter was unopened and returned to Essex, where the postmaster looked at it, and knew the handwriting.

Turpin was now known to the authorities and the trial and sentence of death were inevitable. It is entirely typical of the man that he wanted something dramatic for his exit from the world. Knipe explains: '... he purchased a new fustian frock and a pair of pumps in order to wear them at the time of his death and on the day he hired five poor men, at ten shillings each, to follow the cart as mourners. He also gave hat-bands to several other persons, and left a ring and some other articles to a married woman in Lincolnshire...'

(Dr Johnson's Dictionary defines pumps as 'shoes with a thin sole and low heel')

Even in death Turpin caused a disturbance and some drama. His body was exhumed and carried away so it could be filled with unslacked lime, and then re-buried. His remains had been stolen once, and retrieved.

V

Van Der Elst, Violet (1882–1966)

During the final years of hangings in Britain, the grand black vehicle of arguably the most famous anti-hanging campaigner on record in the twentieth century was a familiar sight outside the prison gates on the day of an execution. Her name was Violet Van Der Elst.

Mrs Van Der Elst is surely one of the unsung heroes of Lincolnshire. She was so set against any kind of judicial hanging that she busied herself with leading demonstrations against the sue of the noose. Her car was often filmed being used as a road block and an obstruction by prison gates. If there was a hanging, she would be there stirring up trouble, and she wrote to every dignitary she could think of to gather support in her humanitarian cause. Eventually she wrote a book with an account of her campaigns and the stories behind the condemned people she worked for and indeed prayed for. *On the Gallows* was published in 1936, and she included letters from people who had refused to support her, including one from the Bishop of London.

Violet was always in the centre of controversy. In 1936 she appeared before the magistrate in Manchester after refusing to stop her car during scenes following the execution of Dr Buck Ruxton. She told the court that an officer had said to her, 'You will get prison this time. We are going to have you medically examined.' Clearly, she had been in a ruck. A doctor who examined her the day after the Manchester demonstration told the court hat she had two bruises on her hip and, 'He suggested they were due to an act of violence.'

A year before she had been robbed: a maid at her flat stole four pieces of carved Chinese ivory. A detective had found these figures in her room, wrapped in leaves. The maid said to him, 'I am fed up with all this and I will find some peace... if I have to commit suicide.' Poor Violet was always involved in affairs of this kind.

She was born Violet Dodge in Surrey, the daughter of a coalman and a washerwoman and, incredibly, she started as a scullery maid, before going into business, making her fortune with 'Shavex' a brushless shaving cream. She married a Belgian painter – hence her very exotic name. With her money, she bought Harlaxton Manor, but such was the intensity of her campaigning and her foray into politics that she lost her fortune and was forced to move to live in a London flat. Happily for her, the year after her death in 1966, the death penalty was abolished. Given her personality, we can well imagine that a ghost reported to be seen in Harlaxton is indeed her restless shade, still out to disturb the peace.

W

Wallace Mystery, The

F.J.P. Veale, writing in the preface to his study of the Wallace murder in 1950, asserted that 'In the opinion of many, the trial of William Herbert Wallace may be regarded as the most famous case in English criminal annals.' It is hard not to agree with that.

The events of the case could be a plot for an Agatha Christie mystery, and every little circumstance and footnote to the narrative between Wallace receiving a phone call at his chess club in Liverpool to his trial and death soon after avoiding the noose are open to several interpretations. The spine of the story is straightforward. Wallace, an insurance agent, received a call from a Mr Qualtrough at his chess club; the message is passed on that the man wants to meet with Wallace, and the address given is at Menlove Gardens East. There is no such address, as Wallace finds out when he sets off to meet the caller that day.

A few hours later, Wallace arrives home at Anfield, where he finds his wife Julia, brutally battered to death. Two neighbours are with him, as he had some difficulty getting inside. Who would do such a thing, and why?

Wallace was a man of culture. As well as his love for chess, he played the violin, read philosophy and enjoyed well-informed conversation. He was sociable and gregarious, although he could amuse himself with reading and listening to music. He and Julia seemed happy and fulfilled to their neighbours. What motive could he possibly have to kill his wife?

It was the circumstances of the attack and the killing itself that generated these questions. Julia was lying by a mackintosh which was stained with blood on a small part of the material; there were witnesses who had seen Julia between 6pm and 6.40pm on the evening of the murder. Wallace had left the house not long after the last witness sighting of his wife. This means that he would have had to dress for the appointment, and look impressive as the 'man from the Prudential' in a very short time.

Did anyone else in their lives have a potential motive? The answer was no. Every line of thought led to Wallace himself – a man whose statements about the fateful night appeared to sound like a thinly fabricated sequence of alibi material. He had made a point of speaking to a number of people on his journey to the nonexistent address. Surely, it had to be asked, this was a case of wife-murder?

There have been numerous studies of these actions and events over the years, but at the time, Wallace was charged and tried. He was sentenced to hang, but an appeal court decided that the verdict could not be supported on the nature of the evidence. He was freed, but he had little time left. He wrote a diary, and this passage is significant: 'Can you wonder that when I sit alone in the evenings with my chess-board... the shadow of the dock, the shadow of the judge in the black cap – yes, even the shadow of the scaffold itself – rise up before my very eyes?' He died on 26 February 1933. His reputed last words were, 'Do good with your life.'

Weare Murder, The

This case, the murder of Weare by two ruthless killers called John Thurtell and his friend Hunt, is celebrated in crime narratives for many reasons, but surely the most curious of these is that Thurtell designed his own gallows. A publication of the 1940s explains: 'It is not at all likely that his design was adopted but certainly the new type of gallows with a "drop" was used, for he is reported to have said to the prison Governor, "I understood that when you rounded here you put them in a tumbrel and sent them out of the world with a *Gee up, gee up* but this is rather an ungentlemanly way of finishing a man."'

Few would have been sympathetic to this complaint. The murder he had committed was savage and brutal. One of the very first published accounts of the killing was in an anonymous publication, and this provided a dramatic account of the proceedings. The publisher claimed: 'Containing the examinations before the magistrates, the coroner's inquest... with the whole of the evidence, the confessions of Hunt... to which is prefixed an introduction containing anecdotes of the deceased... and full particulars of the horrible association formed by them.'

The murder arose from a fight over a gambling debt. Another man, Probert, was also involved. Following the trial, Thurtell was hanged and Hunt was transported to Australia. The barrister, Serjeant Ballatine, gave the most cogent summing-up: 'Probert and Hunt turned King's evidence. The former was subsequently hanged for what in any other person would have been treated as borrowing a horse, but the jury were only too glad to make him pay the penalty of his former crime. Hunt was transported and I have heard was killed by the crew upon his outward voyage.'

Wearside Jack (See Also Yorkshire Ripper)

This is the story of a thoughtless and horrendous hoax, but it is also a tale of a detective and two linguistics experts. During the murderous regime of the Yorkshire Ripper, later discovered to be Peter Sutcliffe, a man who was later arrested and charged, John Humble, was held responsible for a tape submitted to the police which purported to be produced by the Ripper. The public thought they were listening to the serial killer who had cruelly murdered several women around West Yorkshire. The accent on the tape was that of a Geordie, but Humble himself was not a Geordie: he was, as the nickname says, from Wearside. He sent his tape, along with three letters, to the police, and a campaign followed which had the public experiencing a terrible paranoia, meaning anyone with a north-east accent would be suspicious in the eyes of some of the general populace, especially in the Yorkshire area.

In one letter sent to George Oldfield, one of the lead officers, Humble had written: 'I am the Ripper. I've been dubbed a maniac by the press but not by you. You call me clever and I am. You and your mates haven't a clue that photo in the paper gave me fits...'

The tape itself was given to two academics at Leeds University. One of them was a lecturer in Dialectology (and was my tutor in that subject in 1974). He was Stanley Ellis.

Stanley Ellis was born on 18 February 1926, in Lidget Green, Bradford. With a scholarship, he went to Corpus Christi, Cambridge, and then did National Service. He was in India at the time of Partition, and there he was working with the United Free Church. His academic career followed that global experience, and at Leeds he produced a study of Lincolnshire dialect for his Masters degree. He was the ideal fieldworker for the Survey of English Dialects, and Harold Orton was his mentor, as Stanley had been mine.

At the time, he married, and his dedication to the dialect survey was such that he took his wife and first child with him, using a caravan, into several areas of England, to administer the standard questionnaire and to conduct long interviews with local people. He had the common touch; Stanley could talk to anyone. He put people at their ease and used humour and anecdote to great effect. I was told that on his fieldwork trips, the sponsors, Ringtons Tea, had supplied him with tea, so that a small gift could break the ice and start a conversation in a friendly way.

After his death in October 2009, several people wrote to the papers with memories of Stanley, and these tend to confirm what was often said about him, that he was to Linguistics what Desmond Morris was to Zoology. Cecily Mills, for instance, recalled meeting him at the Leeds Playhouse where they started chatting and he said she was from the North East. Cecily added,

'I quizzed him as to where more particularly? After several seconds he decided on Tyneside and eventually Newcastle....I desisted from trying to pin him down to North West Jesmond.' He probably could have located that place.

We know this because of Stanley's notoriety regarding the infamous 'Ripper Tapes' and Wearside Jack. He and his colleague Jack Windsor Lewis worked on the tape of that Geordie voice which was played across the land at the time as police hunted for the Yorkshire Ripper. The tape was available to the media in 1979 and the experts soon were set to work on it. Stanley and Jack concluded that it was more than likely a hoax. We now know that the voice was that of John Humble, who was convicted at Leeds Crown Court in 2006 for perverting the course of justice.; despite the academic conclusions, the search for the Ripper was still focused on Tyneside. As to the accent on the tape, well Stanley had that right: Wearside, and Castleton.

Before he retired from teaching in 1983, Stanley Ellis became a media personality. This was largely because his voice was heard, answering questions and explaining language use, on BBC radio, when he figured prominently in *Take a Place Like* and *Talk of the Town, Talk of the Country*. His relaxed manner, as he carried his learning lightly, made the study of language fascinating, and of course, the study of dialects always reveals a mass of intriguing information about social history as well, just as such things as farmyard implements or long-forgotten kitchen equipment opens op the past so that it comes closer to us.

In 2004 he was awarded honorary life membership of the International Association for Forensic Phonetics and Acoustics, the first person to be given the award. At the same time as he was contributing to the success of forensic phonetics in the courts, he was still very much a presence in the Yorkshire Dialect Society, and for some time he edited the *Transactions* of the Society.

As for Humble: he was arrested and charged, and he died in July 2019 after being released. As the focus of the Ripper investigation moved to Wearside, women continued to be killed in West Yorkshire at the hands of the real Ripper.

Whiteley: A Double Fatality

On 24 January 1907, wealthy businessman William Whiteley and a young man called Horace Rayner came face to face. The young man thought he was talking to his estranged father; the older man thought he had a lunatic in front of him. Then the lunatic pulled out a revolver.

This all happened in Whiteley's store in Westbourne Grove in London, and it related to events far back in time; young Rayner, it was claimed, had been taken as a small child to that address to meet his father, and that was the root of his burning resentment against the old man on that January morning. The conversation had been odd from the start. Rayner had been shown into the office, and Whiteley had no idea of the level of resentment and desperation seething inside his visitor.

Rayner had earlier been to Russia to learn the language; after that he had jobs in Leeds and in Worcestershire. Now here he was in London, living a life of poverty, with a sick wife, and it is on record that he told his landlord at the time that he was at the end of the tether. J.P. Eddy, the barrister, explains: 'So it was not surprising, in view of his dire predicament and his wife's condition, that Rayner bethought himself of his reputed father, Mr Whiteley, whom he had described to one witness as one of the richest men in London. Why was he in the dock? He had shot and killed his putative father, as the two men stood outside the office.

Whiteley had left his office and asked a secretary to call a policeman, as Rayner had pulled out the gun. The conversation had opened with a simple exchange on the issue that was at the base of the problem for Rayner:

'What is it I can do for you?' Whiteley asked. The reply was direct and candid. Rayner asked, 'I believe I am right in stating... that your son is speaking to his father?' Then Whiteley turned the talk towards offering some kind of help in the realm of employment, rather than any immediate offer of anything tangible. Whiteley even directed things towards the topic of working abroad. All this should have distracted the young man. But then Rayner said something that changed the pattern of the whole confrontation. He said, 'Then I must tell you I made up my mind before I came here that I would blow out my brains if unsuccessful in my application to you.'

By this point, Whiteley, though worried, was cool. His assistant went to find a police officer, meanwhile, Rayner appeared and shot directly at Whiteley; Rayner also collapsed, and it was later found that there was a bullet hole in one of his eyes.

There was no defence to a charge of murder at the Old Bailey. But in spite of witnesses and testimonies, and a clear history of what we would now see as depression, the jury found Rayner guilty and he was sentenced to hang. There was, however, a commutation, and he was released in 1919.

Wilde, Oscar (1854–1900)

It is comparatively rare to have a major literary figure in Britain feature prominently in the history of crime as well as in literature, but that distinction applies to Oscar Wilde. In my book, *Jane Austen's Aunt Behind Bars* (Thames

River Press, 2013) I explained several criminal connections around well-known literary figures, including Daniel Defoe and Leigh Hunt, but Wilde's unfortunate experience in the teeth of the Victorian criminal law system led him to a horrendous prison sentence. He spent most of that time in Reading Gaol, where he wrote his great poem, *The Ballad of Reading Gaol* (1898), his last work in print.

Wilde, born in 1854, had made a name for himself in the cultural hub of London, after being an outstanding Oxford scholar; in 1894 he married Constance Lloyd, but his true proclivities led him to the use of rent boys, hence he stepped over the line into criminality under Victorian laws. At the height of his success, writing hugely successful plays such as *The Importance of Being Earnest* (1895), his friendship with Lord Alfred Douglas, whose father, the Marquess of Queensberry) hated Wilde, led him steadily towards accusations of sodomy, and finally he chose to face the enemy, as it were, and take his accuser to court for slander. Once in the public eye, his fall from grace accelerated; evidence revealed by Queensberry's defence led to a warrant for Wilde's arrest on the same day that it was decided Queensberry was innocent.

Wilde was tried at the Old Bailey for 'gross indecency', to which he pled 'not guilty', in April 1895. This first trial reached an impasse but at a second trial, the prosecution had tightened their case and Wilde was found guilty; he was sentenced to two years of hard labour in Her Majesty's prisons.

His time at Reading Gaol was described in his magisterial work, *De Profundis*, and as time went by, more and more was learned about his time behind bars. A comprehensive account of this was written by Anthony Stokes: *Pit of Shame: The Read Ballad of Reading Gaol* (Waterside Press, 2007).

Wise, Thomas J. (1859–1937)

Wise was a specialist in forgery, and he had a particular penchant for literary materials; he had the right credentials for forging valuable works, as he was a bibliophile, and he was also a wealthy man. In that milieu, what has the capability of generating plenty of profit is of course specialist bookselling. Readers who enjoy the Times Literary Supplement, for instance, will see a back page full of volumes for sale from Forum Auctions, and an example from early 2023 has a first edition of Fleming's *Casino Royale* for £15,000-25,000 as an estimate. A first edition of *A Bear Called Paddington* is estimated to fetch £6,000.

Wise issued catalogues of his wares, and many of his titles were, to readers in the inter-war years, modern classics, such as works by Kipling or John Ruskin. He had always been a book collector, and he needed funds; he would contact collectors who were well-heeled and then work for them, locating what they needed for their collections. There is no doubt that he was a very talented and knowledgeable bibliographical expert but in 1934, John Carter and Graham Pollard wrote *An Enquiry into the Nature of Certain Nineteenth Century Pamphlets* and they set out to show that many of the supposed editions from Wise were forgeries. He died shortly afterwards and so there was no real response.

What had been detected was his skill in extracting lengthy pieces of text from old editions and then transmuting them into supposed separate editions, and as these were of classic highly-rated authors, there would be a market. So therywere forgeries but also transpositions: clever re-workings.

Of course, Wise did have a considerable library – fakes or not – and after his death this was sold for an immense sum of money. The Brontë scholar, Fanny Ratchford, brought copies to the experts in England so that forgeries could be ascertained. It says everything about this book obsessive that his first wife left him as he was far too involved in his old volumes.

Y

*Yorkshire Witch, The (Mary Bateman, 1768–1809)

York Castle has a long, and often grim, disturbing history, and some of the most remarkable tales in the history of crime are set in this formidable and dark place. Not all of these stories have the glamour and myth of Dick Turpin, but they tell us a great deal about a turbulent period in English social history. One of the most evil residents of that dungeon was the Leeds poisoner, Mary Bateman, said by many to be a witch. She was born Mary Harker in 1768 and one writer said, 'From an early age she developed great quickness which, instead of taking a direct course and developing into intelligence, was warped into low cunning.'

The York prison cells housed countless criminals, many poor unfortunate wretches, and some hardened killers, during the years of English history when the number of capital offences was in three figures, and law and order were hard to find. Violence was rife at this time, with highwaymen and footpads everywhere, and riots always likely to break out among the underclass. One of the most heinous cases must be that of the young mother who had murdered to make her way in life, and had even dabbled in black magic.

At 5am on a chill Monday in March 1809, forty-one-year-old Mary Bateman was brought from her cell in York to keep her date with the hangman.

Knowing that pregnant women were spared the noose, she had tried to 'plead her belly' to save her neck, but it was no use. A massive crowd gathered; they wanted their entertainment, and to see justice done.

What had she done, this woman from Aisenby, near Thirsk, to come to such a sorrowful end? The jury were in no doubt that she had poisoned Rebecca Perigo of Bramley, Leeds. Her crime had been carried out in such a protracted and cunningly planned way that her evil was deemed the more outrageous and callous. Mary had schemed to defraud Perigo, and was clearly aiming to poison another victim who was suspecting her of the crime when she was apprehended. When arrested, a phial of deadly poison was found on her.

Her offences were seen as even more devious and damnable when it was learned that she had attempted to practise witchcraft while she was in prison. She had extorted money from a young girl who wanted to see her sweetheart by sewing a charm and coins into her dress: a charm that would mysteriously force the young man she loved to come and visit her in the gaol.

Naturally, when it didn't work, the material was torn open and the coins were gone – in Mary's pocket. She had the knack of being able to put on a performance when required, and also to be as nimble and deceptive as the most skilled pickpocket.

Mary, while living in Leeds, did very well for herself by conning all kinds of people. One Victorian account of her crimes describes a typical ruse:

> The subject of this narrative contrived to ingratiate herself, as she well knew how, into the good graces of a family of the name of Kitchin, two maiden ladies of the Quaker persuasion who kept a small linen shop near St Peter's Square in Leeds. There is every reason to suppose that she had deluded these unfortunate young women with some idea of her skill in looking into futurity… For some time Mary was the confidante of the Misses Kitchin… In the early part of September, 1803 one of the young women became very ill; Mary Bateman procured for her medicines.. These medicines were of a powerful efficacy and in the course of less than one week, Miss Kitchin died…

Mary and her husband had first lived in High Court Lane when they first came to Leeds, and from there she started her life of crime, first stealing from a lodger and then working hard at obtaining property by deception. She even took money under false pretences from a poor widow and callously saw the children of her victim sent to the workhouse.

At the trial, when Mary claimed she was pregnant, the scene almost devolved from solemnity into farce. The judge wanted a group of matrons in the court to examine Mary to prove her condition and, as no one wanted to be involved, the good matrons of York began to shuffle out of the courtroom with some indignation, but the law prevailed. The judge ordered the doors to be shut so that the women had no choice but to comply and Mary was duly inspected, pronounced not with child, and the sentence passed. The trial had lasted for eleven hours. Mary had those harrowing words said to her as she stood there, the judge donning his black cap: 'The sentence of the law is, and the court doth allow it, that you be taken to a place whence you came, and from thence, on Monday next, to the place of execution, there to be hanged by the neck until you are dead, and that your body be given to the surgeons… May Almighty God have mercy on your soul…'

The gaoler, who was with her on her last night, noted that she wrote a letter to her husband and sent her wedding ring home to be given to her daughter. She had her youngest child in the cell with her, to suckle, and it was a scene that the ordinary (the officer who normally interviewed and monitored statements by prisoners) noted with feelings of sympathy. However, he also remarked on her silences regarding the crimes she had committed and felt sure that she knew much more about other suspicious deaths connected with her activities. In the end, these secrets went to the grave with her.

At that time, noted killers and footpads attracted great crowds at their death, and Mary Bateman was no exception. Though there were no friends to swing on her legs and quicken her death, there was, nevertheless, a crowd to prove her status as a local celebrity. A massive crowd had travelled from Leeds, where she had murdered, to see justice done. The hanging took place at the new drop, behind the castle. It was eerily quiet when Mary said a prayer, but a shudder went through the crowd when she begged for mercy and shouted out that she was innocent.

Her body was taken away to be used for medical dissection – all the way to Leeds by hearse – but with all celebrities, death provoked a general curiosity to view the body, and Mary's was a particularly successful crowd-puller. So many people came to look at her corpse that the money raised was £80 14 s – a great deal of money then. It was given to the General Infirmary. This was due to the quick-wittedness of the enterprising William Hey, who saw a chance for some easy fundraising.

Mary Bateman was destined to be the subject of ballads, chapbooks and tales by the fireside for many years to come throughout Yorkshire, at a time when killers and robbers attracted more attention and sensation than conventional heroes. It appears that she was full of tricks and cons, even on one occasion having a hen appear to lay an egg with 'Christ is Coming' written on the shell, and so she became the stuff of myth and tall tales. After all, this is the time when some children were told to be good or 'Old Boney' (Napoleon Bonaparte) would come and get them. Maybe others were threatened with a visit from the restless spirit of 'Mary the Poisoner.'

This Leeds killer is perhaps the best-known of a host of similar criminals, people who saw an easy way to acquire some riches; as insurance developed, the temptations for This particular line of work grew apace, and in Liverpool the infamous case of the 'Black Widows' who killed several members of their own family represents that temptation and its nasty, repulsive results. But Mary Bateman also had that other quality of the worst killer: stealth and subtlety, so that she won allegiance and trust before she struck with her deadly poison.

Young, Graham (1948–1990)

Sometimes, the power of poison gives a person with a sick mind the opportunity of removing anyone they like, and in a very short time. However, poisoners have often taken a twisted pleasure in the slow death caused by prolonged arsenic use (see the allegations against *Florence Maybrick*). Yet some poisoners appear to have a compulsion that outsoars any rational attempt at explanation. Such an example was Graham Young.

As young as fourteen years old, Young was incarcerated in Broadmoor for poisoning his stepfather and sister, along with attempts to kill several others. He was destined for life in an institution but a psychiatrist concluded that he had somehow been returned to a normal state of mind and, in his early twenties, he was employed by a firm in Bovington. From late 1971, the year of his release, employees started to become seriously ill, and some died. There were complaints of extreme stomach pains and then there was an investigation.

Young asked if thallium, a metal similar to lead that Young used, might be responsible and he was soon investigated. His background featured prominently in the attempts to understand him. As Judge Sparrow pointed out in an essay, 'Young was top chemistry pupil at John Kelly Secondary School in Willesden... He started in a simple way putting antimony in a cream biscuit and giving it to his school friend, John Williams.' He was to become a Broadmoor patient as time went on. In Broadmoor, he was clever enough to carry on with more than simple pranks; he could and did still do dangerous things. He was popular with other inmates as he knew such things as how to become drunk without conventional booze. He even managed to borrow books, particularly on extreme deviants such as Christie of *Rillington Place*.

Young died in Parkhurst gaol in 1990. His convictions were for murder, attempted murder and administering poisons. Two of his victims were in Broadmoor and his actions played a part in the creation of the Butler Committee on mental illness.

Contents

A
Acid bath Killer, 1
Adams, Dr. John Bodkin (1899–1983), 2
Aram, Eugene (1704–1759), 3
Assizes, 5

B
Baby Farming, 6
*Bank of England Job: The American Gang, 8
*Baretti and Dr. Johnson, 21
Bentley, Derek (1933–1953), 25
Bills O'Jacks Murder, 25
Blackout Ripper, The, 26
Blazing Car Mysteries, 27
Blood, Colonel Thomas (1618–1680), 29
Bloody Assizes, 29
Boot fetishist-or not?, 30
Bottomley, Horatio (1860–1932), 37
Bow Street Runners, 38
Brides in the Bath, The, 39
Brodie, Deacon (1741–1788), 41
Burke and Hare and Resurrection Men, 42
Burning at the Stake, 45

C
Chicken House Murder, 46
Cotton, Mary Ann (1832–1873), 47
Courvoisier Case, 48
Crippen, Dr Hawley Harvey (1862–1910), 49
Cutlery Eater, 51

D
De Quincey, Thomas (1785–1859), 51
*Detectives, national and local, 53

E
Eliza Armstrong: bought for £5, 56
Euston Square Mystery, The, 57

F
Family Massacre (Ratcliffe Highway, 1811), 58
Flasher to Killer: the birth of DNA forensics, 58
Flogging, 59

G
Garotting Panic, 60
Ghost in the Nick (Fred Nodder), 63

H
Half-Hanged Smith, 65
Hall, Marshall (1858–1927), 66
Hanged, Drawn and Quartered, 67
*Hangman tales, 68
Hangwomen, 73

Hanratty (A6 Murder), 73
Heath, Neville (1917–1946), 74
Highwaymen, 75
Humphreys, Sir Travers (1867–1956), 78

I
Ilchester Gaol Scandal, 78

J
Jack the Ripper, 79
Justice Godfrey: Slain, 80

K
Kiszco, Stefan, 81
Kray Brothers, 82

L
*Lags and the Library, 83
Lee, John, 'The man they couldn't hang', 88
Lord Haw Haw (William Joyce 1906–1946), 89

M
Macaroni Parson, The (Dr Dodd), 90
Martin, Jonathan: Arsonist (1782–1838), 93
Maybrick, Florence (1861–1942), 94
*Messengers (Kings' and Queens'), 95
Moat Farm Mystery, The, 97
Moll Cutpurse (Mary Frith c. 1584–1659), 98
Moors Murders, The, 98
Murder that never was: Beverley Nichols, 99
Musical Milkman, The, 100

N
Naked on a Ladder (*R. V Collins*, 1975), 101
Newgate, 101
Newgate Calendar, 103

P
Palmer, William, Prince of Poisoners (1824–1856), 104
Peace, Charles (1832–1879), 105
Penny Dreadfuls, 105
*Phonetics, forensic, 106
Pirates, 109
*Poaching, 110
Poison Everywhere: Thomas Overbury, 118
*Police Murders: the very first and a typical death, 124
Pressing, 123
*Prison Escapes, 123
*Prison Mutinies, 126

Q
Queen Victoria: Edward Oxford, would-be assassin, 131

R
Rillington Place, 131
*Riots: Politics and Dripping, 132
Road Hill House Murder, The, 138
Roughead, William (1870–1952), 139
*Rowland, Walter: Twice Condemned, 139
Rush, James: Slaughter in Norfolk, 141
Ruxton, Dr. Buck (1899–1936), 142

S
Sheppard, Jack (1702–1724), 143
Slater, Oscar (1872–1948), 144
Smethurst, Dr., (1805-unknown), 144
Sweet Fanny Adams, 148

T
Teeth Say it All (The Dobkin Murder), 148
Thompson/Bywaters Murder, The, 149
Tichborne Claimant, The, 150
Treason Tales, 151
Turpin, Dick (1705–1739), 153

V
Van der Elst, Violet (1882–1966), 155

W
Wallce Mystery, The, 156
Weare Murder, The, 157
Wearside Jack (*see also* Jack the Ripper), 158
Whiteley: A Double Fatality, 159
Wilde, Oscar (1854–1900), 160
Wise, Thomas J. (1859–1937), 161

Y
*Yorkshire Witch, The (Mary Bateman, 1768–1809), 162
Young, Graham (1948–1990), 165

Bibliography and Sources

1. A Reading Guide to the Major Subjects

A very useful first stage reference work for an overview of sources here is Ruth Paley and Simon Fowler's *Family Skeletons* (National Archives, 2005) This contains a very detailed reading guide broken down into very specific subjects such as 'Resurrection Men' and 'Children who kill.'

Trials
Birkenhead, Earl of, *Famous Trials* (Hutchinson, 1925)
Birkenhead, the Earl of, *More Famous Trials* (Hutchinson, 1938)
Most useful and thorough of all are the series works published by William Hodge, *Notable British Trials*. Penguin Paperbacks also brought out a paperback series called *Famous trials* throughout the 1940s to the 1960s.

Prisons
Byrne, Richard, *Prisons and Punishments of London* (Harrap, 1989)
Morris, Norval, *The Oxford History of the Prison* (OUP, 1998)
Priestley, Philip, *Victorian Prison Lives* (Pimlico, 1999)

Police
Emsley, Clive, *The English Police: A Political andSocial History* (Pearson, 1991)
Reith, C.A., *Short History of the British Police* (OUP, 1948)
Shpayer-Makov, Haia, *The Ascent of the Detective* (OUP, 2011)

Punishment
Abbott, Geoffrey, *Execution* (Summersdale, 2005)
Eddleston, John J., *The Encyclopaedia of Executions* (John Blake, 2002)

2. General Bibliography

Note: Dates of the first published editions are in brackets after the title.

Books Cited

Abbott, Geoffrey, *William Calcraft: Executioner Extraordinaire* (Eric Dobby, 2004)
Anon., *Life of Jack Sheppard the Housebreaker* (Glover & Co., 1840)
Anon. *Life of Richard Turpin A Most notorious highwayman* (Thomas Richardson, 1834)
Ballantine, Serjeant, [sic] *Some Experiences of a Barrister's Life* (Bentley & Son, 1883)
Bidwell, George, *Forging His Chains* (Scranton, 1888)
Birkett, Lord, *The New Newgate Calendar* (Folio Society, 1993)
Browne, Douglas, and Tullett, E.V., *Bernard Spilsbury: His Life and Cases* (Companion Book Club, 1952)
Byrne, Gerald, *Neville Heath* (Headline, 1946)
Chambers, Robert, *Traditions of Edinburgh* (W & R Chambers, 1931)
Charles, Barrie, *Kill the Queen! The Eight assassination attempts on Queen Victoria* (Amberley, 2012)
Connon, Bryan, *Beverley Nichols: A Life* (Timber Press, 2000)
Cullen, Pamela V., *A Stranger in Blood: the case files on Dr. John Bodkin Adams* (Elliott and Thompson: no date)
Deans, R. Storry, *Notable Trials: Romances of the Law Courts* (Cassell, 1906)
De Quincey, Thomas, *On Murder* (OUP, 2009)
Diamond, Michael, *Victorian Sensation* (Anthem Press, 2003)
Donaldson, William, *Brewer's Rogues, Villains and Eccentrics* (Phoenix, 2004)
Eddy, J.P., *Scarlet and Ermine* (William Kimber, 1960)
Fielding, Steve, *Pierrepoint: A Family of Executioners* (John Blake, 2006)
Fielding, Steve, *The Executioner's Bible* (John Blake, 2007)
Flanders, Judith, *The Invention of Murder* (Harper Press, 2011)
Gilbert, Michael (editor), *The Oxford Book of Legal Anecdotes* (OUP, 1990)
Greville, Charles, *The Diaries of Charles Greville* Edited by Edward Pearce (Pimlico, 2006)
Haining, Peter (editor), *Hunted Down: The Detective Stories of Charles Dickens* (Peter Owen, 1996)
Hall, Jean Graham, and Smith, Gordon D., *R v Bywaters & Thompson* (Barry Rose, 1996)
Hibbert, Christopher, *The Roots of Evil* (Sutton, 2003)
Humphreys, Sir Travers, *A Book of Trials* (Pan, 1953)
Irving, Ronald, *'The Law is an Ass'* (Duckworth, 2000)
Jones, Richard Glyn (editor), *True Crime Through History* (Magpie Books, 2004)

Kennedy, Ludovic, *Ten Rillington Place* (Victor Gollancz, 1961)
Knight, Stephen, *The Killing of Justice Godfrey* (Granada, 1984)
Knipe, William, *Tyburn Tales* (1867) (History Press, 2010)
Lee, John, *John Babbacombe Lee: The man they could not hang* (Devon Books, 1995)
Lefebure, Molly, *Murder on the Home Front* (1954) (Sphere, 2013)
Lobban, J. H. (editor), *Dr Johnson's Mrs Thrale* (T.N. Foulis, 1910)
Marjoribanks, Edward, *The Life of Sir Edward Marshall Hall* (Victor Gollancz, 1929)
Mayhall, John, *The Annals of Yorkshire* (Joseph Johnson, 1861)
Mehew, Ernest (editor), *Selected Letters of Robert Louis Stevenson* (Yale University Press, 1977)
Nichols, Beverley, *Father Figure* (Heinemann, 1972)
Nichols, Beverley, *Twenty-Five* (Penguin, 1926)
Pierrepoint, Albert, *Executioner: Pierrepoint* (Coronet, 1974)
Priestley, Philip, *Victorian Prison Lives* (Methuen, 1985)
Robinson, Bruce, *They All Love Jack* (Fourth Estate, 2016)
Roughead, William, *Classic Crimes* (NYRB, 2000)
Rowe, John G., *The Scaffold and the Dock* (Mellifont, No date)
Seddon, Peter, *The Law's Strangest Cases* (Robson Books, 2007)
Sharpe, James, *Dick Turpin* (Profile Books, 2004)
Simpson, Keith, *Forty Years of Murder* (Harrap, 1978)
Taylor, Rev. R. V., *Yorkshire Anecdotes* (Whittaker & Co., 1883)
Vandome, Nick, *Crimes and Criminals* (Chambers, 1992)
Veale, F.J.P., *The Wallace Case* (Merrymeade Publishing, 1950)
Ward, Charles E., *The Life of John Dryden* (University of North Carolina, 1961)
Watson, Katherine, *Poisoned Lives: English poisoners and their victims* (Hambledon, 2004)
Whittaker, G.H. *Bills o' Jack's: A Moorland Mystery* (Whittaker, 1932)
Wilkinson, George Theodore, *The Newgate Calendar* (Edited by Christopher Hibbert) (Cardinal, 1991). This was first printed as *The Malefactors' Register* in the late eighteenth century.
Wilson, Colin, and Wilson, Damon, *Illustrated True Crime* (Parragon, 2006)

Ephemera

The New Newgate Calendar (A. Ritchie, No Date) six issues used for quotation.
The Strangeways Murder (Sporting News, reprint from Clifford Elmer Books, 2004)

Reference Works

A Full Account of the Atrocious Murder of the Late Mr W. Weare (Sherwood Jones, 1823)
Anon. *Palmer the Rugeley Poisoner* (Daisy Bank, 1912)
Anon. *The Bloody Assizes* (E. and G. Goldsmid, 1890)
Anon. *The Case of Thompson and Bywaters* (Newnes, No Date)
Anon. *The Great Crippen Horror* (Daisy Bank, 1912)
Anon. *The Life and Career of Mrs Cotton* (W.J. Cummins, 1873)
Anon. *The Moat Farm Mystery* (Daisy Bank, 1912)
Anon. *The Tichborne Trial: the summing-up by the Lord Chief Justice of England* (Ward Lock and Tyler, 1874)
Beadle, Jeremy, and Harrison, Ian, *First, Lasts and Onlys: Crime* (Robson Books, 2007)
Berry, James, *My Experiences as an Executioner* (David and Charles, 1972)
Byrne, Gerald, *John George Haigh, Acid Bath Killer* (Headline, 1949)
Cox, David J., *A Certain Share of Low Cunning: a history of the Bow Street Runners 1792-1839* (Willan Publishing, 2010)
Cyriax, Oliver, *The Penguin Encyclopaedia of Crime* (Penguin, 1996)
Doughty, Jack, *The Rochdale Hangman and his Victims* (Jade, 1998)
Douglas, Hugh, *Burke and Hare* (Robert Hale, 2003)
Hudson, Roger, *Hudson's English History: A Compendium* (Weidenfeld and Nicolson, 2005)
Hunt, Henry, *Investigation at Ilchester Gaol* (Thomas Dolby, 1821)
Jackson, Lee, *A Dictionary of Victorian London* (Anthem Press, 2006)
James, P.D., and Critchley, T.A., *The Maul and the Pear-Tree* (Faber and Faber, 1971)
Keily, Jackie, and Hoffbrand, Julia, *The Crime Museum Uncovered* (I.B. Tauris, 2015)
Linebaugh, Peter, *The London Hanged* (Verso, London) 2003
Lyons, Frederick J., *George Joseph Smith: The Brides in the Bath Case* (Duckworth, 1935)
Marks, Laurence, and Van Den Bergh, Tony, *Ruth Ellis, A case of Diminished Responsibility* (Macdonald and Jane's, 1977)
Morris, Norval, and Rothman, David J., *The Oxford History of the Prison* (OUP, 1998)
Nash, Jay Robert, *World Encyclopaedia of 20th Century Murder* (Headline, 1922)
Parris, John, *Scapegoat* (Duckworth, 1991)
Plowden, Alison, *The Case of Eliza Armstrong* (BBC Publications, 1974)
Rede, Leman Thomas, *York Castle in the Nineteenth Century* (John Bennett, 1831)

Rose, Jonathan, *et alia*, *Innocents* (Fourth Estate, 1997)
Roughead, William, *Trials of Burke and Hare* (William Hodge, 1948)
Russell, Lord, *Deadman's Hill: Was Hanratty Guilty?* (Secker and Warburg, 1965)
Saunders, John B., *Mozley & Whiteley's Law Dictionary*, 9th edition (Butterworth's, 1977)
Scott, Sir Harold (editor), The Concise Encyclopaedia of Crime and Criminals (Andre Deutsch, 1961)
Sharpe, J.A., *Crime in Early Modern England 1550-1750* (Longman, 1984)
Stephen, Sir James Fitzjames Stephen, *A History of the Criminal Law of England* (Macmillan, 1883)
Taylor, Bernard, and Clarke, Kate, *Murder at the Priory* (Grafton Books, 1988)
Trow, M.J., *The Wigwam Murder* (Constable, 1994)
Whittington-Egan, Richard, *A Casebook on Jack the Ripper* (Wildy and sons, 1975)
Whittington-Egan, Richard, *Jack the Ripper: The Definitive Casebook* (Amberley, 2013)
Whittingtom-Egan, Richard, *Speaking Volumes* (Cappella Archive, 2004)
Wynn, Douglas, *The Crime Writer's Handbook* (Allison and Busby, 2003)
Younghusband, Sir George, *The Tower of London* (Herbert Jenkins, 1924)

Essays and Articles

'Moorland Murder Riddle of 1832 Baffles Jury of 1959', *Yorkshire Post* (19 June 1959)
Siveking, Paul, 'The Undead', *Sunday Telegraph*, 12 November 2000
Webster, Mike, 'Lady Betty Sugrue' *Ireland's Own* (July 2002) p.18

Internet Material

Hansard report: Horatio Bottomley 30 July 1924 Vol. 176 cc2061-3
http://www.capitalpunishmentuk.org/
https://pubmed.ncbi.nlm.nih.gov 'The Conviction of Dr Crippen: new forensic findings in a century-old murder' Foran, David R., et alia (American Academy of Forensic Sciences)
www.supremecourt.uk/docs/speech -121009 *The High Sheriff of Oxfordshire's Annual Law Lecture given by Lord Wilson 9. October, 2012*
www.unsolved-murders.co.uk/murder-content